New Perspectives on Social Class and Socioeconomic Development in the Periphery

New Perspectives on Social Class and Socioeconomic Development in the Periphery

EDITED BY
NELSON W. KEITH
AND
NOVELLA ZETT KEITH

HN
981
.S6
N48
1988
West

CONTRIBUTIONS IN ECONOMICS AND ECONOMIC HISTORY, NUMBER 77

GREENWOOD PRESS
NEW YORK • WESTPORT, CONNECTICUT • LONDON

Library of Congress Cataloging-in-Publication Data

New perspectives on social class and socioeconomic
  development in the periphery.

  (Contributions in economics and economic history,
ISSN 0084-9235 ; no. 77)
   Bibliography: p.
   Includes index.
   1. Social classes—Developing countries.
2. Capitalism—Developing countries. 3. Peasantry—
Developing countries. 4. Urban poor—Developing
countries. 5. Informal sector (Economics)—Developing
countries. 6. Ethnicity—Africa, Sub-Saharan.
7. Church and social problems—Catholic Church.
8. Church and social problems—Latin America.
I. Keith, Nelson W. II. Keith, Novella Zett.
III. Series.
HN981.S6N48   1988   305.5'09172'4   87-25113
ISBN 0-313-25688-8 (lib. bdg. : alk. paper)

British Library Cataloguing in Publication Data is available.

Library of Congress Catalog Card Number: 87-25113
ISBN: 0-313-25688-8
ISSN: 0084-9235

First published in 1988

Greenwood Press, Inc.
88 Post Road West, Westport, Connecticut 06881

Printed in the United States of America

The paper used in this book complies with the
Permanent Paper Standard issued by the National
Information Standards Organization (Z39.48-1984).

10 9 8 7 6 5 4 3 2 1

Copyright Acknowledgment

The editors and publisher gratefully acknowledge permission to use the following:

A. Portes and J. Walton, *Labor, Class and the International System,* © 1981 the Academic Press,
Inc.

Contents

New Perspectives on Social Class
and Socioeconomic Development
in the Periphery

Introduction

NELSON W. KEITH and NOVELLA ZETT KEITH

This volume is built around two interrelated themes which have become signposts of a kind amidst the peculiar features of peripheral social formations: the systemic "weakness" of the two basic capitalist classes (the bourgeoisie and the proletariat), and the persistence and relative resilience of the noncapitalist classes.

The class structure of peripheral social formations provides the background against which emerge institutions and practices that are quite at variance with those of developed social formations. Differences in the structure of domination and authority are visible, for example, in the roles of the state and the military. In turn, at both the political and the cognitive levels, we observe the prominence of certain noneconomic and nonproperty phenomena such as ethnicity and religion. These variables are often supported by their association with noncapitalist practices, which still hold a central place in peripheral social formations.

The "articulation of modes of production" approach is, in our view, a most promising starting point for the development of analyses that fully account for the peculiar socioeconomic features addressed in this volume. Briefly, this approach holds that capitalist relations are unable to assimilate the various modes of production often coexisting in a single peripheral social formation. Rather, the capitalist mode of production becomes meshed with these other modes, spawning hybrid socioeconomic forms and structures which are both mutually accommodating and antagonistic. These phenomena are not merely precapitalist remnants, staging a valiant but hopeless battle against the inevitable victory of capitalism: the reality is far from it. Indeed, as with the informal sectors of urban centers, some of these phenomena postdate capitalism, and their resilience seems to deepen with time.

The concept of articulation allows us to grasp these processes in relative freedom from the distorting effects of established theoretical models. Meaning both "to join <u>and</u> to give clear expression to something" (Post, 1978: 18), articulation entails the emergence of new expressions of social structures and forms, which are then further developed in the course of the relationship. Land and labor, for instance, may be shared between two competing modes of production. As the articulation is effected through the medium of classes, it involves the entire social formation: cognitive and political, as well as economic practices become joined and further developed in the process.

Two important issues emerge here. First, these processes do not merely create variants of capitalist classes. When noncapitalist modes of production become articulated with capitalism, the determinate role does not automatically belong to the capitalist mode of production. There are cases, for instance, where noncapitalist practices function almost completely outside the impact of capitalist relations, leading to developments that cannot be understood if the capitalist mode of production is used as the main point of reference. Even more importantly, the discussion cannot be allowed to revolve exclusively or even principally around a debate framed in terms of the determinacy of one mode or another. Inasmuch as it is the articulation of modes of production which is integral to peripheral capitalism, it is far more fruitful to explore the forms which articulation assumes and their overall relationship to the formation of given social classes and agendas for political action.

Second, the exploration of the different forms that articulation assumes brings to greater prominence what has been a constant point of contention for Marxist theorizing: the significance of noneconomic and nonproperty variables. The persistence of ethnicity and kinship in peripheral social formations, for example, provides the empirical ballast for reopening the question of the relative autonomy of consciousness and ideology. As the concluding chapter asserts, if we are to move toward more fruitful theory construction, we must begin by approaching these variables as phenomena sui generis, rather than confining them to the role of ephiphenomena.

The contributors to this volume attempt to grapple with some of the crucial questions raised above. For convenience of presentation, they are divided into two sections. The first section consists of a single chapter by one of the co-editors, which addresses the central theoretical and conceptual issues linked to the themes of weak basic capitalist classes and persistent noncapitalist classes, and which provides a conceptual framework for the entire volume. This chapter should be used as a point of reference, as the wide range of emphases and geographical spread of the other chapters might superficially obscure the common themes and cohesiveness of the volume as a whole. All the contributions touch--some centrally, others peripherally--on the determinants of class structures and their sociopolitical ramifications, and on the place of nonproperty variables relative to that of the economic determinants of the classical Marxist schema. The relative importance of these variables is a thorny question which does not admit any categorical conclusions given the current state of research, and thus the position of our contributors on this issue is far from uniform. The reader will also encounter some theoretical and methodological eclecticism, underscoring our belief that the theoretical development and systematization which this area of research still needs can best be pursued through openness to insights derived from differing approaches.

The opening chapter, "Class Analysis in the Periphery," sketches the historical and structural causes for the weakness of the basic capitalist classes in the periphery, locating this condition within the peculiar structures and relations of peripheral capitalism. Author Nelson W. Keith argues that this species of capitalist relations, though located within the overarching form of the capitalist mode of production, exists as a pure type. This ensemble of structures and relations is not transitional; rather, permanent partial development is a regular feature, endemic to peripheral capitalism.

The state of permanent partial development originates in the differential socioeconomic patterns through which the center and the periphery were capitalized: the former, largely from within and on its own steam; the latter, from without and with hardly enough capital to transform unfree into free labor. Two main sets of consequences stem from this pattern of capitalization. First, the state in the periphery tends to enjoy a pronounced relative autonomy. This quality arises directly from the condition of capital scarcity which does not permit the emergence of hegemonic bourgeoisies. Absent is the rough-and-tumble of laissez-faire principles which presupposed both ample capital resources and strong capitalist classes. Second, permanent partial development ensures the continuing existence of many noncapitalist economic practices and, concomitantly, a stronger play for what we refer to as the nonproperty variables: religion, ethnicity, kinship, culture, and the like.

So far, these remarks would attract some support from many writers in the field who, like the author, argue compellingly for a more determinate place for these noncapitalist classes in the spheres of class consciousness and political action. Certainly, the Chinese and Vietnamese revolutions lend their support. There is, however, a respectable body of writing that is prepared to make concessions to the classes involved (the peasants, the agricultural laborers, and so forth) but still sees their political and ideological practices as dependent for leadership on the proletariat.

Nelson Keith takes issue with that formulation. The specific form of consciousness required to effect socialist transformation is revolutionary consciousness, and not working-class consciousness. Working-class consciousness is but one of a cluster of ideologies, which ultimately coalesce into revolutionary form. Although working-class consciousness remains a powerful instrument for socialist transformation, the noncapitalist classes are largely integrated into world accumulation in a way that may permit the leadership of their ideological practice in the forging of revolutionary consciousness.

The contributors to Part II address, in their respective ways, some of the major consequences of permanent partial development. As a whole, they find their starting point in the peculiar evolution of classes and institutions in the periphery, which they illustrate by outlining varying processes of articulation.

As discussed in the opening chapter and elsewhere, noncapitalist classes are an integral part of peripheral capitalism. The stubborn persistence of peasantries (variously defined) has not escaped the notice of commentators, and neither has the growth of urban-based "informal sectors"-- that group of independent workers and petty commodity producers which forges often ingenious solutions to the lack of permanent wage labor. Thus, if the volume betrays a preoccupation with noncapitalist classes, that bias is encouraged by the developmental patterns of the periphery. Nevertheless, the evolution, relative strength, and political role of these classes are at great variance; the social structures do not provide the continuities in analyses of peripheral social formations as much as do the processes through which the structures become articulated.

Contributors Curtain, Mandle, and Johnson provide useful insights into the articulation of peasantries within the social totality (whether capitalist or socialist), an articulation with quite different consequences in terms of the evolution of the class. They attempt to answer questions such as how, specifically, the colonial state may contribute to the process of arrested proletarianization and, conversely, to the maintenance of peasant modes of production; the nature and sources of the resilience of peasant modes of production; and the best relationship between a socialist state and peasantries in developmental socialism. Howard and Skinner's chapter is similarly grounded, but focuses instead on noncapitalist, ethnically based classes around which the articulation of capitalist and noncapitalist modes of production revolves.

We will now discuss in more detail each chapter in Part II, beginning with Richard Curtain's contribution, "The Colonial State, Migrant Labor, and Class Formation in Papua New Guinea." Curtain's central focus is on the role of the state in class formation through its control of labor. The state in colonial Papua-New Guinea established its control over labor by instituting a migrant labor system (MLS). Curtain points out how state action was directed both at the provision of a labor force for capitalist enterprises and at the maintenance of the noncapitalist mode of production which ensured the reproduction of this labor force. Laws served to preserve the basic structure of the noncapitalist classes by combining the requirement that the worker's family be left behind in the village with compulsory repatriation. Not incidentally, as Curtain aptly observes, we encounter here one of the mechanisms responsible for the arrested development of a large proletariat in the periphery.

Does the noncapitalist mode of production have in itself the dynamism necessary to resist the encroachments of capitalism and contribute in a positive sense to the process of change? The answer, as found in Curtain's data, is mixed. The rate of outmigration from villages in Papua New Guinea varied considerably, depending on factors such as geography, accessibility, and the role played by men in the domestic economy and cultural life. Curtain also notes "the tenacity of the closely knit, well-integrated social systems of some 700 different language groups." Nonetheless, while the noncapitalist mode is not merely reactive, capitalism and its institutions remain the prime moving force. True, an intricate articulation is established between the two modes, leading to a dual dependence rather than obliteration of the one by the other. Nevertheless, the noncapitalist mode remains subordinate. "The peasant economy of a labor reserve area such as the East Sepik Province has retained a degree of self-reliance, but it is within the framework of a subordinate relationship to the capitalist economy, subsidizing the latter at the cost of its own development."

Curtain's analysis has as its point of departure the functions that articulation plays for the dominant mode of production and political system. The presentation of data is necessarily selective, giving less prominence to the social actors who are the carriers of the noncapitalist mode of production. This mode's persistence and potential for generating transformative impulses are not subjected to an intense scrutiny. Other chapters, such as those by Johnson, Howard and Skinner, and Forbes, focus more closely on the noncapitalist classes and nonproperty variables, thus contributing to our understanding of the persistence and position of these classes from a different vantage point. The authors' research uncovers sufficient dynamism within these sectors to serve as a warning against hasty generalizations on the all-pervasive determinacy of the capitalist mode of production.

Mandle's chapter, "Agricultural Transformation in Developmental Socialism," raises the issue of the control of labor by socialist states and, in doing so, makes a potential contribution toward broadening the concept of articulation to include the articulation of the peasantry with a socialist mode of production. Since articulated modes of production are central to peripheral formations, socialist states which develop in these formations must also encounter noncapitalist forms and classes. These states have not always been the saviors of the peasantry, as Mandle notes. What is in store for agriculturalists in the periphery if they must contend with a state obeying the requirements of socialist transformation instead of those of capital accumulation? Agricultural production must play a central role in developmental socialism. Mandle argues that the needs of development are best served when agriculturalists are willing participants in the process; thus cooperatives are the preferred form of organization for agricultural production, both in order to promote economic development and to institute socialist relations of production. However, what is logically sound is not always politically acceptable. Mandle is well aware that the decentralized power structure that must accompany the creation of cooperatives runs counter to the prevailing preference for centralized planning in socialist countries. The articulation of peasantries with a socialist mode of production may lead to their integration into socialist relations of production, but only if economic pressures are strong enough to compel their leaders to accept a relative loss of power.

The following chapters explore more fully the role of certain noncapitalist and nonproperty variables in fashioning peripheral social structures and political action. Ethnicity is often counterposed to class in studies of African social formations, providing as it does a major organizing principle for consciousness and political action along vertical rather than horizontal lines. Howard and Skinner's chapter, "Ethnic Leadership and Class Formation in Freetown, Sierra Leone," demonstrates the complex interweaving of these variables with each other and the broader socioeconomic totality. The authors unravel a wealth of historical data, from which ethnicity emerges as a fluid adaptation and response to the broader environment, as well as a force in its own right. Ethnicity is not a given, but one possible way of structuring identity and organizing around values and interests. In this sense, then, ethnicity is counterposed to class.

Howard and Skinner carefully examine economic, political, and cultural variables as they relate to the process of ethnic group and class formation and transformation. From its founding in 1792 as an abolitionist project, Freetown expanded into an important center for trade and, later, extraction of iron and gold. Leading us through three periods of colonial rule as well as developments in the postcolonial era, the authors focus on the evolving role of the headmen as political, cultural, and economic intermediaries. The account uncovers five interrelated historical processes which are of importance for analyses of ethnicity and class:

1. the impact of capitalism on noncapitalist economies;

2. the composition and policies of the power bloc (colonial and postcolonial);

3. the ability of particular communities to forge an identity and position of dominance which influence later communities;

4. the class position of ethnic leaders and their ability to draw on capitalist and noncapitalist resources; and

5. the capacity of workers and others to organize along class lines.

In Sierra Leone, noncapitalist relations of production and exchange were only slowly and incompletely transformed through articulation with capitalism and colonialism, a fact which appears to account for the continued importance accorded to the headmen. Are capitalist structures and relations pushing their way through, and is ethnicity destined to lose its centrality to class? The issues do not admit of easy answers. Though the headmen have been losing ground in recent times, the persistence of ethnicity is not so directly linked to the persistence of traditional or precapitalist practices and relations. Ethnic organization has shown its adaptability in urban settings. For instance, younger members who are responsive to the needs of the large numbers of casual and semiskilled workers have been allowed to assume leadership roles. Its viability is further supported by the fact that many ethnic leaders have remained peripheral to the bourgeoisie, retaining close geographic, paternalistic, and kinship ties with their communities.

In the sphere of political action, however, ethnicity has fanned out into cross-ethnic forms: while there are signs of an evolving class or trade-union consciousness, other developments, such as the urban youth culture and its dance societies, strongly suggest the continued vibrancy of nonproperty variables as foci for identity formation and organization. "The saliency of ethnicity may decline over time," conclude the authors, "but it could also take new forms."

While the chapters are united in their central concern with the role of nonproperty variables in the dynamics of political action and social change, the key variables to be examined cannot be uniformly the same, as they must emerge organically from the specific historical circumstances of the social formation in question. In the context of Sierra Leone --generalizable perhaps to much of the African continent--the joint evolution of ethnicity and class is a key variable of interest. For much of Latin America, especially for revolutionary or prerevolutionary social formations, the role of the Catholic Church (always of some importance) has assumed new dimensions of late, as liberation theology has raised the possibility of support for revolutionary movements.

Thomas Bamat, in "Political Change and the Catholic Church in Brazil and Nicaragua," discusses the role of religion within the context of a concrete revolutionary situation. The Sandinista revolution in Nicaragua and political restiveness in other Catholic-dominated countries in Latin America have posed a fundamental question for Catholicism: can the Catholic Church be in the forefront of revolutionary change? Bamat outlines in a progressive way the gradual integration of the Church with revolutionary practice, which eventuated in the crafting of liberation theology. However, the high degree of practical commitment evinced by the leadership of the Church splintered into dissent, strong support, and reaction. Why has this been so? Bamat explains the dilemma in terms of fundamental contradictions between the main organizing principles of the Church and those of radical and socialist politics; or, in other words, between exacting obeisance and the ideas of governance animated by popular will.

These contradictions are not easily resolved, as the structures of domination in Latin America remain formidable. Bamat's discussion does, however, highlight the revolutionary currents flowing around grassroots pastoral efforts. They are Christian to the core, but are prepared to bend these doctrines to the revolutionary cause: "the Church's development of organizational abilities, leadership, and critical consciousness among grassroots Christians is far more important [than the Church's institutional intervention] in terms of the prospects for . . . some form of socialist future in Latin America." Bamat does indeed introduce some exciting possibilities for the transformative role of religion as a stimulus to revolutionary consciousness and action.

Johnson's chapter, "Ideological Dimensions of Peasant Persistence in Western Kenya," focuses not on revolutionary situations but on the factors that enable the peasantry to persist and even flourish while articulated well and truly with capitalism. Some research findings had already adverted to a symbiotic relationship between the peasants and the capitalist economy, ensuring the former's persistence (see, for instance, Stavenhagen, 1978, on the Mexican peasantry). However, the process was characterized as "progressive decapitalization," with capital being transferred out of the peasant sector. Johnson's microeconomic research, conducted from the perspective of the economic anthropologist, found the peasants of the Migori Division of Western Kenya far more independent and able to chose the desired degree of involvement in the capitalist economy: "if pressured too much by the state (on behalf of capital) they can disengage and still meet their basic needs through subsistence production and reciprocal exchange with neighbors and kin." The peasants Johnson studied actively participate in shaping the social formation.

Utilizing a carefully assembled grid of structures and relations (circulation, means of production, and the like), Johnson makes an attractive and often compelling case for the prevalence and determinate role of nonproperty variables. These are "cultural forces" working against capitalist relations: obligation to kin, patterns of generalized reciprocity (the "economy of affection"), the ideology of egalitarianism, and the "needs ideology" linked to the peasant's desire to remain in control of land. As Johnson sees it, capitalist relations of production will be kept at bay as long as the defining values predominate. His conclusion is supported by more recent research by Christopher Leo (1984), who contends that the Kenyan peasantry is indeed expanding and flourishing.

Dean Forbes' chapter, "Conflict, Class, and the Urban Poor in the Third World," extends the general line of thinking of the introductory essay to an analysis of one of the seedbeds of noncapitalist classes and their political practices: the informal sector in Third World cities. It thus provides a fitting conclusion for the volume. In an acute and persuasive way, Forbes takes issue with the strong structural-functional tendencies that have become a part of class analyses in the periphery. After a thoroughgoing critique of the main offending positions, he settles into applying a recursive class analysis to the behavior of wage and nonwage labor in Jakarta. In the course of his analysis, he stresses the central place of human agency in political action; not as actors merely shunted around at the pleasure of shifting structural rearrangements, in the worst traditions of applications of Althusser, or as individuals spurred \on by expressions of voluntarism outraged into some form of remedial political action by universal ethics. As he puts it, "the critical missing elements [in class analysis] are struggle and conflict, and the historical and spatial context in which these processes occur."

Forbes' notion of discursive class analysis emphasizes the paramount importance of the human agency. In the presence of peripheral social structures such as are found in Jakarta, where one-half of the workforce is located in the noncapitalist informal sector, we cannot insist on classical notions of consciousness and political action. Where peculiarities in class relations are compounded by differential patterns of proletarianization and a highly repressive political milieu, Forbes suggests, we must seek the sources of change within the interstices of day-to-day situations. Both informal sector workers and the urban proletariat, Forbes informs us, have participated in broad social protest movements within Indonesian cities. Nevertheless, outfitted with classical Marxist spectacles, one would indeed be hard-pressed locating, let alone understanding, these phenomena. The participation of the rickshaw riders in these protest movements is a case in point. Their political action (the specificities of their ideology, for example) must be abstracted from linkages with semicriminal activities and other factors defined by customs and culture; there are no direct causal connections between these class dynamics and formal commodity production.

The conclusion by Novella Zett Keith, "Notes on Theory and Method for Third World Studies," selects some of the threads that are woven through the volume and provides suggestions on directions to be taken in the process of theory construction. The historical moment seems to place special attention on matters of consciousness and religion in generating social change. How precisely these factors should be inserted into the realm of theory remains to be seen. However, the chapter counsels that the rethinking of ideology and the inclusion of a modicum of methodological eclecticism would make for good starting points.

Thus we reach the end of the volume. We would like to remind the reader, before he or she plunges on, of a statement we made earlier in this introduction. We pointed out that this field of scholarship tends to be either narrow and historically specific or broad and general. Our aim in shaping this volume was to convey a sense of the similarities of themes and processes without sacrificing the richness of social and historical experience as it enlivens every social formation, rendering it unique. These contributions are not, then, scattered leaves in the wind, but represent an unbounded unity. We hope they will succeed in provoking probing thought and discussion, and so raise new questions as we attempt to grasp the complexity of the Third World.

BIBLIOGRAPHY

Leo, Christopher
 1984 Land and Class in Kenya. Toronto: University of Toronto.
Post, Ken
 1978 Arise Ye Starvelings; the Jamaican Labour Rebellion of 1938 and Its Aftermath. The Hague: Martinus Nijhoff.
Stavenhagen, Rodolfo
 1978 Capitalism and the Peasantry in Mexico. Latin American Perspectives 5 (3): 27-37.

Part I
THE SETTING

1
Class Analysis in the Periphery: A Partial Evaluation

NELSON W. KEITH

The literature on class analysis in the periphery is abundant. It is, however, all too often hampered by overly narrow confines inherent in existing models of development. Whether derived from linear western models of growth or Marxist schemas of successive modes of production, predominant approaches to peripheral social formations have tended to emphasize the presence of anomalies, aberrant cases to be corrected as necessary by the intervention of market forces, governmental policies, or revolutionary bourgeoisies or proletariats. By and large, these biases are present not only in conceptualizations falling squarely within the models, but also in those elaborated as critiques; thus critiques provide a counterpoint, but are still located within a framework in which these models are the primary referent. As a case in point, dependency theory, developed as a critique of neoclassical development economics, could not entirely overcome the confines of this framework and fully address on their own terms, broader questions couched in terms of global processes of capital accumulation.

Fruitful theory construction requires that we progress beyond center-based models, with their emphasis on the periphery as the aberrant case. The articulation of modes of production is undoubtedly the most promising of the new approaches. Enriched by the early efforts of anthropologists like Meillassoux and Rey, we now have the tools to approach peripheral social formations as entities with singular developmental patterns which need not--indeed, do not--ape or merely passively respond to impulses from the center. At the same time that it highlights these particularities, the approach asserts a commitment to globality. By situating peripheral social formations within the global context of capitalism, it provides a special vantage point from which to abstract and interpret the evolution and relations of classes in the periphery. A new global process of capital accumulation is dynamically linked to the interpenetration and transformation of social formations at the center and the periphery. According to the thesis, social structures and class relations encompassed by this articulation are shaped predominantly by two sets of forces: those set in motion by incorporation of center and periphery into the world capitalist system, and those associated with the pre- or noncapitalist social formations existing prior to articulation.

The specific questions of exploitation and emancipation lying at the heart of this volume lead us to the crucial issue on which the thesis of articulation sheds new light. The focus is on revolutionary consciousness and revolutionary change. As we know, historical materialism locates exploitation at the level of production relations. Emancipation originates from within the capital-labor dialectic, with the proletariat at the very cutting edge of the process of transformation. In other words, revolutionary consciousness and action radiate from the proletariat.

The capital-labor orbit in the periphery, however, betrays crucial divergencies from its counterpart at the center. Most noticeably, it is inhabited by "weak" bourgeoisies and "weak" proletariats. Historically, the bourgeoisie has been correctly viewed as a transformative dynamo, as it concentrates and centralizes capital in ways that lead to the sharpening of the contradictions between capital and labor out of which revolutionary change results (Dobb, 1975). In the periphery, these characteristics are overshadowed and minimized by state action. For the bourgeoisie, "weakness" translates mostly into the lack of economic resources and the consequential inability to generalize capitalist social relations and ideology within the class structures of these social formations. For the peripheral proletariat, weakness surfaces largely in terms of class size and the relative absence of a transforming consciousness. In the end, the determinate contradictions are not restricted to the capital-labor orbit and the relations of production; in fact, the social relations and practices of other classes (the peasants, for example) are brought more directly into the fundamental processes of change.

While I agree, overall, that the major source of differentiation between center and periphery resides in politico-economic factors, I think that this approach needs to be broadened to include a greater play for sociocultural factors indigenous to the peripheral formation. Here cultural factors assume greater importance than they have in formations at the center. The thesis of the articulation of modes of production has much to commend it, though its implications for examining the noneconomic aspects of noncapitalist forms have not been fully aired. We need to be more eclectic in borrowing freely from across paradigmatic boundaries to arrive at an understanding of peripheral class structures which gives cultural forms their due importance.

In summary, the introductory comments above prompt two related questions. First, is the weakness of the basic capitalist classes in the periphery a factor that undermines their revolutionary missions? Second, if so, where is the locus of revolutionary consciousness and action to be found? We shall have to seek appropriate answers in the manifestly different formulas of capitalization to which each sphere (that is, the center and the periphery) was exposed in its formative development under capitalism. In so doing, I shall demonstrate that the first question requires the consideration of other sources impacting on revolutionary consciousness and action. Let us now turn our attention to the contrasting forms of capitalization to which each sphere was exposed.

CONTRASTING CAPITALIZATION: CENTER VERSUS PERIPHERY

Contrasting capitalization describes a phenomenon originating in the asymmetrical process of capitalist development. Stripped to its essential features, the notion is at once definitional and explicative. First, it makes a profound distinction between those social formations which have been able to maximally transform their economies to the extent that the inner logic of the capitalist mode of production will allow, and those that have not done so. Second, contrasting capitalization exposes the pivotal processes transforming unfree into free labor. In more technical terms, it exposes the qualitative capitalization of labor, which assures the development of the forces of production and the concomitant qualitative changes in the social relations of production.

In turn, the capacity to convert one form of labor into the other engages the interplay of the entire ensemble of political, economic, and ideological relations, fashioning the key elements that shape agendas of development and change. Central to these agendas are dynamic capitalist classes—bourgeoisie and proletariat—whose impact on development and change varies inversely with the progressive erosion and modernization of pre and noncapitalist structures, forms, and social relations, or in other words, the proletarianization process. Of course, while many of these structures and social relations can be traced to the existence of unfree labor, others, such as those originating within the deeper recesses of culture, cannot be so defined. Applied to the development of social classes at the center, the Marxist dictum that culture is epiphenomenal carries some force. However, it fares less well in the periphery—an important distinction which will evolve more fully as this chapter unfolds.

I trust that my pursuit of brevity has not done undue violence to the classical notions of the Marxist theory of social change. The point is that orthodox Marxism confronts seeming anomalies in the periphery, as the movement from unfree to free labor has been impeded. There is an abundance of unfree labor, typified by a burgeoning Third World peasantry. Indeed, there is hardly a reasonable chance, as I will discuss below, that the classical Marxist project sketched earlier will ever come to pass.

Nevertheless, the asymmetries come together in the world system, underscored by accumulation on a world scale. This global process is indeed a horse of a different color, displaying much that is at the heart of the capitalist mode of production but betraying at the same time enough to render it significantly different. Samir Amin (1976: 360) describes the new global capitalist form in the following way:

> Capitalism has become a world system. The contradiction is not between the bourgeoisie and the proletariat of each country considered in isolation, but between the world bourgeoisie and the world proletariat. But this world bourgeoisie and this world proletariat do not fit into the framework of the capitalist mode of production —they belong to a system of capitalist formations, central and peripheral. Therefore the problem is: what

constitutes the world bourgeoisie and the world proletariat, respectively.

The important point here is that the two capitalisms now
articulated do not fit into the conventional framework of the
capitalist mode of production. I will argue that this is due
to the chronically unfree character of labor in the periphery, which runs contrary to the orthodox notions of social
classes with historic missions: bourgeoisies and proletariats in the periphery are endemically weak. Thus I suggest
that Amin's analysis, in spite of its useful insights, avoids
the important class implications of the globalization of
capital accumulation. It remains quite a puzzle both that
there is a main contradiction to these articulated capitalisms which are, in crucial ways, quite disparate; and also
that the contradiction originates between the world bourgeoisie and the world proletariat. The real issue is avoided, as
the characteristics of the peripheral bourgeoisie and proletariat are apparently explained away by a change of name.
The discussion of contrasting capitalization in the periphery
and the center will shed some light on these questions.

The ensemble of factors giving rise to the asymmetries
sketched above derives predominantly from a historical form
of undercapitalization. This process set in motion a complex
interplay of historical, structural, and cultural forces
which assisted in erecting barriers to the autonomous development of the periphery. Concretely, the shortage of investment capital from the original capitalist economies (England,
Germany, and France) played the major part in the backwardness of the periphery but was only one of several compenetrat-
ing agents of causation. Undercapitalization is therefore an
umbrella, under which resides a whole cluster of causal factors. The defining matrix remains the process of capital
accumulation, of which undercapitalization is one feature.
Both processes describe much more than quantitative patterns
of investment and rates of profit. Accumulation requires,
for instance, the institution and maintenance of certain
social relations, such as those attendant to the private
ownership of the means of production; further, ideological
structures, such as the lionizing of private enterprise are
as intrinsically part of the process as economic ones. These
general comments apply to undercapitalization, which has,
therefore, both quantitative and qualitative features. The
amounts of capital available to the periphery and its deployment patterns are not the lone referents of undercapitalization. We must include as part of a broader picture the sociocultural structures with which capital and capitalist institutions become articulated. Both the paucity of capital and
the resistance of pre and noncapitalist forms, for instance,
have contributed in an ever-evolving process to the development of social formations which are only incompletely and
partially transformed. Examining these factors will enable
us to understand why the basic capitalist classes in the
periphery cannot be the most prominent actors in revolutionary change and also why we need to focus greater attention,
as a matter of theory, on the noncapitalist and nonproperty
features of peripheral structures and social relations.
Briefly, these factors may be summarized as follows:

1. capital inflows to the periphery were insufficient
    to completely transform these social formations;

2. indigenous social structures impeded the inflow of
    investment capital or, when capital was present,
    displayed sufficient tenacity to influence the mode
    of its deployment;

3. under these circumstances, peripheral capitalism
    tended to aid and abet existing local practices
    which were inimical to the development of these
    economies;

4. as capitalism entrenched itself and moved from phase
    to phase, other noncapitalist features developed,
    which varied over time and place.

Without attempting to be exhaustive, I will now discuss some
of the more lasting patterns that emerged with undercapitalization.

THE IMPACT OF UNDERCAPITALIZATION

In the main, undercapitalization, as I have defined it,
did not occur at the center. As many analysts have shown
(Terray, 1972; Rey, 1973; Anderson, 1979), the articulation
of feudal Western Europe with the capitalist mode of production resulted mainly from the interplay of internal forces
transforming feudal relations into capitalist ones. These
forces were of two principal kinds: property relations and
the concomitant dynamics of social class.

In the first instance, changes of a capitalist complexion clustered around landownership, the institution of rent
payments, and the generalized conversion of labor into capital. From the perspective of social class, the rapid pace of
capitalist development which followed was due largely to two
factors: the peculiar transformation of investable capital
on site and the incestuous relationship that it bore to the
class structure. At the upper reaches of the class structure,
the process often involved individuals of vastly contrasting
social ranks (nobility, merchants, and usurers) but there was
little escaping the convergence of factors within English
society, for example, which would necessitate the one displa-
cing the other (Dobb, 1975: chs. 3-4; Bendix, 1964: 55-104).
At the lower reaches of the class structure, labor organized
as the necessary and structural outgrowth of its relationship
to capital. Increasingly, violence against the employer and
his property gave way to the rise of labor organizations:
"When the industrial capitalist appeared, the trade union
also appeared" (Beales, 1958: 85). There surfaced, in other
words, what has been termed a form of indigenous development
in which capital meshed with agreeable mixes of political,
ideological, and cultural factors (Bendix, 1964: 177).

When I speak of indigenous development, my intention is
hardly to underplay the significant role of colonial trade.
There is, however, an important distinction involving economic theories and practices and their implications for a systematic form of unequal relationship between the colonial

powers and their colonies, between the center and the periphery. In fact, the glorious years of colonial trade coincided with the glorious reign of mercantilism. It was a system of exploitation which hardly contemplated colonies as entities to be harmoniously integrated. The dynamics of trade and economic development were cast in the mold of a zero-sum game: the economic prosperity of England was hardly a dialectical process allowing the colonies to be integrated into a dynamic system of economic growth, made more effective by more rational institutional forms and agreeable ideologies. Implicit in this body of formulations and practice is a "bleed them dry" policy, equally disastrous, in the end, for the colonial power as well as the colony, as the examples of Spain and Portugal amply illustrate (Stein and Stein, 1970; Wesson, 1982).

The notion of indigenous development emerges from that combination of ample capital stock, rational institutional forms, and agreeable ideologies mentioned earlier. In England, which was the first capitalist economy in the developed sense of that term, the Bank of England and the National Debt were among the prime institutions to coordinate the monetary and credit system. This made capital resources available, as and when required, and in sufficiently mobile form (Gibbins, 1916; Beales, 1958). An abundance of concrete wealth, as the examples of Spain and Portugal also testify, is just one ingredient required for economic growth. The impact of the institutions mentioned above was to widen the sphere and redefine the bases of this growth: the fruits of colonial labor on agricultural plantations became complementary to the fruits of the labor employed in manufacturing and industry. Consequently, the intrinsic connection between the capitalist class, wealth, and the exertions of the worker took on a systematic, rational, and dialectical form.

Again, taking England as our example, the complementary ideological forms flowed out of the principles of laissez-faire and democracy, and from cultural peculiarities. Laissez-faire and democracy had instilled the tendency to convert inequality into abstract democratic principles, through, for example, the political fiction of the collective will. This elaborate ideological device brought to heel the capitalist as well as the worker relative to freedom, fair play, and similar matters. It served to couch exploitation in a form that could promote capitalist interests as well as those of the worker. In fact, the rise of the trade union movement in Europe owes a great deal to the principles of democracy. The canonized egalitarianism associated with this principled application of democratic practices promoted tendencies favoring popular struggle (legal emancipation, a free labor market, and so on). As Therborn has remarked, "these were all intrinsic tendencies which simultaneously lay the basis for a working class movement of a strength and stability inachievable by the exploited classes of the precapitalist modes of production" (1977: 29).[1]

The role of culture here is quite interesting. Is there something endemic to culture which typifies attitudes to life redounding at once to the benefit of democracy and capitalist development? Tom Nairn (1977) found this to be the case in the rise of capitalism in England. Prodemocratic tendencies flowing from the English ethos were immeasurably responsible for the emergence of the liberal state. It was this liberalism which promoted civil conventions of self-regulation, adding (by inference) cultural forces to the systemic ones shaping the antagonism between the capitalist and the worker.[2]

Overall, these patterns contrast rather vividly with events accompanying the rise of capitalism in the periphery. Contrary to the confident declarations of Marx himself and of many early Western-oriented development theorists as well, the periphery does not seem likely to ever emerge as a carbon copy of the developed capitalist economies. Equally faulty, however, were the later, Third-World oriented predictions of perennial underdevelopment and dependency, based largely on distinctions between foreign and local capital and on the destructive properties of the former.

We are better able now to understand that the capitalization of the periphery occurred on a meeting ground of the laws of motion of capital and local circumstances, which would here aid and abet, and would there resist, the encroachments of capital. This created the patterns that would provide the foundation for peripheral capitalism as a distinct form spawned from the parent model. While the variations created by historical circumstances are enormous, there is agreement on the processes which shaped the class structures of peripheral social formations, thereby giving them a degree of regularity. As I stated in my introductory comments, three sets of related processes have had a defining impact on these formations:

1. the relatively sparse quantities of capital deployed from the center and the restricted economic avenues into which this capital flowed;

2. the resulting hybrid social forms and their impact; and

3. the effect of those structures and processes which remained largely unchanged by outside intrusion, either because of the marginal effect of incoming capital or by reason of an intrinsic resistance to it.

Let us begin with capital deployment to the periphery. First, capital resources were hardly deployed in the form and quantities to promote a sustained reorganization of peripheral class structures. It has been suggested that during the early stages of industrial capitalist development, the bulk of available capital was required at home, where it was absorbed in the task of industrializing the home base (Lublinskaya, 1968: 75). In periods of demonstrable excess, this policy of restrained capital outflow to the periphery remained seemingly unchanged. Throughout the nineteenth century, for example, the discovery of gold in California and Australia increased the coinage issued by Britain, France, and the United States nearly six-fold, from £ 4.9 million to £ 28.1 million (Hobsbawm, 1975: 35). Nevertheless, these changes hardly affected traditional investment patterns.

If we take England as an example, we find considerable selectivity in investment patterns. Up to World War I, the bulk of investments (nearly 80 percent) were concentrated in some seven countries or regions, with little apparent discrimination between colonial possessions and independent countries. Three of these--India-Ceylon, Argentina, and Brazil --were part of what is now termed the periphery, a fact that will require some comment later. The others--the United States, Canada-Newfoundland, Australia-New Zealand, and South Africa--are now all within the developed sphere. The vast majority of the countries of the world, the prized possessions of European colonial powers, received very little capital as investment (Feis, 1965: 23).

While we remain in the strictly economic sphere, I should also remind the reader that the selectivity exercised with respect to geography was also at work in the type of venture likely to receive support. While the occasional peripheral forays into sugar refining, meat packing, rubber production, and similar manufactures were not substantial or successful enough to attract even modest support (Rippy, 1959: 159-60), the bulk of investment in the pre-World War I period (85 percent) went to railway securities, loans to governments, and infrastructural projects (Feis, 1965: 27). The point is not that such investments are bad in themselves but that, in becoming inserted in a particular socioeconomic structure, they may serve to complement and entrench existing forms of production which are inimical to further development along the route followed by the center. The enforced specialization of the periphery in agriculture and other primary goods is a case in point. Railroads in Latin America served to open up the country to more production of cattle and other food stuffs destined to feed the hungry workers of Birmingham, but they did nothing to stimulate the manufacturing industries so important for the growth of the Center.

While there is no question that laws and policies were deliberately employed to promote the economic growth of the colonial powers at the expense of the colonies if need be (the destruction of India's textile industry is a case in point), it is also true that investors' decisions were dictated largely by the tripartite "golden rule": opportunity for profit, security, and familiarity. It is here that such factors as the presence of virgin land versus land encumbered by ancestral rights, political stability, compatible customs and cultures, and a sound financial and commercial infrastructure come into play in directing the investment process. If capital went to turbulent parts of the world like Latin America, it was because the lure of profits and the presence of gunboats off the coast served to comfort all but the most timid hearts (Hagen, 1976: 428).

In all cases, these factors and the constant competition for capital from the center combined to spell a general scarcity. Unable to sweep aside or mold existing economic and social practices to its image, capital found easy accommodation by promoting partial modifications--migrant labor systems, for instance--which filled its needs without at the same time contributing to the advancement of the peripheral formation to a higher level of development. Articulated with such pre- and noncapitalist practices during its formative stage, capitalism in the periphery established a base which is entirely different from that of the center, and which continues to this day.

In this way we begin to grasp the main ingredients of a systematic structure of unfree labor and hybrid social classes (the "peasantariat" is perhaps the latest coinage in this realm: see Parson, 1984). However, in order to fully grasp the processes involved in this creation and its significance for agendas of emancipation, we must take into account the broader meaning of undercapitalization, that is, its qualitative, cultural dimension. The fact of the matter is that capital is not money or wealth but a social relation. Its deployment and accumulation call into play all social realms, broadly defined, through the agency of people joined in classes--people with ideas, social mores, attitudes, and beliefs that cannot be entirely defined by their class location.

Some ideological perceptions inimical to capitalist development were taken, along with capital, to the periphery, where they flourished in contact with local forms. Paternalism is one such ideology, inimical because it fosters particularistic social relations tending at once to inhibit the emancipation of the bourgeoisie and the construction of working class consciousness. The familiar motto of the Brazilian bourgeoisie that "industry is unnatural" (Frank, 1967: 161-63) makes the point. Conspicuous consumption becomes the norm, or even the social duty of the bourgeoisie, while severely undermining the habits of thrift on which economic development depends.

Yet capital and ideologies from the center also met with peripheral practices and ideologies which reacted in varying ways to the encounter. Many peripheral features impeded development almost to the degree that they permitted easy access to the investor. For the most part, these features are the other ingredients of undercapitalization as I described it. The continuing backwardness of India can in large measure be attributed to the cumulative impact of many such phenomena. Religion is one example. Compared to Islam or Buddhism, the Hindu religion evinced an openness to capitalist penetration by being at once largely apolitical, in the general sense of the term, and other-worldly. Hinduism stresses transcendent purity as being prior in time and importance to the social standing of the individual. This process of purification is rooted in the immanence of a hierarchical order (the caste system), which is sustained by ascriptive ritual activities serving in part as an otherworldly guide to the social order. The rootedness of ascription largely ensures the nonpolitical dimension, inasmuch as a form of religious absolutism becomes preemptive: "It is fairly established in the Indian's mind that Parmeshwar (the Almighty) has decreed his existence and condition from the beginning of time; it is futile to try to change His Will" (Rangnekar, 1958: 66). The other-worldly takes precedence over and guides the direction of mundane activities. Patterns of social mobility, for instance, are all related to the dynamics within and between castes without undermining the structure of the sociocultural order (Eisenstadt, 1978: 120). Of course, these arrangements form part of a heterogenous network of structural-organizational factors rendering the social order more tolerant of foreign influences (Eisenstadt, 1965: 668).

Another example is the persistence of tradition which
remains quite coercive even in the face of structural
change. Let us glance at landlord-tenant relations in
contemporary Bihar, India:

> A group of tenants of a big landlord in Almora district
> vehemently protested against my suggestion that no land-
> lord should be allowed to keep more than he could culti-
> vate with his family labor. They remarked, "In this
> village we are all small people and if that landlord
> were reduced to our level, whom shall we approach in
> times of need and who would protect us against outsi-
> ders?" I attributed the villagers' reply to fear of the
> landlord and to their backwardness. But as my under-
> standing of village life became deeper I found their
> answer realistic, because no alternative source of help
> was yet available for the villagers. (Joshi, 1981: 472)

Of course, a good portion of these attitudes can be traced to
the peculiar social definitions of land under the Moguls and
later, the zamindars (Moore, 1967; Ray, 1975). Their most
persistent remnants exist in the form of an ingrained paternalism which is not significantly affected by the arrival of
more observable forms of bourgeois landed property (Alavi,
1980).

Let me now give a synopsis of British economic policy.
The colonies as well as the independent Latin American countries were merely markets and farms. The accompanying economic theory systematized by Ricardo reasoned that capital
accumulation and the maintenance of high profits depended on
the existence of cheap sources of food. As labor employed in
industrial pursuits is more productive than agricultural labor, it was prudent to maximize the former at home, leaving
the colonies and the rest of the world to provide food for
the industrial worker. As Ricardo put it, "If . . . in the
progress of countries in wealth and population, new portions
of fertile land could be added to such countries, with every
increase of capital, profits would never fall, nor rents
rise" (Gonner, 1966: 231). This task of finding adequate
supplies of food for the industrial proletariat of Birmingham
and Manchester was exacting. Indeed, the rate of population
growth far outstripped agricultural production by 1911
(Hobson, 1927: 450).

It is therefore quite obvious that investment policies
were structured around discrete patterns of capital accumulation. Countries such as Argentina and Brazil were merely
pieces of fresh fertile land appended to Britain's economy.
The huge investments in railways, bridges, and the infrastructure of these economies were associated with a particular
formula: the periphery must repay its debts "by feeding the
rapidly growing populations and industries" (Kahn, 1946: 43).

There was hardly a more effective recipe for entrenching
backwardness. First, confining the periphery to agriculture
and mining hampered the maximal capitalization of labor. Had
industrialization and manufacturing been encouraged, the resulting network of linkages would have pushed these economies
toward greater self-propulsion. Instead, laws were enacted
preventing the production of certain agricultural crops in
England, doubtless based on the proposition that British

labor and land could be more productively utilized through industrialization.[3]

Second, the development of dynamic social relations (aggressive bourgeoisies and vibrant proletariats) was also impeded. Promoting agriculture to a large degree encouraged pre- and noncapitalist forms and relations (peasantries and a variety of arcane tenancies, for example) which frustrated higher levels of development. These patterns would have invariably involved the progressive transformation of unfree into free labor. Overall, the periphery may have produced its Alexander Hamiltons, but the necessary conditions for forcing the hand of the British investor, as Hamilton indeed did, were hardly opportune.[4] Instead, the periphery labored under mounting constraints, some of which legislated against the deployment of skilled personnel and technology for its development (Court, 1967: 55). It is not surprising to learn that only 2 percent of British capital investment actually went into Latin American manufacturing up until the First World War (ECLA, 1965: 17).

Let us now turn to the more illustrative aspects of contemporary capital accumulation. Assuredly, the trek of global socioeconomic events from the late nineteenth century to the present is a journey from the competitive phase to the so-called monopoly phase of capitalism. It is also true that while structures, relations, and institutions have altered over the period, they have done so largely to accommodate the fundamental principles of capitalism. We may characterize the situation as one that produces variables within a matrix held together by invariable principles.

At present, capital shortages in the periphery remain a fact of life, and foreign investment invariably feeds into production-consumption cycles which are nothing more than variations on an old theme. Perhaps this contention can best be illustrated with reference to the so-called "semiperiphery" --the most developed of the underdeveloped economies. Overall, their case is quite interesting, both because the impact of undercapitalization is more visible and also as they reveal a glaring contradiction with profound implications for development and social change: the increasing development of the forces of production does not result in a corresponding development of the social relations of production as the growth and entrenchment of the basic capitalist classes is curtailed by the activist policies of the state. In these social formations, the combined force of state and foreign capital coalesce into what one commentator termed "repressive capitalist development from above and outside" (Petras, 1981: 50). The phenomenon, which remained quite evident throughout the late 1970s and the early 1980s, entrapped the historic missions of bourgeoisie and proletariat by dismantling the political mechanisms through which the interests and positions of these classes were articulated: the state had abolished politics (Evans, 1979: 265-66).[5] It was also an abolition carrying a more than subtle form of chastisement, as these classes were ridiculed for their inability "to generate either an electoral consensus or charismatic leadership" (Horowitz, 1982: 101).

My brief, largely economic analysis will explore the manner in which the profits of characteristically small inflows of capital to the periphery are maximized. At the same time I will give a sense of the seemingly fixed nature of these arrangements, substantiating the proposition that undercapitalization is consistent with a kind of permanent partial development of the periphery.

Analyses of the performance of foreign capital in these economies over the period of bureaucratic authoritarianism are well known and require little elaboration (O'Donnell, 1973; Canak, 1984; Stepan, 1978; Philip, 1984). The period witnessed a significant movement of foreign investment accompanied by rapid increases in production. In the notable example of Brazil, the economy maintained an average increase of 19.3 percent annually for the period 1969-1972--the most difficult years of bureaucratic authoritarian rule. Countries like Argentina did not boast such impressive growth, but the levels were still significant (Kaufman, 1979:231). These figures faltered somewhat in the succeeding years due to the effects of the energy crises and the outmodedness of import substitution, but the overall performance was quite creditable. The growth rate fell dramatically between 1976 and 1979, to an average of 4 to 5 percent, and dropped even more precipitously in the 1980s due to the combined impact of negative growth rates and mounting debt-servicing difficulties. On the financial front, the share of external financing in foreign capital inflows doubled for the two decades up to 1970, while direct investment declined at an identical rate. Indeed, the anticipated breakthroughs calculated to minimize the openness of these economies to metropolitan capital had not been realized (Kaufman, 1979: 234).

This pattern of growth without development is traceable, in large part, to specific formulas of capitalization. The revitalized investment climate to which these economies were attracted was part of a larger phenomenon: the accelerated rate of capital exports after the Second World War, in which public capital was destined to play a crucial role.

Up until World War I, capital exports had been overwhelmingly of private origins, with the bulk of capital (some 69 percent) going to Europe and the "newer" colonialized countries (the U.S., Canada, and the "colonies of settlement"). After the Second World War, the periphery began to receive a large flow of capital. In fact, some 64 percent of long-term capital exports between 1951 and 1961 went to the periphery. The pattern of distribution of private and public capital, however, has much to tell us about the phenomenon of permanent partial development. Table 1.1 summarizes this pattern, which has continued beyond the period for which figures are provided.

Viewed more closely, the figures are quite revealing. Private direct investment, the most dynamic of the three types, was conspicuously low in the periphery. In fact, the ratio of public to private capital flowing to the periphery and the metropolis was almost exactly reversed: three to one for the periphery (75 percent public capital) and one to three for the metropolis (76 percent private capital). Indeed, the share of the private capital invested in the periphery, as opposed to the industrial economies, declined further over the succeeding years. What is more, a sizeable portion of this direct investment consisted of reinvested earnings, with 43 percent of the periphery's direct investment coming in this form (Jalee, 1973: 72).

TABLE 1.1
LONG-TERM CAPITAL EXPORTS, 1951-1961 (billions of $)

		Exports To Periphery	Exports to Metropolis	Total Exports
Public Capital	Grants	22	1	23
	Loans	12	5	17
Private Capital	Investments	11.5	19.5	31
TOTAL Capital Exports		45.5	25.5	71

Source: Adapted from Jalee, 1972: 69-70.

While these data refer to the 1960s, the pattern seems to have entrenched itself over time. Brazil provides a good example: by 1972, direct private investment exceeded $2 billion and was increasing at the rate of 25 percent annually. At the same time, however, the other two categories of investment seemed to have kept pace. Public capital (U.S. economic and military assistance) amounted to $4.2 billion, while long-term capital of public origin (disbursements from multilateral banks, and so on) contributed another $4.7 billion. A total public investment of $9 billion was pumped into the Brazilian economy for the period 1962 through 1976 (Petras, 1981: 75). Table 1.2 gives us a sense of the traditional investment patterns that are generalizable throughout the periphery.

TABLE 1.2
CAPITAL FLOWS TO AND FROM THE UNITED STATES
AND LATIN AMERICA (millions of dollars)

	Net Capital Flow from United States	Reinvested Earnings	Interest Dividend Remitted to United States	Fees & Royalties
1966	303	309	708	175
1967	311	202	918	211
1968	708	361	825	247
1969	385	331	906	267
1970	579	453	514	274
1971	696	373	688	269
1972	272	645	270	259
1973	645	991	529	269
1974	2,208	1,109	927	341
1975	1,215	1,621	-21	376
1976	145	1,302	796	299
TOTAL	7,476	7,697	7,061	2,987

Source: Selected Data on U.S. Direct Investment Abroad, 1966-76. U.S. Department of Commerce, Bureau of Economic Analysis. Petras, 1981:76.

Some fifty-one percent of total U.S. direct investment in Latin America results from reinvested earnings. The additional point is that while the major portion of invested capital in Latin America is derived from outside sources, quite often these funds are obtained from within the Latin American economies. Over eighty percent of the capital financing of U.S. majority-owned corporations originates from non-U.S. sources (Petras, 1981: 76).

Now to the consequences. First, these three types of seemingly different capitals work in tandem and are largely responsive to the existing requirements of capital accumulation. As is well recorded, the bulk of public capital gets to the periphery in the form of loans, grants, and other types of aid, which are not directly introduced into productive economic ventures. This species of capital functions mainly to reproduce the conditions favoring capitalist relations. Whether geared to the peripheral infrastructure or associated with education, public health, or other public sector investments, these capital outlays are invariably tied to technical assistance packages having more to do with the principal objectives of the donor countries than those of the recipients. In the end, these funds get fed into Keynesian pump-priming mechanisms, which more often than not have little to do with the expansion of the productive capacity in the periphery. It is also well recorded that recipient countries which attempt to place their own developmental priorities over metropolitan directives often come in for a good deal of punishment.[6]

Capital disbursements from multilateral banks serve an almost identical purpose. Lending institutions like the World Bank and the IMF (International Monetary Fund) tend to operate religiously within orthodox capitalist guidelines. The IMF, for example, still bases its lending on restrictive monetary policies and a free-market system of prices. The centerpieces of the IMF's formula for success are devaluations and prices and income policies which penalize labor in favor of capital, while devices such as protective tariffs and import licensing are condemned. Overall, this approach limits local capital formation, increases unemployment, and places the economic advantage in the hands of foreign capital (Petras, 1981; Robinson, 1979).

These two types of capital perform a supportive role which can be aligned to the expansion of productive capacity in the periphery only in a most indirect sense. Combined, they function to shore up the revenue bases of peripheral economies, thereby enabling the generation of profits of the kind reflected in Table 1. Public capital writ large merely prepares the ground for direct capital investment, which is richly rewarded in spite of its comparatively small volume.

It is primarily this small volume which promotes backwardness in the periphery. The causal factors derive from three different directions. The state of the periphery accounts for the first. Much of the earlier discussion on the structural and ideational unpreparedness of the periphery for maximum capitalist "take-off" applies here. It is beyond serious dispute that the structural organization of the periphery does not to this day command larger outlays of direct private investment and, even to the extent that it does so, the socioeconomic framework is simply not equal to the task required by capitalist principles. Local capital has been prevented from participating in the more productive sectors in any of a number of ways. Where it was not too small and disorganized, it suffered from a low intrinsic profitability vis-a-vis its foreign counterpart, which was invariably of a higher organic composition; at times it could even be excluded unilaterally by the policies of the foreign investor.

It seems ironic, then, that the greater the outlay of public capital (in the sense that I have defined it), the greater the incidence of underdevelopment and the more varied the modes of economic theory and practice within the two spheres. In the net, direct private capital remains comparatively small--a feature which forces it into a deepening instead of a widening of strategies to maximize profits.

The second factor associating backwardness with the limited volume of direct private investment is derived in part from the prevailing rules of capital deployment. In the inevitable competition for investment capital the center prevails. Of course, this results from the principles of uneven development inherent in the capitalist mode of production. However, in the short term, this structural tendency forces an imperative on the limited direct investment going to the periphery: it must seize every opportunity to maximize profits within the limits set by this competition and it must further bend every socioeconomic structure of the periphery toward that end.

This explains in part the flurry of activity aimed at creating, modifying, or rehabilitating anomalous structures and social relations in the periphery. Often these new forms are clearly at odds with the dynamics of capitalism at the center. As I indicated earlier, the emasculation of the bourgeoisie as well as the proletariat, the abolition of politics and the overbearing role of the state are typical examples.[7]

Third, the phenomenon of scarcity is further buoyed in its consequences by certain structural features in the periphery. It should be evident that these economies do not need to be carbon copies of the metropole for enormous profits to be realized. In the process, it would appear that the dialectics of labor, so central to the Marxist conception of revolutionary change, is compromised.

Labor relations, as I will later demonstrate, have taken a variety of forms which in the end dovetail into capital accumulation. For example, it is no longer necessary to proletarianize the peasant in order to extract profits and generally support an economy's productive capacity. Through unequal exchange, labor can create surplus without the worker being reduced to the status of a wage laborer (Amin, 1977; Roemer, 1982).

The immediate consequences for revolutionary change via class action are twofold. First, to the extent that proletarianization promotes political action, arresting that process tends to retard collective action. Richard Curtain's essay in this volume points to the earlier practice of German colonialism in Papua New Guinea, in which the flow of proletarianization was arrested by legislative fiat. Similar policies aimed in the main at minimizing or preventing political instability are part of contemporary metropolitan calculations. Second, to the extent that the commoditization of labor is stymied, so too is the economy's capacity to increase the rate of capital formation and ultimately to reduce the incidence of unfree labor.

Before summarizing the main positions of this section, I will comment further on the state activism to which I referred earlier. Under the conditions described, the state in the periphery, unlike its counterpart at the center, is forced into remedial work: its main task is to structure the entire ensemble of socioeconomic relations in the periphery to meet the special requirements of the pattern of capital deployment I described above and to generally promote capital accumulation. As often, therefore, as it penalizes and even represses the basic capitalist classes in the interest of overall accumulation, the state rushes in to create or resuscitate, promoting a bureaucratic bourgeoisie in Tanzania (Saul, 1979) or in Jamaica (Keith and Keith, 1985); a middle class in Chile (Grant, 1983); or elements of a national bourgeoisie in Colombia (Mayorga, 1978). Of the other classes, we see, for example, a strengthened working class in Argentina under Peron (Corradi, 1974) and the resuscitation of the peasantry in Colombia to maintain political stability (Galli, 1978).

It is easy to see the abundant weaknesses in these class-state relations--particularly for the classes involved, but for the state as well.[8] Classes created and supported by the state tend in large measure to be subject to its whims and fancies--a fragility originating in the weak and unstable economic and political conditions out of which these classes emerged. Parenthetically, the weak basic capitalist classes here should be contrasted with their counterpart at the center. Many of the distinctions between strong, vibrant bourgeoisies and proletariats (at the center) and their enfeebled counterparts (in the periphery) can be traced to the role of the state in civil society, where state action is prompted largely by class directives arising from a robust economic base and highly self-centered political mechanisms; this should be counterposed to the authoritarianism in the periphery where the conditions for class hegemony of that kind never existed (see the chapter by Bamat in this volume).

I will now summarize the main points of this section in the following way:

1. The flow of capital to the periphery came into a natural and inevitable competition with indigenous investment and development at the center. Overall, the tug-o'-war was resolved in favor of the center, precipitating two crucial results: first, capital to the periphery was in chronically short supply and second, the capital so deployed was forced to employ ingenious methods to maximize profits. While the process of investment encountered a variety of historical situations in which to promote accumulation, the fundamental principles of profit maximization remained largely intact.

2. As a flexible, rational system, capitalism, if denied optimal conditions for entrenchment and expansion (that is, conditions which support the productive flow of capital-labor relations), will create suitable alternatives.

3. The development of capitalism in phases (mercantile, competitive, and monopoly) does not allow the periphery to rebound once the fundamental limits placed on its development, largely through the forces of undercapitalization, have been systematized.

4. Because of the authoritarian character of peripheral societies (as compared to the civil form of their metropolitan counterpart), the state arrogates to itself enormous powers both contributing to and assisted by the systemic weaknesses of social classes, particularly the basic capitalist classes.

I will now discuss the phenomenon of unfree labor which is endemic to the capitalist mode of production itself. A major result here is that these dynamics tend to reinforce the rigidities of peripheral class configurations.

UNFREE AND FREE LABOR

It should be relatively simple to make the connection between meager capital investment and unfree labor. We must, however, get a surer sense of the contemporary structure of the phenomenon and the way in which the capitalist mode of production in its own right promotes its continuing existence.

First, the pivotal role of labor in the cycle of socioeconomic development can hardly be controverted. With regard to process, the formation of agricultural surplus and its realization into commodity form are directly linked to labor. At the heart of cognate formulations about labor and its relationship to profits is the theory of value. Among other things, the theory states that, depending on the level and intensity of exploitation and domination, basic capitalist classes will emerge whose potential for fundamental change (that is, toward socialism) will vary with the sharpness and intensity of the contradictions between capital and labor. It is primarily in this sense, according to the theory of value, that the change from unfree to 'free' labor is so important.

The initial impact of chronic capital shortage on the periphery frustrates the designs of socialism, partly as the levels of invested capital are insufficient to fundamentally transform the other modes of production to commodity production. This quantitative explanation is at best partial, however, and must be conflated with others. Indeed, it should be noted that the capitalist mode of production possesses a natural tendency to create unfree labor. The gist of this position is that accumulation is structured from a systemic interpenetration of the so-called extended reproduction (social production) and subsistence production. The first of these defines the transformation of labor into commodity form, while subsistence production is related to the "reproduction of life and of living capacity" upon which the former unalterably depends (Bennholdt-Thomsen, 1982: 241).

The labor employed in extended reproduction is compensated by wages, but that of subsistence production, apart from being unremunerated in a good many cases, serves to shore up pre- and noncapitalist practices and relations.[9]

The labor of the peasant, which is seen mainly as producing use values, is invaluable to extended reproduction.

Overall, the peasant's subordination takes three major forms:

1. Family members who work in agriculture are, inter-mittently, wage earners on large agricultural es-tates. This preponderance of seasonal or occasional wage employment (casual labor) is most inimical to the peasant's interests. Among its effects are low wages, weak organization, restricted development of the peasantry, and the maintenance of arcane belief systems.

2. When a peasant migrates to the urban areas, it in-variably leads to a life of petty trading, car washing, shoe shining, and the like--occupations instilling and maintaining precapitalist tendencies and ideologies (Saffiotti, 1977: 31).

3. Capital tends to exercise increasing control over the process of peasant production through such de-vices as credit agreements. In this way, many of the basic relations associated with unfree labor are extended or preserved.

Thus in the periphery the development of the productive forces involves artisan work, production for direct consump-tion, and exploitation under nonwage forms. We should hardly wonder, then, that peasantries are a regular and unyielding feature of our contemporary socioeconomic landscape. Of course, this situation cannot be totally ascribed to the ca-prices of capitalism, as in some instances the inner resili-ence of that mode of production makes its own contribution, often through cultural means, to the continuing existence of the class (see Steven Johnson's chapter, in this volume). In other cases, the peasantries may have been able to maintain themselves through successful agitation for land reforms--a success which in some cases can be traced directly to the weakness of the bourgeoisie (Marini, 1976; Montoya Rojas, 1978).

What are quite noteworthy, however, are the concerted efforts of foreign capital and international institutions, such as the World Bank, to assist in this rehabilitation pro-cess. While the World Bank and International Labor Organiza-tion (ILO) recommend supporting existing peasantries as well as injecting new blood into the informal sectors of Third World cities, multinational corporations lend a hand in keep-ing peasantries alive by manipulating credit arrangements and restructuring tenancies (Tobis, 1980; Taussig, 1978).[10]

The mechanisms that promote unfree labor within the schema of extended reproduction-social production discussed above, do so largely in an indirect way. However, there are more direct ways which at once entrench this form of labor and frustrate the development of the basic capitalist classes. This is the case, for instance, with the Colombian peasantry, in areas where peasant farming proves more efficient and pro-fitable than its capitalist counterpart. The resulting effi-ciency advantage enjoyed by the peasant farmer translates into an appreciable decrease in maintaining and reproducing wage labor, with a noticeable consequence being the arrested development of the working class:

> This structural feature of peripheral economies, whose market lies at the centers of the world capitalist system, means that concern with increasing workers' purchasing power is secondary to the drive for unlimited expansion of production. Hence, reducing the value of labor or maintaining it at a low level makes for less contradictions than in advanced capitalist economies, and semiproletarianization of the peasantry as opposed to complete proletarianization is in keeping with such a structure. Moreover, this same structural feature precludes the conditions necessary to sustain a fully fledged, "pure" proletariat. (Taussig, 1978: 67)

Even when conditions allow the creation of a pure proletariat, the commoditization of labor itself carries tendencies which limit proletarianization. One of these tendencies is embedded in the requirement of high technical efficiency coupled with the need to constantly replace living labor (wage labor) with "dead" labor (machinery and other technical innovations). Singly or in combination, both requirements betray a low capacity for absorbing labor. Theoretically, there should be little cause for alarm, as significant profits would normally be expected to move horizontally into other sectors rather than moving out vertically. However, the undeveloped state of the periphery and the mobile nature of capital tend to propel capital outward in pursuit of more attractive opportunities. There appears to be little surcease from appealing to the foreign investor as a good corporate citizen or applying strong-arm tactics.

In any event, the transformation of labor is impeded along with the development of basic capitalist classes. A couple of examples should suffice. The first of these revolves around worker-per-factory densities. In his studies of the Jamaican working class, Munroe (1981: 70-71) found that this ratio held steadily over a thirty-year span (the years of rapid industrialization) even though the absolute numbers of factories and workers increased over the period. Low worker-per-factory densities impede political organization and, in Munroe's view, this contributed handily to the lack of development of the working-class movement in that country.

Subcontracting and off-shore assembling of light manufactures provide the other example. The impediment here is the decomposition of the labor process, that is, the utilization of technology under the new international division of labor to break down complex processes into relatively simple functions which require unskilled and semiskilled workers only. On the whole, the wage laborforce increases but its political and ideological practices are often thrown into disarray. The unskilled, the semiskilled, the reserve army of labor, the active and passive political elements, and the classical proletariat all come together. However, the process of reconciling this motley aggregation and forging a collective consciousness is often quite elusive as there is an abundance of factors inhibiting the consolidation of working-class consciousness, such as balkanization and impediments to unionization.[11]

This form of production of industrialized goods for a small or reduced market tends to recreate and reinforce precapitalist activities (domestic servants, yardboys, car washers, shoeshine boys) alternating with petty commodity production where possible. Such situations betray peculiar ideological and political forms: for instance, it is not unusual to find the politics and ideology of the subordinate classes (the lumpen and the subproletariats, for example) swinging wildly between fascism and socialism, depending on the vagaries of the moment (Taylor, 1979: 237-40). It is no surprise that the forcible emasculation of labor by the state progresses the farthest in peripheral economies.

My final comment in this section will be directed to the state. Already I have hinted at its peculiar role in peripheral social formations. I will now summarize the main features of this role, particularly with reference to its mediations within and among articulating modes of production. Foweraker (1981: 102) captures the essence of this role quite well:

> What is important to emphasize is that with the dominance of capitalism, a capitalist State is founded historically on the basis of a heterogeneous economic base, where different modes of production are present. This implies, in turn, that the State has the historical task not only of articulating the growing world capitalist market for goods and capital with the domestic economy . . . but also of underpinning politically the articulation of different modes of production, to guarantee, for example, both the reproduction of the relations of appropriation within the different modes themselves and the reproduction of the mechanisms for the transfer of surplus from the subordinate modes to the dominant capitalism.

The principal functions of the peripheral state may be summarized as follows:

1. To promote capital accumulation. The interests so promoted, of course, are both local and foreign, and are not always identical. The function of the state here is to mediate in accordance with the principles in the quote above.

2. To be sensitive and accommodating to the totality of class interests in the social formation. The state is not merely an instrument of capital or the capitalist mode of production; it arises from the processes by which precapitalist forms become integrated into international capitalism. This is a crucial distinction which separates the peripheral state from its metropolitan counterpart, whose role is hardly that of mediating and harmonizing the dynamics of different modes of production coexisting in a single geographical space (Vergopoulos, 1983: 43). If it owes its forms and function to this special type of articulation, then the state must mediate two broad sets of structures and relations with an eye on some measure of balance: it must promote the

accumulation of foreign capital as well as responding to or mediating the contradictions associated with various pre- and noncapitalist forms peculiar to the lesser modes and which remain as central features of the overarching process of articulation. The lesser modes can be best brought into metropolitan designs by this process, and a master strategy actually ensures the continuing existence of a good portion of their intrinsic characteristics. In fact, many peculiarly pre and noncapitalist forms command state mediation, but not in a fashion that is partial to metropolitan designs, as Frank and others would have it; in a way, these pre and noncapitalist forms also command equal time. It is mainly for these reasons that the state must be seen as the most important social relation in the periphery--even more important than the capitalist mode of production (Vergopoulos, 1983: 44). The logic of the peripheral state is rooted in the materiality of articulations, which embraces cardinal questions of exploitation and emancipation relative to all the articulated modes of production, acting singly or in combinations.

3.   To ensure the state's own continuing reproduction. This process involves a complex system of mediations among classes and other interests competing for scarce resources and political power. Here laissez-faire principles hover at best at the margins, as the state preempts the spotlight: civil society is dominant at the center, but it is the state that flourishes in the periphery. In social formations where state action has verged toward authoritarianism, mediation has led to the emasculation of both basic capitalist classes, pushing them back (especially the working class) in the direction of their precapitalist origins.

This brief summary by no means exhausts the functions of the peripheral state. I have merely isolated those features immediately relevant to the two overlapping concerns of this chapter, namely, weak basic capitalist classes and the central place of nonproperty and noneconomic factors in the practices of social classes in the periphery. Immediately, it should be noted that the all-embracing process of articulation over which the state presides has taken disciplined notice and yielded ample time to the pre- and noncapitalist classes and their practices. Inasmuch as this is the case, the production and emancipation features of the parent modes of production of these classes are pivotal in their own right--a fact borne out in large measure by their prominence, as well as by the intermodal balancing undertaken by the state.

I have attempted in this segment to make the case for unfree labor as a kind of perpetual condition under peripheral capitalism. Unfree labor, as I discussed it, is kept intact by the dynamics of center-periphery contact and, structurally, by the logic of the capitalist mode of production in association with the peripheral state. The net result of the persistence of this form of labor is the determinate role of nonproperty and noneconomic factors which I will now discuss.

NONPROPERTY AND NONECONOMIC PHENOMENA

In this section, I will move beyond the conceptual limits set by most contributors to this volume. Some of the pieces, notably those of Curtain, and (less so) Johnson, have admittedly addressed some of these phenomena, but have not departed in any significant way from the main principles of the proletarianization theme. There remains some devotion to the role of the working class as the principal agent of change.

I think that the working class thesis is somewhat overworked. While it can be stressed that history and experience support this position, there is much in current area studies that questions the automatism involved here. My own queries on the subject will be raised in three specific contexts: the direct consequences of permanent partial proletarianization; cultural-anthropological issues; and collective consciousness and action. The analysis will not transgress the principles of historical materialism as a method, though my particular use of cultural-anthropological factors will not sit too well with the unrepentant materialists within the Marxist fold.

Finally, the reader should not expect an exhaustive treatment of these topics. My immediate hope is twofold: First, to attempt to indicate the source of tensions in some of the chapters between religion, ethnicity, and race, on the one hand, and the structural determinism of wage labor. Secondly, I wish to remind the researcher of a fertile area of investigation which is unceasing in its invitation of probing analyses.

Permanent Partial Proletarianization

Samir Amin's perceptive observations on the structure of contemporary capitalism are a convenient starting point. He does well to distinguish between the two "capitalisms" (peripheral and advanced) now constituting a world system. To quote him again, "the world bourgeoisie and the world proletariat do not fit into the framework of the capitalist mode of production--they belong to a system of capitalist formations, central and peripheral."

After making this vital distinction, Amin appears to lapse into ironclad determinism and monocausality: the principal contradictions associated with generating collective consciousness and social change flow from the tensions existing between the bourgeoisie and the proletariat. The two capitalisms conflate, but the factors distinguishing one from the other are not sufficient to fundamentally affect the loci of these contradictions. Of course, revolutionary leadership remains the preserve of these basic capitalist classes, even though they may be chronically weak and ineffectual. Implied here also is the notion that revolutionary change will have to depend on the development of the productive forces to augment and release the transformative potential of labor.

A significant portion of my earlier analysis is at odds with this line of reasoning, however, while a careful look at the structure of these articulated capitalisms reveals other related difficulties. If my general thesis on the basic capitalist classes holds, then it can be forcefully argued

that the proletariat may be an essential but not necessarily
a significant condition for collective action and change.
The paucity of its numbers, the structural impediments to its
sound and effective political organization, and like factors
--all these are drawbacks contributing to a marked undiffer-
entiation in the practices of the proletariat and other subordinate classes. As is widely reported in the literature
(Cohen, 1982; Lloyd, 1982), the average worker in the periphery is often simultaneously and unambiguously proletarian
and peasant, with the result that "working-class" movements
become difficult to identify in terms of the practices of the
proletariat, peasantry, or those of other classes. Indeed,
some authors now even speak of a "peasantariat" (Parson,
1984).

If we look at this conflation of interests and practices
between worker and peasant, much can be explained by the accumulation on a world scale so aptly described by Amin. The
mechanism at work is unequal exchange. The crucial point of
convergence between worker and peasant is the provision to
the former of stable and relatively cheap supplies of food by
the latter. It is well documented (Long, 1975; Castells,
1982) that peasant labor engaged in food production provides
a subsidy for the worker's wages, as the employer fixes wages
against this background. The identity of interests between
all three classes usually surfaces with food shortages and
agitation for wages: the worker realizes the smallness of
his wages vis-a-vis the increasing prices for food, the peasant farmer takes stock of the role of his undervalued labor
in the process of production, and both worker and peasant
point the collective finger at the employer. The overall
conflation of these and other noncapitalist class interests
may be represented in the following way:

1. The interests of the worker and the peasant are more
    tightly drawn together, in a structural sense, even
    though ideological compatibility may prove difficult.
    If we agree that fundamental change has more to do
    with internal and institutional ruptures than with a
    poised and ready revolutionary consciousness, then
    these discrepancies do not necessarily stand in the
    way of collective consciousness and action. Again,
    this situation seems fairly stable, as capitalism no
    longer requires the proletarianization of peasants
    to effectively exploit them; and peasantries, instead
    of disappearing, are threatening to become a perman-
    ent fixture on the socioeconomic landscape.

2. The level and visibility of exploitation are system-
    atically unmasked when traditional patterns of self-
    sufficiency are undermined. In the past, it was not
    often that the peasant farmer could make the connec-
    tion between his labor and international trade; for
    one thing, his ability to provide for himself, lar-
    gely outside of the market, created a cushion from
    the vagaries of market forces but carried with it
    certain blinders. With the increasing participation
    in the market (now to buy goods that were procured
    largely within self-sufficient arrangements, such as
    food, medicine, clothes, farming implements), the

class nature of exploitation loses its opaqueness. Economic nationalist techniques like those that pit exploited country versus exploiting country are still employed, but they tend less and less to be instruments of obfuscation and deception.

3. The other noncapitalist classes operating immediately outside of commodity production (lumpens, subproletariat, and so on) are being brought closely to the central antagonisms of the class structure. This results from the progressive intervention of the state--a process which, because of scarce resources, often means less than a tight control over the class structure, as the trade-offs endemic to state governance lead inescapably to concessions to differing classes, class fractions, or social groups.

There is, however, continuing controversy over the leadership of the class coalition to initiate revolutionary change. Indeed, the support for proletarian leadership is quite strong (Roxborough, 1979; Taylor, 1979; Cohen, 1982). The line of support travels through Lenin who, it should be remembered, stated that the proletariat possessed "the moral and political authority" to lead, which the peasantry and other noncapitalist classes "could not but recognize." Today, working-class political and organizational superiority are supposedly even more crucial to peasant political action in quite the same way that urban social movements (those of petty commodity producers, lumpens, squatters) are hopeless without this vital ingredient (Petras, 1978, 1981). The same reasoning is extended to rural peasant activities (land seizures in Bolivia and Mexico, for example); there are strong and frequent expressions of doubt as to the ability of the class to hold the larger vision required for leading a socialist offensive (Rude, 1980: 68-77).

Castells (1982), Hardiman (1981) and Handleman (1975) are among a growing number of writers attempting to draw contemporary peripheral class analysis closer to the current realities. Castells, for instance, found a very high level of organization among squatter associations--in Peru, Chile, and Brazil. Furthermore, this was tempered with marked activist and revolutionary tendencies, which regimes were quite careful in viewing with care. On display also was a certain political guile which stemmed from clearly defined self-interests not easily disturbed by other influences, even those of other social classes (Castells, 1982: 263-69).

Is there a clear leadership role for these subordinate classes and social groups? Are the highly pronounced militancy and revolutionary strains found among the Peruvian peasants (see Handleman, 1975) incapable of developing into some form of autonomous popular movement? Castells is prepared to admit that a leadership role can emerge independent of proletarian auspices, but he stops short of ascribing any permanence to the role; where success has been achieved, he notes, the results have been invariably short-lived, as the enabling circumstances were quite often "exceptional" (Castells, 1982: 269). Although he avoids the unyielding Leninist position on proletarian leadership, Castells maintains that the development of these associations into an autonomous popular movement will depend on their ability "to establish a stable and flexible link with the overall process of class struggle (Castells, 1982: 262). Nevertheless, there is a hint suggesting an alliance with (or possibly subordination to) working class perspectives.

In my view, these formulations do not go far enough. For the most part, the periphery, as I discussed above, is hardly reducing its quota of unfree labor. This is not conjunctural; as Portes and Walton note (1981: 105), we are not confronted here with "a lag from pre-capitalist times, but rather a very modern and expanding creation. It is an integral component of peripheral capitalist economies and its development is mandated by the conditions in which these economies are incorporated into the contemporary world-system."

The working class remains quite important to the overall process of change, inasmuch as the commoditization of labor persists in the periphery. Agendas of emancipation must continue to rely on working class impulses in generating collective consciousness and its organizational capacities in the area of trade union action and political party organizing. However, the systemic limits placed on the development of the class yield greater amplitude to the other classes in the social formation. It is largely for these reasons that proletarian leadership may be essential, although it is not a conjunctually significant condition for revolutionary theory and practice. If the single most important aspect of the proletarian ethic is its organizational efficacy, can it not be suggested that with the noncapitalist classes displaying equal inventiveness and political tact, such efficacy is now less crucial to the success of collective political action?

I will end this segment with a brief note on contradictions. Even if we accept the position that the major contradictions of capitalism are located within the capital-labor dialectic, the matter does not end there. Capitalism embraces two overlapping and interpenetrating aspects, production and consumption: can the basic contradictions related to fundamental change emerge from either of these aspects? If so, what are the implications for the specificity of class action, particularly the primacy of proletarian involvement?

The trouble is that far too narrow a construction is usually employed. Here the basic contradictions are those between the productive forces and the social relations of production. The results tend to be threefold: first, the term "basic" assumes exclusiveness, as if these are the only contradictions of note; second, the central contradictions reside within the practices of the bourgeoisie and the proletariat; and third, the practices of the noncapitalist classes eventuate as mere bit players.

The fact is that Marx did accord pride of place to the working class in revolutionary action, but he was careful to stress the limits placed upon it by social forces, though he did not always state his caveats explicitly. In Capital he states repeatedly, for example, that the fundamental cause of all real crises is the poverty and restricted consumption of the masses and not the drive of capitalist production to develop the productive forces (Marx, 1975). He further goes on to make crucial distinctions between production and consumption. As he notes, the production of surplus value is only the first part of capitalist accumulation. The second part is the realization of the surplus value through the sale of the commodities. Both carry different consequences: "the conditions of direct exploitation, and those of realizing it, are not identical. They diverge not only in place, but also logically" (Marx, 1975, Vol.3: 244).

Let us look at some of the more compelling conclusions here. First, it can be argued that there is nothing wrong with formulating the basic contradictions within capitalism writ large. The periphery is now integrated via accumulation on a world scale, albeit in a special way. It might be so, but the irritating glosses which automatically give a determinate character and pride of place to the working class must be eliminated. That characterization applies only to the classical capitalist model (for example, Western Europe). I have already stated my objections to this line of analysis.

Of greater interest is the relationship between the interpenetrating realms of production and consumption. As spheres which do not necessarily have identical consequences for the agenda of emancipation, they can function in combination or independently. There can hardly be a "pecking order" of contradictions, with those from the one (production) always taking precedence over the other (consumption). In fact, the contradictions radiating from consumption (from the market) might be even more crucial and more often encountered in revolutionary situations. Why might this be so? On the narrow plane of production, the worker is indeed exploited before the commodities he produces are sold. It must be conceded that crises based on exploitation can develop before consumption amd before the play of market forces and other monopolistic mechanisms (unequal exchange, for instance) takes effect.

Crises would seem, however, to occur more in relation to consumption than production proper. This is so because the overall impact of market forces and other monopolistic mechanisms can so easily upset the delicate balance between prices and wages at the point of production. What often stands between exploited workers and their involvement in collective action is the regularity of their pay which, however small, forces workers into certain stable relations largely associated with their family's welfare.

The discords at the level of consumption, that is, retrenchment, cutbacks in production, lay-offs, deflated prices, reduction in sales, often thrust these pent-up tensions into the open. However, it should be realized that these political expressions are not merely extensions of working-class discontent. Indeed, many are so influenced inasmuch as the fragile structure of worker exploitation sketched above is shattered. Nevertheless, other class forces, with no less of a revolutionary fervor than that of the working class, surface within the allowable theoretical framework expressed explicitly by Marx.

These class expressions spring predominantly from non-capitalist origins which are often linked to working class dynamics, yet this is hardly as a matter of course. We may return to the peasantry. This class, as I have shown, continues to be a viable entity, and is drawn more and more into the class struggle as consumers, that is, via consumption.[12] In this way, the peasants will more likely than not see the merchants as sellers of imported goods or as the middleman handling their produce as the target. Only in a derivative sense will they see the manufacturer or industrialist as the immediate enemy. To that degree they are unlike the wage workers, yet the distinction which would normally set them apart, (that is, exploitation which supposedly occurs at the level of production and so gives the working class the edge in the revolutionary enterprise) is rendered nugatory. It is nugatory first because exploitation actually takes place in connection with the production process and, second, because the contradictions propelling change do not have to originate at the level of production but can conceivably do so in the realm of consumption.[13]

If my line of analysis holds, then the peasantry, from a structural standpoint, is as imbued with intrinsic revolution- ary elan as the proletariat. If the class succeeds in its continuing efforts to upgrade its organizational machinery, the longstanding arguments in support of proletarian leader- ship will be further undermined.

Cultural Anthropological Issues

These issues have not sat well with the classical tradi- tions of Marxism and positivism, for that matter. Tensions continue to exist between the etiology of certain cultural activities (philosophy, for example) and the supposedly de- terminate character of the economic base. Other nonmaterial- istic phenomena (race, religion, and nationalism, for example) have been suffering the identical fate, as the historical materialist strives to locate them within the superstructure, describing them as mirroring, being determined, or reproduced by the exigencies of economics.

Much of the problem of subordinating these phenomena to the vagaries of a materialist base can be traced to the rise of capitalism. It is well known that its development in the metropole (with the notable exception of the United States) had escaped the full force of these phenomena. It is not that the European experience was spared the collective impact of nationalism, race, and ethnicity: after all, structural pluralism was a common enough feature of these societies. Of course, these structural alignments are also a feature of peripheral societies, but there is a difference. In the me- tropole, majoritarian democratic tendencies came more quickly into being, due to two principal factors: the confluence of forces ushering in the capitalist mode of production and the existence of certain cultural orientations, which themselves were not necessarily peculiar to the European setting as they were quite amenable to capitalist contagion.

The impact of the forces ushering in the capitalist mode of production is reflected in well-known accounts and need not bother us here. On the other hand, the blending of cul- tural strains as diverse as the Judeo-Christian ethic, and Greek, Roman, and tribal orientations into a singular tradi- tion illustrates crucial points of departure between the cen- ter and the periphery. As Eisenstadt (1978: 139-43) cogently argues, European civilization betrayed a number of distin- guishing characteristics, most of which celebrated the autonomy of the individual and his relatively open access to a social order, whether it was fashioned in the mold of the transcendental or the mundane. These tendencies were supported by high levels of activism, again stressing a commitment to autonomy and individualism.

Moving somewhat beyond Eisenstadt, we should note that the forces directing a choice between the transcendental and the mundane were hardly peculiar to the region. The peculiarity came in the form of the existing forces--capitalism-- which gave the largely anthropological underpinnings to the expression of individual autonomy some distinct theoretical and praxiological twists based on their dominant place in defining social reality. However, while these capitalist forces foisted a choice upon the polity--the mundane rooted in the rational as against the irrationalism of the transcendental--the process was less a structural reconstitution of the cultural-anthropological than the provision of a medium of expression compatible with the main patterns of social life. It is interesting that many Marxists have gradually abandoned the once seemingly impregnable rule of the dependence of the superstructure on the base; now there is repeated reference to concepts like "homologous structures" positing structural relationships "where there may be no direct or easily apparent similarity, and certainly nothing like reflection or reproduction, between the superstructural process and the reality of the base, but in which there is an essential homology or correspondence of structures, which can be discovered by analysis" (Williams, 1982: 33). I will return to some of the consequences of this statement later.

In the periphery, these phenomena as well as others (ethnicity, for instance), are more pronounced in form and effect. Of course, a good deal of the difference is attributable to a far less dramatic incursion of the original capitalist forces than was witnessed in the European case. My earlier observations on the differential capitalization of each bloc make the point. Were the capitalist agenda the only orchestrator of emancipation, then the ensuing prominence of these cultural-anthropological phenomena could be seen as fatal to that enterprise, due to the critical place that commodity production holds in Marxism. However, this is not the case. While much is made of the shortcomings of 'consociational' democracy, notably its restrictedness to segments of the social structure, its impact on emancipation and change is structurally partial (Lijphart, 1977). It is partial to the extent that commodity production is associated with the periphery, and its impact on the development of the productive forces and the working class is vital to a Marxist revolutionary program. It is not crucial if, as I suggest, those emancipatory cultural-anthropological strains informing thought and action not only predate capitalism but also employ its structures and relations as carriers, albeit in a complex, dialectical form. It is this distinction which allows us to understand how the consciousness underlying certain forms of political action in the periphery betrays a marked individualistic quality that has little to do with property (Onselen, 1976). It also helps to explain the fact that when violence breaks out (in some African cities, for example) "it is more often between ethnic and religious groups than between occupational strata or social classes though economic rivalry may well be the root cause of the conflict" (Lloyd, 1972: 101).

Also caught within this explanatory sweep is the phenomenon of migrants to the advanced countries carrying certain "aspects of peasanthood not only in the traces of the past in the present, but also in terms of actual relations and contacts, both real and imaginary" (Shanin, 1978).[14]

It comes as no surprise that the autonomous character of these cultural-anthropological phenomena is now receiving increasing support. Prominent Marxists, such as Debray (1977), Poulantzas (1978) and, to some extent, Seve (1975, 1978), have all raised crucial queries about the automatism of the economic base even in the developed social formations.

While Poulantzas, retreating from earlier positions, questions the location of the state in the materiality of economic relations and chooses to clothe it in a rather anthropological garb, Debray renders an identical service to nationalism, which for a considerable time enjoyed the status of an epiphenomenon. He speaks of its origins in a certain archaic structure, definitely predating the fineries of capitalism, and existing as "a fundamental psychoanalytic and historical datum" (Debray, 1977: 34).[15]

Although space does not allow more than a cursory comment, a fair portion of the supporting analyses derive from the continuing influence of "original causes." For example, while religion, like philosophy, has been getting more and more autonomy (Williams 1980: 40-42) conceding much to its "residual" form, it can be seen across time as a determinate force whose effect, though greatly influenced through its association with wealth and power, essentially operates from the van of autonomy. Thinkers as far apart in time and political circumstance as Montesquieu (1905) and Schumpeter (1942) have reflected tellingly on this quality which, hardly as an act of political consensus, emerges at once as a binder of the populace and a conscience that just as easily sanctions social and political change, whether directly or indirectly.

In the case of despotism, with its absence of codified laws, it was religion that ultimately provided legitimation and a basis for the laws. It might well have become the servant of the forces of oppression, perhaps too readily playing a part in the nefarious schemes of many a monarch, but its original sanctions sprang from a timeless human requirement lying at the very heart of existence itself. It is a chronic fear of the profoundly disruptive effects of arbitrariness that follows in the wake of a lack of systematic laws and sanctions.

Of course, the ultimate fusion of the religious with the political has not resulted in the eclipse of religion. It waxes itself into many quasi-religious traditions of which paternalism is a good example. While it has been exposed to the corrosive influence of, say, nationalism and secular thought, it maintains a supranational presence, interacting with economic, political, or artistic thought, and infecting them with basic anthropological demands which quite often become embedded in sanctions and other forms of generalized behavior, of which freedom and democracy are excellent examples (Hertz, 1944: 134-35).[16]

Time has not dulled the immediacy of religion nor diminished its impact on social processes. Where must appropriate answers be sought for many of the conundrums of contemporary political theory and practice? How should we, for instance, explain the agreeable disposition of the citizen who is not for one moment taken in by the pretense of equality? Schumpeter suggests that the answer lies in a continuing embrace of religious precepts, the original religious idea, even though rationalist thought preempts that terrain. The entire political enterprise is anchored to a profoundly religious commandment: "everyone to count for one, no one to count for more than one" (Schumpeter, 1942: 266). There is, in spite of a preponderance of secular and rationalist thought, an immutable order divined by the Creator which remains largely unsullied by the calculations of humanity.

We should add that where religious and other cultural forms necessarily take on crucial political importance, their visibility may largely be a function of the rational or non-rational mechanisms of thought to which they are exposed. In the developed economies these forms are invariably mediated by successive layers of rationalism. Here religious and cultural factors are invested with the trappings to account for and legitimate the changing conditions as well as the alternative ideological demands created by a complex social order in the name of freedom. Nonetheless, the rationality of the system can hardly obscure the naked religious underpinnings when systemic contradictions surface.

In settings such as the periphery where a good deal of "primary process" thinking occurs, religion holds sway. It lies at the center of a constellation of myths and rituals to which political practices adhere. Along with other cultural forms, religion lies at the heart of dynamic ideologies and world views, often inhibiting or promoting change-related action with a certain facility that derives from its autonomy. This is true because, like nationalism, religion lacks a predetermined class position or content. The content assumes a class complexion largely through its appropriation by class elements, whose success depends on their specific location within the class struggle.

Collective Consciousness and Action

That the consciousness required for revolutionary action need not be proletarian in origin may be inferred from my analysis. The leadership of what must now be seen as a coalition of ideologies has the proletarian component as one ingredient. Is this proletarian component (working class consciousness) the most important, and does it occupy a leadership role as a matter of course?

Perhaps the most cogent theoretical explication may be found in the works of Althusser (1971) and Laclau (1979). By employing the concept of "interpellation," that is, discrete fragments of ideologies (class, religious, and so on) whose involvement with political action is not determined a priori by specific class interests outside of themselves, we get the sense of a complex interplay of ideological forces in the process of change. Interpellations, we discover, have a certain freedom of movement, supporting and articulating with other ideologies in ways which allow us to speak of working class consciousness and its ideological complements as one set of many consciousnesses and ideologies constituting revolutionary consciousness (Laclau, 1979). Working-class

consciousness and revolutionary consciousness are not inter-
changeable. They might have been under the ideal conditions
of classical Marxism, but such conditions have never obtained
in the periphery.

If working class consciousness dominates the coalition
of ideologies comprising revolutionary consciousness, then it
is fair to infer that commodity production has penetrated
deeply into that social formation or that it has managed to
attract the support of other interpellations. However, there
is nothing automatic about this process, and this is why the
interpellations massing around the leadership role of the
coalition of classes have the capacity, singly or in combination, to assume such a role. In other words, the leadership
of the coalition can emerge from the direct practices of the
noncapitalist classes.

CONCLUDING REMARKS

I began this introductory chapter by raising several
questions about the appropriateness of orthodox Marxist analyses for peripheral social formations. In particular, I
pointed to the need to reconsider the theory of revolution in
light of the insights produced by recent, more sophisticated
theoretical approaches, as well as mounting empirical evidence. For peripheral social formations, integration within
the global capitalist system has chiefly been characterized
by undercapitalization. A complex phenomenon which calls
into play sociocultural as well as economic variables, undercapitalization entails the incomplete transformation of these
formations by capitalist incursions and the persistence of
pre and noncapitalist forms of production and social relations. It is the articulation of these forms with capitalist
ones that constitutes the predominant features of peripheral
social formations; chief among them are the weakness of basic
capitalist classes, the persistence of unfree labor, and the
emergence of altered forms of the state, which generally
assumes the place that civil society occupies in central
social formations. The inescapable conclusion is that peripheral capitalism must be understood as a phenomenon sui
generis, with its own change processes.

It is crucially important to reassess theories of revolution and social change in the light of these facts. I have
argued that this reassessment must accord renewed importance
to hybrid and noncapitalist class formations as well as to
cultural and nonproperty phenomena. On the one hand, the
patterns through which the periphery is integrated with the
center assign a structurally determined place to noncapitalist
classes in the overall scheme of exploitation, a place which
may enable these classes to play a leading revolutionary role.
On the other hand, there is now an increasing recognition
that classical Marxism has downplayed the importance of cultural phenomena in the advent of capitalism in the West. The
vastly different and persisting cultural patterns present in
peripheral social formations raise profound questions for
traditional base-superstructure schema. Recognizing the possibly autonomous character of some of these cultural phenomena is a prerequisite for less hidebound and more fruitful
analyses.

Admittedly, this brief treatment requires a good deal of theoretical refinement aided by ample case studies. Nonetheless, there can be little doubt that this theoretical line holds much promise for the analysis of class consciousness in the periphery.

NOTES

1. Schumpeter (1954: 185) ascribes this in part to the notion of "natural liberty" for these orderly patterns which are "logically determined." See also C. B. MacPherson (1975: 9-10); K. R. Perry (1972: 73-79).

2. However, change was not always a matter of "spontaneous emancipation." Often the parties had to be violently dragged to the trough--see Polanyi (1944: 250). Stephens (1979: 115) reminds us that strong, emancipated working classes have emerged only recently, in the 1940s-1950s, in spite of century-long agitation.

3. A good example of this was tobacco, which home-based British farmers were prohibited from growing (Heckscher, 1955).

4. Hamilton was a fierce supporter of protectionism. His "Report on Manufactures" to Congress in 1791 was not immediately successful but most of its provisions appeared in the Tariff Act of 1816.

5. On March 15, 1985, Brazil (one of the so-called bureaucratic-authoritarian states) reintroduced democratic elections. The evidence so far suggests that it is too early for enthusiasm, as the old military regime continues to hold superordinate power (see Scott Mainwaring, 1986). For a more analytical treatment (if somewhat overly deterministic), see James Petras (1986).

6. The 1976 attempt by Michael Manley to introduce democratic socialism in Jamaica is a good example. The IMF removed the ability of the state to participate in productive ventures. There is some evidence also that the Jamaican economy was actively "destabilized" by the U.S. government. Cheryl Payer (1982: 358) notes that the World Bank uses its considerable resources to block progressive change, whether the changes are incremental or revolutionary.

7. In peasant societies, these constraints take forms such as predatory systems (Coquery-Vidrovitch, 1976); encouraging nonbeneficial forms of economic production as in Indonesia (Taylor, 1979); the forcible alteration of economic production to meet new priorities though the old ones were not detrimental to local interests (Weiskel, 1980). These patterns fall in line with Leland Jenks' famous critical line: "[British] activity aided and abetted the tendencies that were already there, and in the case of Argentina, seemed to have given them renewed strength" (1951: 388).

8. Quite often classes are drawn into coalitional relations tending to impede their inner consistency, as under populism. The practice of bartering is said to lie at the heart of the fragmentary and unstable state of revolutionary movements in countries like Venezuela (World Marxist Review, 1983). A major weakness of the state results from its constant competition with the bourgeoisie for surplus to be taxed to finance its activities. This competition draws the

state into repeated crises, often exacerbating class conflict (see Offe and Ronge, 1975). For an enlightening account of state-class reciprocal weakness, see Florestan Fernandes (1981).

9. These theoretical formulations have been extended to women in the periphery and advanced economies as well. See Beneria and Sen (1981); Meillassoux (1985); Friedman (1980).

10. Many euphemisms and obfuscations are used to cover up these exploitative devices. One is the notion of "associated producers," whereby major landholding companies (such as United Fruit Company in Central America) sell or lease their holdings to local farmers with the proviso that they produce and sell only to the company. Arnold Bauer (1979) also discusses other mechanisms used by capital to coax and coerce the peasantry into the labor force. Interestingly, some writers such as Bernstein (personal correspondence, 1979) formulated a theorem that as capitalism so intricately defines the peasants' roles and economic choices, their labor should be taken as the equivalent of wage-labor. Of course, this is unacceptable, as emphasis is placed on the forms rather than the substance of processes and social relations.

11. See June Nash (1985) who engagingly discusses the effect of the segmentation of the work process and the negative consequences for class solidarity. Another factor affecting the consolidation of class consciousness is ethnicity (see Beer, 1980; Nielsen, 1985). Among the Vietnamese, White (1983) discovered a "lineage consciousness"--pride of descent from a common ancestor--which prevented mobilization against exploitative relatives.

12. This results largely from a combination of modernization, physical displacement, and economic changes. As self-sufficiency is lost or eroded, the peasant now comes face-to-face with the classes or fraction(s) forming a part of the chain of exploitation. An important class is that of the middlemen (fraction of the bourgeoisie) acting as buyers of produce and providers of the wares the peasant could once grow or produce. Often the class nature of this exploitation is realized in the course of the usually unequal exchange of peasant produce for manufactured goods.

13. It has been suggested that the fall of Allende might have been directly related to a "realization" problem which generated crises at the level of consumption (Valenzuela, 1976: 1014). See also Paul Sigmund (1986).

14. There is a growing movement among scholars of advanced capitalism to the effect that revolutionary consciousness cannot be confined to the industrial proletariat: see Wright (1980), Katznelson (1981), and Therborn (1983).

15. In particular, Seve's work, with its emphasis on an improved Marxist epistemology that establishes a dialectical relationship between "people-in-relations" and more representative definitions of materialism, forms an encouraging beginning. It is a vastly complex body of theory. More insights on Seve's work are provided in the concluding essay in this volume, along with bibliographical references.

16. If we trace the role of religion back to the Hammurabi dynasty (circa 2500 B.C.) we find that although religion was roughly thrust aside, political rule was still encased in it. It was, for example, used to justify hereditary succession to office. Although the power of the priestly class was

greatly curtailed, all kinds of compromises had to be made with religion because of its important role in defining reality, not the least of which was the very being of the individual.

BIBLIOGRAPHY

Alavi, Hamza
  1980 India: Transition from Feudalism to Colonial Capitalism. Journal of Contemporary Asia 10 (4).
Alavi, Hamza and Teodor Shanin, eds.
  1982 Introduction to the Sociology of "Developing Societies." London: MacMillan.
Althusser, Louis
  1971 Lenin and Philosophy. New York: Monthly Review.
Amin, Samir
  1974 Accumulation on a World Scale (Vol. I). New York: Monthly Review.
  1976 Unequal Development. New York: Monthly Review.
  1977 Imperialism and Unequal Development. New York: Monthly Review.
Anderson, Perry
  1979 Lineages of the Absolutist State. London: New Left.
Bauer, Arnold J.
  1979 Rural Workers in Spanish America: Problems of Peonage and Oppression. Hispanic American Historical Review 59 (1) (February): 34-63.
Beales, H.L.
  1958 The Industrial Revolution, 1750-1850. London: Frank Cass.
Beer, William
  1980 The Unexpected Rebellion: Ethnic Activism in Contemporary France. New York: New York University.
Bendix, Reinhard
  1964 Nation-Building and Citizenship. New York: John Wiley and Sons.
Beneria, Lourdes, and Gita Sen
  1981 Accumulation, Reproduction, and Women's Role in Economic Development: Boserup Revisited. Signs 7 (2): 279-98.
Bennholdt-Thomsen, Veronika
  1982 Subsistence Production and Extended Reproduction; a Contribution to the Discussion about Modes of Production. Journal of Peasant Studies 9 (4).
Borodulina, T.
  1978 K. Marx, F. Engels, V. Lenin--On Historical Materialism. Moscow: Progress.
Canak, William L.
  1984 The Peripheral State Debate: State Capitalist and Bureaucratic-Authoritarian Regimes in Latin America. Latin American Research Review 19 (1): 3-36.
Cardoso, Fernando
  1979 On the Characterization of Authoritarian Regimes in Latin America. In David Collier, ed., The New Authoritarianism in Latin America. Princeton, N. J.: Princeton University.
Castells, Manuel
  1982 Squatters and Politics in Latin America: a Comparative

Analysis of Urban Social Movements in Chile, Peru and Mexico. In H. I. Safa, ed., _Towards a Political Economy of Urbanization in Third World Countries_. Delhi: Oxford University.

1986　_The Urban Question_. Cambridge, Mass.: MIT.

Chilcote, Ronald, and Joel C. Edelstein, eds.
1974　_Latin America: The Struggle with Dependency and Beyond_. New York: John Wiley and Sons.

Cliffe, Lionel
1982　Class Formation as an "Articulation" Process: East African Cases. In H. Alavi and T. Shanin, eds., _Introduction to the Sociology of "Developing Societies."_ London: MacMillan.

Cohen, Robin
1982　Workers in Developing Societies. In H. Alavi and T. Shanin, eds., _Introduction to the Sociology of "Developing Societies"_. London: MacMillan.

Collier, David, ed.
1979　_The New Authoritarianism in Latin America_. Princeton: Princeton University.

Coquery-Vidrovitch, Catherine
1976　La mise en dependance de l'Afrique noire: essai de periodisation, 1800-1970. _Cahiers d'Etudes Africaines_ 16: 23-35.

Corradi, Juan E.
1974　Argentina. In R. Chilcote and J. C. Edelstein, eds., _Latin America: the Struggle with Dependency and Beyond_. New York: John Wiley and Sons.

Court, W. H. B.
1967　_Concise Economic History of Britain; 1750 to Recent Times_. Cambridge: Cambridge University.

Debray, Regis
1977　Marxism and the National Question. _New Left Review_ 105 (September-October): 25-41.

Dobb, Maurice
1940　_Political Economy and Capitalism_. New York: International.
1975　_Studies in the Development of Capitalism_. New York: International.

ECLA (Economic Commission for Latin America)
1965　_External Financing in Latin America_. New York: United Nations.

Eisenstadt, S. N.
1965　Transformation of Social, Political, and Cultural Orders in Modernization. _American Sociological Review_ 30 (5): 659-73.
1978　_Revolution and the Transformation of Societies_. New York: Free Press.

Evans, Peter
1979　_Dependent Development; the Alliance of Multinational, State, and Local Capital in Brazil_. Princeton: Princeton University.

Feis, Herbert
1965　_Europe, the World's Banker, 1870-1914_. New York: W. W. Norton.

Fernandez, Florestan
1981　_Reflections on the Brazilian Counter-Revolution_. New York: Sharpe.

Foweraker, Joe
  1981 The Struggle for Land: a Political Economy of the
        Pioneer Frontier in Brazil from 1930 to the Present
        Day. New York: Cambridge University.
Frank, A. G.
  1967 Capitalism and Underdevelopment in Latin America. New
        York: Monthly Review.
Friedman, Harriet
  1980 Household Production and the National Economy: Concepts
        for the Analysis of Agrarian Formations. Journal of
        Peasant Studies 7: 158-84.
Galli, Rosemary
  1978 Rural Development as Social Control: International
        Agencies and Class Struggle in the Colombian Country-
        side. Latin American Perspectives 5 (4): 71-89.
Gibbins, H. de B.
  1916 Industry in England. New York: Charles Scribner's
        Sons.
Gonner, E. C. K., ed.
  1966 Economic Essays by David Ricardo. London: G. Bell
        and Sons
Grant, Geraldine
  1983 The State and the Transformation of a Middle Class: A
        Chilean Example. Latin American Perspectives 10 (2-3):
        151-70.
Hagen, Everett E.
  1976 The Economics of Development. Homewood, Ill.: R. D.
        Irwin.
Handleman, Howard
  1975 The Political Mobilization of Urban Squatter Settle-
        ments: Santiago's Recent Experience and its Implica-
        tions for Urban Research. Latin American Research
        Review 10 (Summer): 35-72.
Hardiman, David
  1981 Peasant Nationalists of Gujarat: Kheda District. New
        York: Oxford University.
Heckscher, Eli F.
  1955 Mercantilism (2 Volumes). London: George Allen and
        Unwin.
Hertz, Frederick
  1944 Nationality in History and Politics. New York: Oxford
        University.
Hobsbawm, Eric
  1975 The Age of Capital, 1848-1875. New York: Charles
        Scribner's Sons.
Hobson, John A.
  1927 The Evolution of Modern Capitalism. London: George
        Allen and Unwin.
Horowitz, Irving Louis
  1982 Beyond Empire and Imperialism. New York: Oxford
        University.
House, William J.
  1984 Nairobi's Informal Sector: Dynamic Entrepreneurs or
        Surplus Labor? Economic Development and Cultural
        Change 32 (2): 277-302.
Jalee, Pierre
  1969 The Third World in World Economy. New York: Monthly
        Review.
  1973 Imperialism in the Seventies. New York: Monthly
        Review.

Jenks, Leland H.
1951 Britain and America's Railway Development. _Journal of Economic History_ 11 (4): 375-88.
Johnson, Dale, ed.
1985 _Middle Classes in Dependent Countries_. Beverly Hills, Calif.: Sage.
Joshi, P.C.
1981 Fieldwork Experience Relived and Reconsidered; the Agrarian Society of Uttar Pradesh. _Journal of Peasant Studies_ 8 (4): 455-84.
Kahn, Alfred
1946 _Great Britain in World Economy_. New York: Columbia University.
Katznelson, Ira
1981 _City Trenches: Urban Politics and the Patterning of Class in the United States_. New York: Pantheon.
Kaufman, Robert
1979 Industrial Change and Authoritarian Rule in Latin America: A Concrete Review of the Bureaucratic-Authoritarian Model. In David Collier, ed., _The New Authoritarianism in Latin America_. Princeton, N.J.: Princeton University.
Keith, Nelson, and Novella Keith
1985 The Rise of the Middle Class in Jamaica. In Dale Johnson, ed., _Middle Classes in Dependent Countries_. Beverly Hills, Calif.: Sage.
Laclau, Ernesto
1979 _Politics and Ideology in Marxist Theory_. London: New Left.
Leo, Christopher
1984 _Land and Class in Kenya_. Toronto: University of Toronto.
Lijphart, Arend
1977 _Democracy in Plural Societies: a Comparative Evaluation_. New Haven, Conn.: Yale University.
Lloyd, Peter C.
1972 _Class, Crises and Coups_. New York: Praeger.
1982 _A Third World Proletariat?_ London: George Allen and Unwin.
Long, Norman
1975 Structural Dependency, Modes of Production and Economic Brokerage in Rural Peru. In Ivar Oxaal, ed., _Beyond the Sociology of Development: Economy and Society in Latin America and Africa_. London: Routledge and Kegan Paul.
Lublinskaya, A. D.
1968 _French Absolutism: the Crucial Phase_. New York: Cambridge University.
Mainwaring, Scott
1986 The Transition to Democracy in Brazil. _Journal of Interamerican Studies and World Affairs_ 28 (1): 149-79.
Malloy, James M.
1977 _Authoritarianism and Corporatism in Latin America_. Pittsburgh: Pittsburgh University.
Marini, Ruy Mauro
1976 La reforma agraria en America Latina. _Cuadernos Agrarios_ 1: 14-19.
Marx, Karl
1975 _Capital Vol. 3_. New York: International.

Mayorga, Rene Antonio
  1978 National-Popular State, State Capitalism and Military
        Dictatorship in Bolivia: 1952-1975. <u>Latin American
        Perspectives</u>, 5 (2): 89-119.
Meillassoux, Claude
  1985 <u>Maidens, Meals and Money</u>. Cambridge: Cambridge Univer-
        sity.
Montesquieu, Baron de
  1905 <u>The Spirit of Laws</u>. London: George Bell and Sons.
Montoya-Rojas, Rodrigo
  1978 Changes in Rural Class Structure under the Peruvian
        Agrarian Reform. <u>Latin American Perspectives</u> 5 (4):
        113-26.
Moore, Barrington
  1967 <u>The Social Origins of Dictatorship and Democracy</u>.
        Boston: Beacon.
Mouzelis, Nicos
  1978 Ideology and Class Politics: A Critique of Ernesto
        Laclau. <u>New Left Review</u> 112 (November-December):
        45-61.
Munroe, Trevor
  1981 <u>Social Classes and National Liberation in Jamaica</u>.
        Kingston, Jamaica: Vanguard.
Nairn, Tom
  1977 The Twilight of the British State. <u>New Left Review</u>
        101-2: 3-61.
Nash, June
  1985 Segmentation of Work Process in the International
        Division of Labor. <u>Contemporary Marxism</u> 11 (Fall):
        25-45.
Nielsen, Francois
  1985 Ethnic Resurgence in Advanced Countries. <u>American
        Sociological Review</u> 50 (April): 133-49.
O'Donnell, Guillermo
  1973 <u>Modernization and Bureaucratic Authoritarianism</u>, in
        the series, <u>Studies in South American Politics</u>.
        Berkeley, Calif.: University of California, Institute
        of International Studies.
Offe, Claus, and Volker Ronge
  1975 Theses on the Theory of the State. <u>New German Critique</u>
        6 (Fall): 137-47.
Onselen, C. Van
  1976 <u>Chibaro: African Mine Labour in Southern Rhodesia,
        1900-1933</u>. London: Pluto.
Parson, Jack
  1984 The Peasantariat and Politics: Migration, Wage Labor,
        and Agriculture in Botswana. <u>Africa Today</u> 31 (4):
        5-25.
Payer, Cheryl
  1982 <u>The World Bank; a Critical Analysis</u>. New York: Month-
        ly Review.
Perry, K. R.
  1972 <u>The Bourgeois Century</u>. New York: Humanities.
Petras, James
  1978 <u>Critical Perspectives in Imperialism and Social Class
        in the Third World</u>. New York: Monthly Review.
  1981 <u>Class, State and Power in the Third World</u>. Montclair,
        N.J.: Allanheld, Osmun.
  1986 The Redemocratization Process. <u>Contemporary Marxism</u>
        14 (Fall): 1-15.

Philip, George
1984 Military-Authoritarianism in South America: Brazil, Chile, Uruguay and Argentina. Political Studies 32 (1): 1-20.
Polanyi, Karl
1944 The Great Transformation. New York: Rinehart.
Portes, A., and J. Walton
1981 Labor, Class and the International System. New York: Academic.
Poulantzas, Nicos
1978 State, Power, Socialism. London: New Left.
Rangnekar, D. K.
1958 Poverty and Capital Development in India. London: Oxford University.
Ray, Rajat, and Ratna Ray
1975 Zamidars and Jotedars: a Study of Rural Politics in Bengal. Modern Asian Studies 9 (1): 81-102.
Rey, Pierre-Philippe
1973 Les Alliances de Classes. Paris: Maspero.
Rippy, J. Fred
1959 British Investments in Latin America, 1824-1949. Minneapolis: University of Minnesota.
Robinson, Joan
1979 Aspects of Development and Underdevelopment. Cambridge: Cambridge University.
Roemer, John
1982 A General Theory of Exploitation and Class. Cambridge, Mass.: Harvard University.
Roxborough, Ian
1979 Theories of Underdevelopment. London: MacMillan.
Rude, Georges
1980 Ideology and Popular Protest. New York: Pantheon.
Safa, Helen I., ed.
1982 Towards a Political Economy of Urbanization in Third World Countries. New Delhi: Oxford University.
Saffiotti, Heleieth I. B.
1977 Women, Mode of Production, and Social Formations. Latin American Perspectives, 4 (1-2): 27-37.
Saul, John
1979 The Dialectics of Class and Tribe. Race and Class 10 (4): 347-72.
Schumpeter, Joseph
1942 Capitalism, Socialism, and Democracy. New York: Harper and Brothers.
Seve, Lucien
1975 Marxism and the Theory of Human Personality. London: Lawrence and Wishart.
1978 Man in Marxist Theory and the Psychology of Personality. Atlantic Highlands, N.J.: Humanities.
Shanin, Teodor
1978 The Peasants Are Coming: Migrants Who Labour, Peasants Who Travel, and Marxists Who Write. Race and Class 19 (3): 277-88.
Sigmund, Paul E.
1986 Development Strategies in Chile: the Lessons for the Future. In Ilpyong J. Kim, ed., Development and Cultural Change: Cross Cultural Perspectives. New York: Paragon House.

Stein, Stanley J., and Barbara H.
  1970 The Colonial Heritage of Latin America; Essays on
        Economic Dependence in Perspective. New York: Oxford
        University.
Stepan, Alfred
  1978 The State and Society; Peru in Comparative Perspective.
        Princeton: Princeton University.
Stepan, Alfred, ed.
  1973 Authoritarian Brazil: Origin, Policies, and Future.
        New Haven: Yale University.
Stephens, John D.
  1979 The Transition from Capitalism to Socialism. London:
        MacMillan.
Taussig, M.
  1978 Peasant Economics and the Degelopment of Capitalist
        Agriculture in the Conca Valley, Colombia. Latin
        American Perspectives, 5 (3): 62-90.
Taylor, John
  1979 From Modernization to Modes of Production. Atlantic
        Highlands, N.J.: Humanities.
Terray, Emmanuel
  1972 Marxism and "Primitive" Society; Two Studies. New
        York: Monthly Review.
Therborn, Goran
  1977 The Rule of Capital and the Rise of Democracy. New
        Left Review 103: 3-41.
  1983 Why Some Classes are More Successful Than Others. New
        Left Review 138: 37-55.
Tobis, David
  1980 United Fruit's Contribution to Underdevelopment. In
        Ingolf Vogeler and Anthony de Souza, eds., Dialectics
        of Third World Development. Montclair, N.J.: Allan-
        held, Osmun.
Valenzuela, Carlos J.
  1976 El Nuevo Patron de Accumulacion y sus Precondiciones:
        el caso Chileno, 1973-1976. Commercio Exterior 26
        (September 9).
Vergopoulos, Kostas
  1983 L'etat dans le capitalisme peripherique. Tiers Monde
        24.
Weiskel, Timothy
  1980 French Colonial Rule and the Baule Peoples: Resistance
        and Collaboration, 1889-1911. New York: Oxford Uni-
        versity.
Wesson, Robert
  1982 Democracy in Latin America: Promise and Problems.
        New York: Praeger.
White, Christine
  1983 Mass Mobilisation and Ideological Transformation in
        the Vietnamese Land Reform Campaign. Journal of Con-
        temporary Asia 13 (1): 74-90.
Williams, Raymond
  1982 Problems in Materialism and Culture. London: New Left,
        Verso.
World Marxist Review
  1983 The Arduous Road to Unity. World Marxist Review 26
        (1): 41-47

Wright, Erik Olin
  1980 Varieties of Marxist Conceptions of Class Structure.
        Politics and Society 9 (3): 323-70.
  1985 Classes. London:Verso.
Yudelman, Montague
  1964 Africans on the Land. Cambridge: Harvard University.

Part II
CASE STUDIES

2

The Colonial State, Migrant Labor, and Class Formation in Papua New Guinea

RICHARD CURTAIN

Papua New Guinea is a former colony of Australia which gained its independence in 1975. The country has a population of nearly four million people who live in an area slightly larger than the Philippines or New Zealand. The mainland of Papua New Guinea lies about one hundred miles north of the eastern half of Australia, in the eastern portion of the island of New Guinea. (The western portion of the island contains the Indonesian province of West Irian.) Although 85 percent of Papua New Guinea's land area is on the mainland, the country also covers some 600 islands. The land has a tropical climate, good soils, and considerable mineral resources, together with forestry and fishery resources.

The indigenous people of Papua New Guinea comprise a variety of distinct ethnic groups, which are predominantly Melanesian. The isolation produced by the country's topography gave rise to unique cultural and linguistic differences among the various tribes. Some 700 distinct languages have been identified. The social systems of the various groups are also markedly different. Patrilineal, matrilineal, and ambilineal descent systems occur.

Before its independence, Papua New Guinea was administered for more than half a century by Australia. Colonization began officially in 1884, when Germany and Great Britain divided the territory that currently constitutes Papua New Guinea along the central mountain range of the island of New Guinea. Papua, the southern section, became a British protectorate and possession and, in 1906, became an Australian territory. New Guinea (the northern section of the mainland) and its neighboring islands were under German control until occupied by Australia during World War I.

The main economic activity promoted by the colonial power was a plantation economy and, in one region, gold mining. Copra production was the main export of the plantation sector. In recent years, however, coffee has become the most important crop. Small landholder production in coffee and cocoa has become important in the postwar period. Despite the inroads of the market economy, about 90 percent of

The empirical data and the analysis contained in this chapter derives from the author's unpublished Ph.D. thesis, Dual Dependence and Sepik Labour Migration (The Australian National University, Canberra, 1980).

the arable land is still devoted to subsistence agriculture, with 60 to 70 percent of the population remaining basically subsistence farmers who are peripherally involved in the cash economy.

This chapter examines the persistence of noncapitalist modes of production in Papua New Guinea and its effect on class formation. This persistence is attributed to two factors: the tenacity of the closely knit, well-integrated social systems of some 700 different language groups, now numbering three million people and, more importantly, the interventionist role of the colonial state. I will demonstrate how, first the German and then the Australian colonial authorities in the territory of New Guinea sought to generate regular supplies of labor for the plantation and mining enclave economy but at the same time also endeavored to preserve the viability of the village-based subsistence economy to enable it to continue to bear the full costs of the reproduction of the work force. The colonial state played a central role in promoting primitive accumulation by extracting what was conveniently assumed to be surplus labor, but this process was not to be at the expense of dissolving the preexisting economy and society. The mechanism for linking the two economies was the migrant labor system (MLS).

The chapter is based on the central notion that the starting point for an understanding of the processes of class formation in the periphery must be a consideration of how capitalism has penetrated the precapitalist system of production. Gunder Frank's (1967) reversal of modernization theory simply assumed that underdevelopment was the product of the destructive incorporation of the periphery into the world capitalist economy. A number of critics, reacting to Frank's polemic, have acknowledged the dominant role played by the expansion of capitalism from the sixteenth century, but nevertheless argue that this expansion has not necessarily destroyed most noncapitalist economies with which it has come into contact (Laclau 1971, Brenner 1977, Bernstein, 1979, Taylor 1979). An alternative analysis based on modes of production and their articulation emphasizes how key elements of noncapitalist economies persist, despite or perhaps because of their widespread involvement in world markets. One benefit to the capitalist economy of the continuing coexistence of two modes of production within one social formation is the release from the obligation to meet the full costs of the reproduction of its work force.

The focus of attention in development theory has therefore shifted to an analysis of the specific nature of this accommodation between the worldwide dominant capitalist world system and the preexisting economy and society of the periphery. It is argued that the most fundamental transformation wrought by capitalism is the dispossession of direct producers from their means of production. However, it is further argued, this has been only partially accomplished in the world today. The persistence of noncapitalist modes of production acts as the major brake on the widespread emergence of a proletariat in many Third World countries.

Burawoy (1976), in a comparative study of Southern African mine workers and Mexican seasonal agricultural workers in California, has outlined a model of the functioning of an

MLS. He has demonstrated how the MLS operates to create and recreate the link between two economies to the overall benefit of one. The MLS arranges, over time and in a systematic way, the transfer of labor and surplus from one economy or mode of production to another. The state, in the interests of the dominant economy, initiates and supervises the MLS to provide low-cost labor to employers, while the alternative economy has to bear the full cost of what is needed to replace the workers in the next generation. Thus the MLS and the context it operates in, force the migrant laborer to develop a dual dependence. This comes about because, on the one hand, alternative sources of cash income are restricted and wage labor becomes the only means of earning money and, on the other hand, the low level of the bachelor wages, the terms of employment, and conditions and rights at the work place make it necessary for workers and their families to maintain a long-term dependence on their home economy. Thus the operation of the MLS requires the physical separation of the worker from his family. This separation is enforced through specific legal and administrative controls which regulate geographical and occupational mobility. The controls operate against a background of social conditions which deny the migrant worker any basic citizen rights of equality before the law.

THE COLONIAL STATE, THE MLS, AND THE CULTIVATION OF A DUAL DEPENDENCE, 1883-1941

The German colonists began to establish a plantation economy in the northeast of the island of New Guinea and the nearby archipelago after 1883, but soon rejected the more demanding plantation crops of rubber, coffee, cocoa and tobacco in favor of the coconut. This was because the latter was particularly suited to cultivation by an unskilled and irregular labor force (Brookfield, 1972: 52). The German planters, however, soon encountered problems in finding and maintaining a supply of low-cost labor, as villagers living close to the plantations found other means of acquiring cash. As the colonists were forced to seek out laborers from farther afield, the colonial state intervened to guarantee a supply of migrant workers by establishing a specific set of regulations dealing with their recruitment, employment, and repatriation. The colonial state, through the institutionalization of a migrant labor system, required the migrant laborer and his family to cultivate a dual dependence on both the home village economy and the enclave wage economy. This came about because, after initial forced recruitment, a demand for a cash income was created by the imposition of a head tax. In the absence of alternative sources of money, able-bodied males had no choice but to sign on as indentured laborers. However, at the same time, the workers' dependence on the wage economy could only be short-term. This resulted from the conditions of employment which included bachelor wages, no married accommodations, compulsory repatriation after seven years, the severe restriction of occupational mobility, and the denial of political rights, particularly the rights to organize and strike.

The Germans first recruited labor within the colony from areas close but still inaccessible to Rabaul (Epstein, 1968: 58). By 1906, however, Aitape on the mainland had to be opened as a government station to regulate recruiting from the Sepik, and by 1912, 22 percent of recruited labor came from the New Guinea mainland (Brookfield, 1972: 51). In this process, "recruiting in German New Guinea was transformed from a labour trade into systematic labour mobilization" (Firth, 1976: 52). The systematic mobilization of labor became institutionalized, in New Guinea as in all the tropical colonies of the European empires from the late nineteenth century, by the adoption of an elaborate set of regulations (Newbury, 1975a: 235). The overall aim of the colonial authority was to preserve the population as "the most valuable asset of the state," yet at the same time "the labour question was seen as the central problem of the colony" (Moses, 1969: 56, 51). As there was growing evidence that large numbers were dying while working on plantations, the two aims seemed in conflict (Firth, 1976: 51). To reconcile these two policy aims, the MLS was established.

The MLS initially provided for the mobilization of workers through recruiters, and for their direction to a prespecified destination for a predetermined employment period. Sanctions were provided to ensure that the migrant worker fulfilled the strict terms of his employment. The colonial government aimed to guarantee the reproduction of the labor force by limiting the period of indenture. This meant insistence on repatriation of contract-expired workers to their home villages, and prevention of over-recruitment by applying various levels of recruiting in specified villages. Thus the colonial state sought to keep intact the viability of the subsistence economy.

In the period up to the Second World War, the colonial state generated a supply of labor by allowing recruiters to operate in areas under minimal administrative control while doing little to discourage the use of force and other less direct inducements.

After the interregnum of the Australian military occupation (1914 to 1920), an elaborate piece of labor legislation was promulgated by the new Australian civil administration in 1922. In place of the previous practice, where recruiting was carried out by government officers, professional recruiters were promised a price for each "unit" delivered. Prices ranged from £3 to as high as £16, or £20 per recruit (Stanner, 1953: 46). Reed, an American sociologist in New Guinea from 1937 to 1938, explained how the price of recruits had hovered around £5 per man, but then suddenly increased to £20 and £25 when the discovery of gold in Morobe in 1926 produced a great demand for laborers (see also Mead, 1977: 64). The cost to the recruiter of "buying," outfitting, feeding and delivering a recruit from the Sepik averaged --3/10/-. The rest, therefore, was profit (Reed, 1943: 222).

Recruiting practices were seldom subject to government supervision because recruiters constantly operated on the margins of controlled areas. The 1922 legislation stipulated that "fraud, willful or grossly careless misrepresentation, intimidation or coercion" in recruiting was punishable by six months imprisonment or a fine of £100 (Mair, 1970: 181).

Nevertheless, at a time of high prices for goldfield recruits, only two Europeans were convicted of unlawfully inducing a "native" to enter a contract. At the same time, 414 New Guineans were convicted of desertion (NGAR 1927: 23).

The payment of bonuses to village headmen to induce their young men to go with recruiters was legally permitted until 1932, when the government admitted that

> it has led to a great deal of extortion . . . The village officials still expect a cut as their prerogative and may actually block the recruiter who tries to comply with the law. More serious breaches of the law are not at all uncommon in the practice of recruiting. Unscrupulous white men may misrepresent the type, place and duration of the work. They have also been known to pose as the 'kiap' and remove boys by deceit. Cases of kidnapping arose as recently as 1937. (Reed, 1943: 183)

Government officers (kiaps) also played an important role by condoning the pressures of the recruiters. Townsend, a patrol officer in the Sepik from the early 1920s, made the following comments on the responsibility of a signing-on officer to satisfy himself of the correctness of the details of the contract and on the willingness of each recruit to enter into the contract voluntarily.

> The difficulties in the way of the conscientious officer were many. In the first place, it was odds-on that the recruiter had not himself visited all the villages where the natives came from, but had sent his boys in to do the recruiting. Secondly, ninety per cent of the recruits would be unable to speak or even understand any words of Pidgin English except the few that the recruiter's boys had drilled into them. His own name, a name for his village and the words 'me like work' were all that were required of a recruit. If a native could not speak Pidgin-English the onus was on the recruiter to provide the interpreter. Invariably amongst his own four or five assistants, he always found an interpreter. Between them they could manage the several hundred languages in the Territory, which was naturally very convenient, if somewhat remarkable. (Townsend, 1968: 52)

Further pressure to initiate a dependence on the wage economy was applied with the imposition of a head tax (to be paid in cash) on only those males who were able-bodied and resident in the village. The state, therefore, used head tax explicitly as an inducement to wage labor, although there is some evidence that individual field officers may have been lenient in collecting the tax.

In 1937 the director of Native Affairs reaffirmed the intention of the head tax, admitting that if it were ended or even lowered "many industries of the Territory would be unable to carry on for want of labor" (Newbury, n.d.: 9). The actual effect of the head tax as a factor in inducing men to become migrant laborers in the interwar period has been commented on by McCarthy (1963), Townsend (1968) and Viall (1938), all of whom were at one time field officers and tax collectors on the Sepik and in the Morobe district. For some villages close to government stations, it was possible to earn the necessary money by occasionally unloading cargo, selling shells to be used as currency by inland patrols or preparing building materials. Others on the coast could collect cowrie shells to sell to the government for use in the buying of food for inland stations. Others still may have been able to sell coconuts or marine products to European traders. These opportunities applied only in a few fortunate subdivisions "but generally the only way a youth of 15 to 20 can earn money is to go away on contract" (Viall, 1938: 391).

Alongside the legislative and administrative arrangements to move village men into wage employment in the enclave wage economy, there was a parallel concern from the German and Australian colonial authorities to preserve the viability of the preexisting subsistence economy. While the planters were often merely concerned with a continuing supply of short-term laborers, the state took the responsibility of ensuring the long-term reproduction of the work force.

The following summary of specific legislative and administrative controls from the inter-war period gives a good idea of the measures instituted to enforce on the migrant worker a continuing dependence on his home economy.

1. Compulsory repatriation of indentured or "casual" labor by the employer was required.

2. The statutory maximum period of employment under indenture was to be seven years.

3. A maximum of three years only (five years for police and other government workers) was to be served before being returned to the home villages for a three-month minimum stay.

4. Nonindentured labor was initially permitted only for men working within 20 miles of their homes and only for periods of up to three months with a six-month period in between. In 1933, the legislation was changed to allow anyone to be employed for an indefinite period without indenture but only within 25 miles of his home.

5. Breaches of contract by employers or laborers were treated as criminal offenses. Deserters were often imprisoned, heavily fined, or both.

6. By 1932, the minimum age of males for recruitment was set at 13 years.

7. The indenture tied the laborer to the sole service and hence the location of his employer.

8. Two-thirds, and later (after 1932) one-half of the laborer's pay was to be deferred and only repaid once he had returned to his home area.

9. The stipulated minimum (and virtual maximum) for bachelors' wages was five shillings a month, plus

keep, and ten shillings a month for those on the goldfields, with elaborate scales of rations, clothing, and so on.

10. Before 1935, wives who did not themselves want to become indentured were not permitted to accompany their husbands.

11. The legislation of 1936 required an employer to issue a laborer's wife, free of charge, clothes, rations, and other articles as prescribed for a laborer and to issue each dependent child half the food rations due a laborer. The employer was also obliged to provide free medical treatment for dependent families, and to meet all the charges of recruitment and repatriation as well as married accommodation during the term of the contract.

12. The viability of the village economy was to be safeguarded by empowering local officers to recommend closing specific villages or areas to further recruiting.

Although the legislation was all-embracing and set out in meticulous detail, one contemporary scholar believed it was observed to a "remarkably high degree" (Reed, 1943: 265). By the late 1930s, only 3.3 percent of the indentured work force were accompanied by their wives. Legislation, backed by field officers on regular patrol, sought to ensure that an area of heavy recruitment retained its capacity to replace its population. Villages were closed to recruiters when it appeared that the number of women of reproductive age greatly exceeded the number of "virile" men.

Finally, an important factor limiting the migrant worker's commitment to his wage employment was the wider colonial situation. The prevailing ideology of racial domination, whereby one race was seen as having a natural right to be treated in all aspects of life as superior, severely restricted the occupational mobility and political rights in the workplace of the indigenous population. This color bar was so pervasive that employers wanting to establish a more stable and skilled workforce were forced to submit to the exigencies of the colonial situation.

The use of migrant labor discouraged occupational mobility for two reasons. First, the high rates of labor turnover made long-term and expensive training impossible. Secondly, the acquisition of advanced job skills for considerable numbers of workers was seen by the colonial authorities as giving migrant laborers a bargaining power based on a relatively scarce resource (Burawoy, 1976: 1060). These reasons for the lack of skill acquisition by the migrant labor force are illustrated by the following account of the events on the Morobe goldfields in the 1930s.

The need for skilled workers in the plantation economy did not arise because its operation was based on a simple division of labor, but a different situation applied in the complex gold mining industry in Morobe. At first, indentured labor on the goldfields was used either for carrying supplies or, in labor gangs, for simple sluicing (later hydraulic sluicing). From 1932 onward the Bulolo Gold Dredging Company (BGD) introduced large and sophisticated machinery into the area. The transition, starting in 1928, from hand-worked claims, meant an upgrading of skills required on the gold-fields. The advanced technology introduced by both BGD and New Guinea Goldfields Ltd. at their respective sites of Bulolo and Wau also resulted in considerable subsidiary employment in construction work, transport, site clearance, and lower-category engineering and management. The semiskilled and skilled positions were filled by expatriate workers, but the demarcation line in jobs between the two groups was not a fixed one. Over time, a growing number of New Guinean workers moved into semiskilled jobs such as driving trucks, firing steam boilers, and working winding gear, at times without European supervision.

This occupational mobility soon began to threaten the indentured labor system, which was based on a low fixed wage and high turnover. This system was particularly appropriate to the simple labor-skill requirements of the plantations, but proved inappropriate and expensive in relation to the complexity of the advanced technology of the mining sector. By 1935, New Guinea Goldfields Ltd. began to experiment with a policy of replacing expensive white workers with trained New Guineans to save on labor costs. However, this resulted in two strikes by the white mine workers of the company. A compromise was reached: the company dropped its scheme for massive labor substitution, and in return the New Guinean Mines and Works Regulation Ordinance of 1935 was relaxed to permit uncertified drivers to operate winding machinery when not used for raising or lowering Europeans in a shaft. Thus, at the expense of the mining industry's more efficient operation, the colonial state acted in favor of the planters' interests to ensure the continuing powerlessness of the migrant labor force and the temporary nature of migrant employment.

The Economic Functions of Migrant Labor

The benefit of the MLS was primarily in the provision of "cheap" labor. However, the question is, "cheap to whom?" The cost to the colonial state of administering and supervising the recruitment and repatriation provisions, together with a host of supplementary regulations, was high. The Commission of Inquiry into Native Labour (1941: 46) claimed that a large proportion of the Territory's revenue was spent directly or indirectly on the administration of the Native Labour Ordinance.

It would appear, therefore, that the cheapness of the labor force was solely to the benefit of the individual employer. By paying very low wages intended to provide merely for the subsistence of a single worker, the planter in particular was able to hold down his operating costs. In the early 1930s, the labor charges for an average copra plantation amounted to about 42 percent of annual expenses, which included marketing overheads, insurance, and the planter's notional salary and living expenses (Newbury, 1975a: 249). Thus labor costs were an important part of overall operating costs. Even the payment of a constant low wage did not mean that labor remained cheap, however. These same low wages

required recruits to be drawn from increasingly more distant
areas. As a result, the planters' recruiting and repatriation costs rose markedly, especially with the competition for
labor after 1926 from the wealthier mining sector. Stanner
(1953) and Reed (1943) have pointed out that recruitment
costs moved from   3 per head in the early 1920s to   20
to   25 per head beginning soon after gold was discovered
and continuing to the late 1930s. Similarly, repatriation
costs varied greatly until the administration undertook to
return all time-expired laborers to their home areas for a
flat rate of   10 per head, paid by the employer.
      Recognizing the ways in which the colonial administra-
tion subsidized the MLS, labor cannot be considered as cheap
as the actual wages might suggest. Perhaps the major reason
for the institutionalization of a low-wage, male migrant work
force was the political benefit to the colonial administration. Its intention was to cultivate European enterprise,
but not at the expense of the "residential" economy. The
colonial authorities insisted that village life must be the
basis of political economic and social advancement and the
government's labor policy has therefore striven to avoid that
wholesale removal or depletion of indigenous groups which has
led to "urbanization" or "detribalization" in much of Southern Africa. (West, 1958: 89)

The Indigenous Response

      The forced cultivation by the migrant work force of a
dual dependence also served to reinforce the resiliency of a
nonhierarchical and localized traditional social structure,
based for the most part on small-scale subsistence agriculture. The reaction of the isolated village societies was
neither passive nor uniform. In reacting to the initial use
of force, the inducements of recruiters and the imposition of
head tax, the villagers responded in a number of ways. These
varied from resistance to manipulation or active participation and collaboration. Warring villages on the Sepik River
used the pretext of the inducements of recruiters to settle
old scores with neighboring villages. The anger of some villagers at being forced to send their young men away contrasted elsewhere with the role of village elders in actively
assisting recruiters. One "big man," Maringini, saw the opportunity to assert his authority over neighboring groups by
working through the patrol officer. Other villagers saw no
harm in acting as recruiters and even using force on neighbors regarded as traditional enemies. In addition, some actively sought out the chance to be transported away to work
in a strange, largely unintelligible world beyond (see Curtain, 1980b: 231-59).
      At a more general level, the different structures of the
subsistence-based economies of the Sepik region of Papua New
Guinea responded in contrasting ways to the demand for labor. Under the effects of colonial pacification, the sexual
division of labor of the traditional social structure limited
male outmigration in some instances and encouraged it in
other situations. One example is provided by the inhabitants
of the Prince Alexander foothills, who are horticultural-
ists. Their subsistence economy is based on the swidden

cultivation of yam and taro, supplemented in lean periods by
sago. The Abelam tribe practice an elaborate ritual whose
centerpoint is the ceremonial cultivation of long yams, which
are sometimes as long as three meters. The long yams represent a fertility cult which demands the men's complete involvement and produces considerable competitive pressure. Furthermore, men play a crucial role in ordinary gardening activity, working in close cooperation with the women.

The river villages have a very different subsistence
economy based on hunting and gathering to provide a diet of
sago and fish. There is also a marked difference in the
sexual division of labor. The work of subsistence production
among the Chambri, for example, is entirely in the hands of
the women, who alone fish and barter their surplus catch with
people inland in return for sago, taro, and other root crops.
Although the men were entirely dependent for their subsistence on the women's fishing and barter markets, the women
were still subservient within a patrilineal organization
which determined the ownership of land and water rights, assigned women to productive roles, and distributed the products of their labor (Gewertz, 1977: 209).

The marked differences between the two areas in the productive role played by men in the domestic economy, particularly for married men over thirty years of age, explain in
part the high rate of return migration among the older Abelam
men. Other factors include the overall low female outmigration, and the permanent outmigration of men and families from
the river villages (Curtain, 1981, Table 8.6).

This suggests that some "traditional" societies are more
susceptible than others to the encroachment of outside forces
inducing males to leave home. The different forms of organization of the precolonial subsistence economies, however, are
only one factor in explaining the dissimilar propensities to
migrate. The easy access for recruiters to large concentra-
tions of population afforded by the Sepik River was certainly
another major factor in explaining the large number of men
recruited from the river villages.

Postwar to Independence, 1975

The conditions that required the vast majority of migrant
workers to maintain a short-term dual dependence were still
very much in force throughout most of the postwar colonial
period. The master-servant contract relationship in law for
all employees made it illegal, until the early 1960s, for
workers to organize among themselves to press for more secure
terms of employment and better pay and conditions. "Casual"
workers who had been employed for less than six months could
be dismissed without notice. Low bachelor wages were paid to
all but a few public servants until 1972, mainly because the
newly formed unions under tight government control were
largely ineffective. A majority of employers provided single
accommodation only. These conditions applied to both agreement and casual labor. Thus, despite a shift away from indentured labor, a variant of the MLS remained in force in the
postwar era, consisting of a set of legal, political, and
social conditions, including guaranteed repatriation, employment of single males only, and restricted geographical and
occupational mobility.

Despite the continuing importance of short-term dual dependence for most migrants, as reflected in the overwhelming predominance of unaccompanied young males in the migration streams, there were changes beginning in the mid-1960s that reflected a shift away from a high-turnover, unskilled urban work force. The colonial state began to provide greater access to education and, at the same time, a number of restrictions on occupational mobility within the Public Service were lifted. The spread of migrant settlements which could provide cheap married accommodations was permitted by the administration. These changes were the result of pressures from an expanding small industrial, commercial, and public sector in the towns, which required a more educated work force with a substantial commitment to long-term employment and the acquisition of skills.

The need for workers to maintain a short-term physical separation from their families was becoming less important. The most dramatic indication of changes in the composition of the urban population was the increase in the ratio of women to men. Between 1966 and 1977 the masculinity ratio in Port Moresby fell from 185 to 139 (males per 100 females).

The Extent of an Urban Proletariat

Contemporary assessments of the emergence of an urban proletariat must start first of all from a recognition of a rural peasantry based on the nonconvertible ownership of land and means of livelihood.

Most urban East Sepik migrants surveyed in 1973-1974 had a continuing close relationship to a rural land base, as was evident from a number of indicators such as length of time in town, gifts sent and received, return visits, propensity to build a rural house, and extent of urban home ownership (see Garnaut, Wright and Curtain, 1977). Nevertheless, a small group of migrants (between perhaps 15 and 30 percent of the total) who were mostly from the poor river districts appeared to be divorced from their home villages. Three groups of East Sepik urban migrants were identified from the 1973-1974 Urban Household Survey: short-term visitors and young men seeking work, permanent urban residents mostly from the poor rural areas, and the educated migrants in stable employment who seem to be merely semi-permanent urban residents.

The first group consisted of a high-turnover, floating population who may represent up to a quarter of the urban population at any one time. These people were still firmly integrated into the rural peasant economy either as visitors or young job seekers. As visitors, they may act as a link between town and country by transferring gifts of food in one direction and money in the other. The young job seekers were not accompanied by a wife. They were most likely to go directly from the village to the nearest town to try their luck and, after a short period of job search, return home. The former were still firmly integrated into the peasant economy, although temporarily absent. The latter group of unskilled young job seekers were engaging in a strategy of short-term dual dependence. At the other end of the spectrum were the permanent urban residents. Apart from the provincial capital's own residents of traditional villages sited within the town's boundaries, permanent migrants appeared to come from the poorly endowed river districts. These areas have few opportunities to partake in a viable peasant economy based on some form of cash cropping.

In general, permanent urban residents were not necessarily part of a proletariat. They may not be compelled to sell their labor to survive if they have managed to gain access to urban land through intermarriage with urban customary land owners and are able to supplement subsistence gardening through the sale of goods or services through the informal sector. The latter case is most likely in the provincial capital, Wewak, where a large number of long-term male residents without wage employment were accompanied by a wife and settled on customary-owned land.

The remaining section of the urban population was generally regarded as likely candidates for permanent urban residence. These are the families supported by a well-educated breadwinner in stable employment. However, temporary proletarian status did not necessarily lead to a permanent status when urban conditions were not conducive to permanent residence and the rural economy did not dispossess even long-term absentees of their land rights. There were a number of indications that many urban migrants are likely to return to their home villages on or before retirement.

The intention of migrants to return home was dismissed as an unreliable and inconclusive indicator (50 percent of respondents were undecided). A high proportion of longerterm urban male residents in wage employment said they sent and received gifts from home (Garnaut, Wright and Curtain, 1977: 69), but other data show that regular remittances were of minor importance. Intents and gifts, therefore, may tell us little about future behavior. Two other concrete indicators were examined: visits to the home village and whether or not the urban migrant had built a house there. Fifty-three percent of all longer-term residents had visited home, but the proportion was much higher (69 percent) for the better educated migrants in wage employment. This closer link for the educated was doubtless encouraged by biennial leave provisions offering return fares home for most middle-level public and private sector employees and their families.

Many long-term urban residents also owned a rural house. Even among the 15- to 24-year-olds with jobs based on their high educational levels, as many as 41 percent had built a rural house. These figures were closely paralleled by a 1977 survey of the urban and rural housing situation of a sample of middle-level public servants (Stretton, 1978). Eighty-two percent of the respondents who were migrants claimed they would return home either on or before retirement. Many had already built their house in their village and most of the remainder intended to do so.

These actions and the attitudes they reflect are not surprising when the contemporary institutional constraints on permanent urban residence are considered. Over 50 percent of urban accommodation was employer-provided or rented. This accommodation was therefore available to the urban migrant only as long as he continued with his employer or received an adequate income to cover the payment of rent. Very few urban residents (only 2 percent) had taken steps to purchase government-built housing. There was little incentive for those

in subsidized government housing to purchase. A large number
of public and private sector employees were posted at regular
intervals to positions around the country. This high degree
of directed movement is likely to greatly hinder a commitment
to permanent residence in any one urban center.

Nelson (1976: 744-47) has discussed the phenomenon of a
long-term circular migration based on dual residence in a
number of Third World countries. The reluctance of Papua New
Guinean urban residents to buy urban housing and their tendency to build a rural house is paralleled by studies from
Uganda, Ghana, Tanzania, and Eastern Nigeria (see also Odongo
and Lea, 1977; Ross and Weisner, 1977). As Nelson (1976:
744-45) has commented:

> Temporary or uncommitted migrants will be reluctant to
> invest more than an essential minimum in housing, even
> if they can afford to spend considerably more. Usually
> they will prefer to rent rather than purchase, or build
> their own shelter. . . . While temporary migrants are
> reluctant to invest in housing in the city they are often
> eager to do so in their homeplaces.

The associated claim that, despite long-term urban residence, many employees will eventually return home, is also
supported by a number of comparative studies. For example,
Elkan (1976) has presented evidence of a more stable work
force developing in Nairobi without the severance of ties
with the rural economy. His conclusion is that despite spending a considerable period of their lives in the city, they
maintain close social and economic links with their villages.
In this sense he sees them as migrants because "nothing that
could conceivably be described as a permanent proletariat is
emerging in Nairobi" (Elkan 1976: 705).

Nelson (1976) makes the point that unfavorable urban
conditions (such as housing, wage levels, and interethnic
conflict) themselves do not explain the strong likelihood of
return movement for many migrants, because it is the more
successful who are likely to return home. In their study of
Nairobi migrants, Ross and Weisner (1977: 367) also conclude
that rural-urban ties, rather than being a transitional phase
for insecure migrants, are actually stronger among the more
established and successful migrants. This is partly because
they could afford the financial burden of such ties and also
seek to win respect and deference from those at home.

The general reluctance of migrants to commit themselves
to a permanent urban residence may also alter if a number of
constraints are lifted. It seems likely that the Papua New
Guinea government will offer much of its stock of housing for
purchase on easy terms. Interprovincial mobility will become
less likely as public servants become tied to employment in
one province (probably their home province). If superannuation payments on retirement are geared toward the urban cost
of living, another major constraint on urban retirement will
have been lifted.

Nevertheless, urban conditions are not the only or even
the main factor in the reluctance of migrants to forsake their
rural base. A crucial factor in high levels of return migration is the importance to absentees of guaranteed access to
land. According to the Rural Survey (Conroy and Skeldon,

1978) village residents claimed that 82.5 percent of male absentees have clear, unchallenged land rights, with a further 13.8 percent having rights which are open to dispute. The conservation of a peasant mode of production by the colonial state is likely to continue to influence attitudes toward permanent urban residence. The viability of the peasant economy will encourage most migrants to maintain a dual dependence on both economies.

This is not to suggest that migration has had little long-term impact on the rural economy, however. There is considerable evidence to show that migration has drained the rural economy of its most capable people at the most productive periods of their lives and laid a corresponding heavy burden on those remaining at home to maintain production. At the same time, little help appears to have been offered through regular remittances as compensation by absentees (Curtain, 1980: 348-55). There is also evidence to suggest that return migration is likely to have accentuated rural inequalities (Curtain, 1980b: 372).

The labor reserve status of the East Sepik Province, for example, has combined with the region's poor physical endowment (which contributed to the use of the area as a labor reserve in the first place) to perpetuate its backwardness. On a composite index of socioeconomic indicators, in 1978 the East Sepik Province ranked some 40 to 50 index points (on a scale of 100) below the three top-ranking provinces (Berry and Jackson, 1978).

Thus the dual dependence fostered by the colonial state and continued today by most migrants (either in the short-or-long-term) has not been to the mutual benefit of the two economies. The peasant economy of a labor reserve area such as the East Sepik Province has retained a degree of self reliance, but it is within the framework of a subordinate relationship to the capitalist economy, subsidizing the latter at the cost of its own development.

The colonial state, through the MLS, was able to provide subsidized labor to the plantation and mining sectors by requiring the subsistence economy to bear the costs of maintaining the migrant worker's family while the employer paid only a minimal wage to the single worker. To cope with an increasing demand for a cash income, while at the same time having to provide for his own and his family's long-term future, the migrant worker was forced into dependence on both the wage economy and the village subsistence economy.

A structure of dual dependence continues as a legacy of the MLS and is manifest in the continuing pattern of circular migration over the migrant's life cycle. The persistence of circular migration over a number of generations results from the conditions of employment and residence in the wage economy, set against the background of the security of rights to land and a guaranteed subsistence livelihood in the rural economy. Where the rural resource base is inadequate, as in the case of a number of villages on the Sepik River, there is likely to be a tendency toward permanent outmigration.

The major consequence of the operation of the MLS has been to inhibit the formation of a large proletariat which accompanied the expansion of capitalism in the metropolitan economies. Labor migration and the increasing commercialization of rural agricultural production transformed the village subsistence economy into a larger peasant economy separate from, but in a dependent relationship to, the capitalist enclave economy.

The future importance of a strategy of dual dependence for migrants will depend on factors in both the rural subsistence economy and the wage economy. The ability of the rural peasant economy to support the reproduction of its population, including absentees, depends on the viability of its subsistence base. Tendencies toward less labor-intensive and nutritious food crops could adversely affect the rural economy's capacity to support a rapidly growing population.

A second factor likely to reverse the capacity of the rural economy to accommodate an expanding population is any change to the current system of communal land tenure. This is likely to occur as a class of rich peasants or rural capitalists develops through the accumulation of land by means of individual ownership. This, in turn, will cause poor villagers to lose their land and become a landless proletariat. Growing rural stratification will transform the rural peasant economy, dispossessing the poor peasants of their land and produce migrants who will become part of a permanent proletariat.

In the wage economy, the postcolonial state has accepted some responsibility for the cost of renewal of the work force through an urban family wage indexed to the cost of living, publicly funded education, health services, worker compensation and superannuation payments to some workers. However, other costs normally provided by the state in metropolitan countries are not met: unemployment benefits, family welfare payments, pensions to unskilled and semiskilled workers, or superannuation payments geared toward the urban cost of living. A continuing reliance on the peasant economy also remains necessary because of the migrants' lack of secure tenure over urban housing and land.

BIBLIOGRAPHY

Bernstein, H.
1979 Sociology of Underdevelopment vs. Sociology of Development. In D. Lehrmann, ed., Development Theory: Four Critical Essays. London: Cass.
Berry, R., and Jackson, R.
1978 Inter-Provincial Inequalities: The State and Decentralization in Papua New Guinea. Paper presented to the Waigani Seminar on Decentralization, Port Moresby, Papua New Guinea.
Brenner, R.
1977 The Origins of Capitalist Development: A Critique of Neo-Smithian Marxism. New Left Review 104: 25-92.
Brookfield, H. C.
1972 Colonialism, Development and Independence; The Case of the Melanesian Islands in the Pacific. London: Cambridge University.
Burawoy, M.,
1976 The Functions and Reproduction of Migrant Labour: Comparative Material From Southern Africa and the United States. American Journal of Sociology 81 (5): 1050-87.

Commission of Inquiry into Native Labour
 1941 Report of a Committee Appointed to Inquire into the
       Matter of Native Labour in the Territory of New Guinea
       1941. Typescript manuscript held in the National
       Library, Canberra, Australia.
Conroy, J., and Skeldon, G.
 1978 The Rural Survey 1975. Yagl-Ambu Special Issue, Port
       Moresby, Papua New Guinea.
Curtain, R. L.
 1980a The Structure of Internal Migration in Papua, New
       Guinea. Pacific Viewpoint 21 (1): 42-61.
 1980b Dual Dependence and Sepik Labour Migration. Unpub-
       lished Ph.D. Thesis, Australian National University,
       Canberra, Australia.
 1981 Migration in Papua New Guinea: The Role of the
       Peasant Household in a Strategy of Survival. In G. W.
       Jones and H. V. Richter, eds., Population Mobility and
       Development in Southeast Asia and the Pacific. De-
       velopment Studies Monograph, Australian National Uni-
       versity, Canberra, Australia.
Elkan, W.
 1976 Is a Proletariat Emerging in Nairobi? Economic De-
       velopment and Cultural Change 24 (4): 695-706.
Epstein, T. S.
 1968 Capitalism, Primitive and Modern. Canberra: Austral-
       ian National University.
Frank, Andre Gunder
 1967 Capitalism and Underdevelopment in Latin America. New
       York: Monthly Review.
Firth, S.
 1976 The Transformation of the Labour Trade in German New
       Guinea, 1899-1914. Journal of Pacific History 11 (1):
       51-65.
Garnaut, R., Wright, M., and Curtain, R.
 1977 Employment, Incomes and Migration in Papua New Guinea
       Towns. Monograph 6, Institute of Applied Social and
       Economic Research, Port Moresby, Papua New Guinea.
Gewertz, D.
 1977 Exchange Spheres Among the Chambri People of Papua New
       Guinea. Unpublished Ph.D. Thesis, City University of
       New York.
Laclau, E.
 1971 Feudalism and Capitalism in Latin America. New Left
       Review 67: 19-38.
McCarthy, J. K.
 1963 Patrol Into Yesterday: My New Guinea Years. Mel-
       bourne: Cheshire.
Mair, L. P.
 1970 Australia in New Guinea. Melbourne: Melbourne Univer-
       sity.
Mead, M.
 1977 Letters From the Field 1925-1975. New York: Harper
       and Row.
Moses, J. A.
 1969 The German Empire in Melanesia, 1884-1914: A German
       Self Analysis. In K. S. Inglis, ed., The History of
       Melanesia. Canberra: Australian National University.

Nelson, J. M.
  1976 Sojourners Versus New Urbanities: Causes and Conse-
        quences of Temporary Versus Permanent, Cityward Migra-
        tion in Developing Countries. Economic Development
        and Cultural Change 24 (4): 721-57.
Newbury, C. D.
  n.d. The New Guinea Labour Force, 1920-1940. Manuscript.
  1975a Labour Migration in the Imperial Phase: An Essay in
        Interpretation. Journal of Imperial and Commonwealth
        History 3 (2): 25-38.
  1975b Colour Bar and Labour Conflict on the New Guinea Gold-
        fields, 1935-1941. Australian Journal of Politics and
        History 21 (3): 25-38.
NGAR (New Guinea Annual Reports)
  1914-1921 to 1939-1940 The Mandated Territory of New Guinea,
        Annual Report to the United Nations. Canberra: De-
        partment of Territories, Commonwealth of Australia.
Odonga, J., and Lea, J. P.
  1977 Home Ownership and Rural-Urban Links in Uganda. The
        Journal of Modern African Studies 15 (1): 59-73.
Reed, S. W.
  1943 The Making of Modern New Guinea, with Special Refer-
        ence to Culture Contact in the Mandated Territory.
        Philadelphia: American Philosophical Library.
Ross, M. H., and Weisner, T. S.
  1977 The Rural-Urban Migrant Network in Kenya. American
        Ethnologist. 4 (2): 359-75.
Stanner, W. E. H.
  1953 The South Seas in Transition: A Study of Post-War
        Rehabilitation and Reconstruction in Three British
        Pacific Dependencies. Sydney: Australian Publishing.
Taylor, J.
  1979 From Modernization to Modes of Production: A Critique
        of the Sociologies of Development and Underdevelop-
        ment. London: MacMillan.
Townsend, G. W. L.
  1968 District Officer: From Untamed New Guinea to Lake
        Success, 1921-1946. Sydney: Pacific.
Viall, L. G.
  1938 Some Statistical Aspects of Population in the Morobi
        District, New Guinea. Oceania 8 (4): 383-97.
West, F. J.
  1958 Indigenous Labour in Papua New Guinea. International
        Labour Review 77 (2): 89-112.

3
Agricultural Transformation in Developmental Socialism: The State and the Peasantry
JAY R. MANDLE

Until the Russian Revolution, Marxists had assumed that the postcapitalist mode of production would be constructed in a society which had already been industrialized. Capitalism would be overthrown only after the industrial working class had become large enough, sufficiently skilled, and organizationally competent to rule on its own behalf. However, these prerequisites require a lengthy period of capitalist development. Modern economic growth would have to precede socialism, for only after that growth had occurred could rule by industrial workers be envisioned. The expansion of democracy implied by the latter was contingent on the prerevolutionary expansion of the forces of production. Engels articulated this assumption graphically when he wrote:

> to accomplish . . . [modern socialism] we need not only the proletariat, which carries out the revolution but also a Bourgeoisie in whose hands the productive forces of society have developed to such a stage that they permit the final elimination of all class distinctions. . . The Bourgeoisie is consequently equally as necessary a precondition of the socialist revolution as the proletariat itself. (Sawer, 1977: 189)

It was not only manufacturing that would advance under capitalism. Capitalist agriculture too would become increasingly productive. Thus, in *Capital*, Marx wrote that with capitalism, "the irrational, old-fashioned methods of agriculture are replaced by scientific ones." As always, Marx saw the contradictory aspects of this process; while capitalism in the countryside would promote an advance in the forces of production, at the same time this organization of agriculture "violates the conditions necessary to the lasting fertility of the soil, . . . crushing out the workman's individual vitality, freedom and independence." Ultimately however, capitalism would set the stage for a higher social order. A basis for a "higher synthesis in the future" would be put in place, in which there would be created a "union of agriculture and industry on the basis of the more perfected forms they have each acquired" under capitalism (Marx, 1906: 554-55).

The Russian Revolution undermined these assumptions, however. The postcapitalist mode of production was to be constructed in advance of the development process or, at

best, simultaneously with it. As a result, policy discussions
in the Soviet Union in the 1920s were not and could not be
concerned solely with the institutional content of working-
class rule. Rather, they had to address the task of economic
expansion and industrialization. These discussions represented a new departure for Marxists: unlike the past, it was
now necessary for Marxists to devise the means to accomplish
a task which it had previously been believed, capitalism would
accomplish for them.

In the effort to achieve rapid economic development in
the Soviet Union, it was obvious from the beginning that
agriculture occupied a strategically important role. It was
called on both to feed the domestic population and to supply
at least part of the savings necessary to help finance the
creation of new industries. The former responsibility was
particularly onerous, since the industrialization process
envisioned would increase the proportion of urban dwellers.
Agriculture, in short, was the base on which growth was to be
accomplished.

However, the development of socialist agriculture is not
concerned solely with economic expansion. Proponents of
socialism also address the kind of society which is under
construction, and particularly the nature of the social
relations of production which are being created. Organizational forms and class relations in rural areas thus assume
relatively great importance. Agricultural policy in such a
setting influences two ends at the same time: advances in
the forces of production and the structure of the relations
of production. Thus, inevitably, the Soviet Union would
ultimately have to face the question of collectivization,
though, as we shall see, this issue did not loom large in the
initial debates concerning Soviet agriculture.

The issues confronted by the Soviet Union in the 1920s
have, in many respects, been reproduced in today's socialist
countries. Aside from the Soviet Union itself and the socialist countries of Eastern Europe, contemporary socialism
exists only in very poor countries. In addition to the
countries mentioned above, there are sixteen countries that
John Gurley identifies as "Marxian Socialist" (see Table
3.1). In no case is the per capita income greater than
U.S.$710. As was the case for the Soviet Union in the 1920s,
low productivity agriculture dominates the economy and
society of most of today's socialist countries. These
countries thus confront the problem of advancing the forces
of production much as the Soviet Union did in the first
decade of its revolution.

In the Soviet Union in the 1920s however, it was economic
development and not class relations which received priority
attention. Thus with respect to agriculture, the question of
the means to achieve cooperative or collectivized units of
production--that is, socialist class relations--did not figure
centrally in the debates between the principal antagonists of
the period, Evgenii Preobrazhenskii and Nikolai Bukharin.
Both assumed that in the long run collectivization was desir-
able, but neither made it the object of short-term policy.
Each tacitly accepted the continuation of the bourgeois and
petty bourgeois class relations characteristic of NEP agriculture. The latter, forced on the Bolsheviks because of the
difficulties of the Civil War period, gave farmers the freedom

TABLE 3.1
GROSS NATIONAL PRODUCT PER CAPITA IN NON-EUROPEAN
MARXIST SOCIALIST COUNTRIES (in 1974 U.S. $)

People's Republic of China	300
Socialist Republic of Vietnam	150
Ethiopia	100
Democratic People's Republic of Korea	390
Cuba	710
Mozambique	340
Cambodia	70
Angola	710
People's Democratic Republic of Yemen	220
Lao People's Democratic Republic	70
Somalia	90
People's Republic of Benin*	120
Albania	530
Mongolia	610
Guyana*	500
Guinea-Bissau	390

* Listed by Gurley but labeled "doubtful inclusion."
Source: Gurley, 1979: 216-17.

to raise and deliver their output in markets of their own choosing and in quantities that they determined. Thus, capitalism in the countryside was accepted even as the Bolsheviks moved to socialism in the cities.

What separated Bukharin and Preobrazhenskii was not, therefore, the issue of the transformation of the relations of production. Rather, their differences centered on the rapidity with which the forces of production could be moved forward. In these discussions, Preobrazhenskii stood for a much more rapid rate of economic growth than did Bukharin. This meant, in turn, that Preobrazhenskii advocated a much more rapid rate of resource extraction from the countryside than did Bukharin. Rapid industrialization required a very large shifting of resources from the agricultural to the industrial sector, and Preobrazhenskii, in his policy formulations, did not shrink from this conclusion.

At one level the debate between Preobrazhenskii and Bukharin was narrow and technical. The former advocated applying more pressure to the countryside than did the latter. Behind this disagreement, however, was a much more intractable problem than merely choosing the correct rate of savings and economic growth, for when Bukharin complained that his opponent stood for an excessive draining of resources from the rural areas, he was really defining a political as well as an economic point of view at variance with Preobrazhenskii's position. The latter wrote in defense of his program that "we should know . . . that we won't be given much time to build. We should expect a drive of rich peasantry united with the world capital which will start an economic as well as military-political offensive" (cited in Erlich, 1960: 37), while Bukharin argued that "a proletarian dictatorship which is in a state of war with the peasantry . . . can in no way be strong" (cited in Cohen, 1973: 165). Clearly Bukharin's unwillingness to accelerate the rate at which resources were extracted from the peasantry was grounded in his concern to retain for the Bolsheviks the goodwill and support of this class. Though Preobrazhenskii did not go so far as to threaten the property rights of the peasantry, he was willing to pressure these farmers for more resources than they voluntarily would contribute to the financing of industrialization--a position which reflected his anxiety that at least a segment of this group was intent on defeating socialism and that real strength lay in rapid growth.

The debate among Soviet policy makers in the 1920s has its counterpart in current discussions concerning economic development in today's impoverished socialist nations. The goal in such countries echoes early Soviet goals: to achieve development with as much self-reliance as possible. Such an approach necessarily assigns a central role to agriculture in the development effort. What is required, therefore, is a careful assessment of the conditions which will allow agriculture to advance in accordance with the requirements of self-reliant growth. Just such a strategy has been advanced by the Guyanese economist C. Y. Thomas.

In taking up the problem of a socialist agricultural strategy today, Thomas is very much alive to the political issues which separated Bukharin and Preobrazhenskii and which ultimately were crystallized by Stalin's forced collectivization. He underscores, for example, the need for agricultural transformation to be carried out with the support of the peasantry itself. In this regard he writes that "the experiences of the Soviet Union have shown that if democracy is not preserved in the rural areas the peasants will be drawn to retaliation and to the sabotage of the transition efforts." Indeed, he argues that the maintenance of voluntarism "is a crucial element in preserving the stability of the worker/peasant alliance" (Thomas, 1974: 154).

Thomas' model of socialist development involves a twin process of convergence. First, there must be convergence between a population's pattern of needs and that population's pattern of effective demand. In practice this means that each consuming unit must receive sufficient income to ensure its ability to gain access to the commodities and services which constitute its basic human needs. Second, it is essential that there be a convergence between this pattern of demand and local production and resource use. In this way an indigenous technology linking needs and resources can be forged and the desired form of autonomous and self-reliant development can be attained (Thomas, 1974:125).

In the immediate context of underdevelopment, the linkage between needs and resource use requires the development strategy to concentrate on agriculture. Thomas advocates a reorientation away from export-specialized agriculture toward the evolving long-term pattern of demand of the local population. Such a shift will not only allow a country to improve the nutritional level of its population, but to avoid dependency as well. As rural incomes rise and demand shifts away from foodstuffs, pressures to industrialize will develop. Again, however, the industrialization which is to occur must be reflective of domestic needs. In this regard Thomas argues for the necessity of "regulating this demand to a country's resource configuration" (1974: 145-49, 195). Thus the process that Thomas envisions is an agriculture-led model in which self-sufficiency in agriculture gives rise to self-sufficiency in manufacturing.

Despite his sensitivity to the possibility that strains might develop between workers and peasants, Thomas goes further than either Bukharin or Preobrazhenskii in one crucial aspect of agricultural transformation. As we have seen, neither of the Soviet writers explicitly addressed collectivization, while such an institutional change is very much a part of Thomas' approach. In his model, Thomas urges the formation of large-scale units of production, to be organized either as state or cooperative farms. He adopts this position for both economic and ideological reasons. On one hand, he argues that productivity advances in agriculture are dependent on the large units of production that can best accommodate modern inputs and technology. At the same time, he insists on the importance of establishing "socialist relations" in the countryside and resisting the rise of a wealthy peasantry or "kulaks." Thus he concludes that during the transition period, establishing "new socialist forms become[s] a matter of top priority" (Thomas, 1974: 153, 155, 163).

Thomas insists that collectivization can be accomplished democratically. He writes that the transformation of social relations must "be achieved in a basically voluntary manner if socialist relations are to prevail," but he acknowledges that this may not be accomplished easily. The basic difficulty, as Thomas describes it, is that to a peasantry "the end of exploitation is frequently seen as occurring by way of greater security of private tenure and real income both of which the peasant believes can only follow from an expansion of holding size and from the preservation and extension of unrestricted rights to the use and disposal of land" (Thomas, 1974: 160, 162). Such attitudes clearly present a major impediment to voluntary collectivization.

Voluntarism and democracy might mean that collectivization will have to be deferred if not removed from the social agenda. This is a possibility that Thomas does not directly address. In fact, Thomas insufficiently specifies the meaning he attaches to the terms "democracy" and "voluntarism." This gap in his analysis is particularly troublesome since the goals of development and socialist reconstruction require specific forms of behavior and therefore imply a limitation on the population's freedom to act as it wishes. For example, economic growth requires the learning of new skills and work habits. Socialism requires a change in the relationship between farmers and farm workers and farmers and peasants. The problem is that rural populations might resist these changes. The question which would then arise, and which is central to the issue of voluntarism and democracy, is what a political leadership should do to encourage the desired behavior, and what limits should be placed on its efforts to obtain behavior consistent with development and cooperation.

Voluntarism does not mean that any form of behavior is as acceptable as any other form, nor does it mean that people are free, in an absolutist way, to do whatever they wish. Inherent in all social settings is the presence of positive incentives and negative sanctions which both narrow the range of options and tend to encourage specific forms of action. These constraints must be acknowledged before the principles of voluntarism and democracy can be meaningfully applied. This is all the more true where a specific pattern of behavior is the goal of the society's leadership, but the leadership hopes that the population will adopt those patterns in the absence of compulsion.

However, if voluntarism is to possess real content, it must mean that the leadership might fail in its efforts to induce change. If this condition is not satisfied--if the leadership's position will prevail, no matter what--then it hardly can be said that voluntarism is present. To be sure, in a voluntary setting leaders are not entirely powerless in attempting to accomplish their goals. The adjusting of incentives and sanctions is not inconsistent with voluntarism. This adjustment process may raise the cost of specific forms of behavior and thus lead to adaptation and change. But resistance to change may also be present, resulting in the continuation of old forms of activity or institutions despite the higher cost attached to them. In such a case, a leadership in a regime of voluntarism must be prepared to accept such a conservative verdict. Under no circumstances is voluntarism consistent with a leadership's use of violence to accomplish its ends. Thus evidence that voluntarism is present takes the form of constraints which are imposed on a leadership's ability to effectuate behavioral or institutional change.

To achieve the kind of transformation envisioned by Thomas in a voluntary context necessitates that the peasantry identify its interests with those of socialist development. Only the careful construction of an appropriate set of incentives and sanctions can lead to the perception of such a convergence of interests. Appropriate policies and actions must at once encourage the peasants to learn and use skills associated with development, and at the same time engage in the kinds of nonexploitative social relations associated with socialism. In the meantime, the peasants must come to believe that in doing this they will advance their own interests as they understand them.

Three requirements must be satisfied for such an incentive system to work. First, the state as the creator of the incentive system must be in sufficiently close contact with the population to ascertain the rewards which will encourage the desired behavior. Second, policy makers must accept those rewards as legitimate and reasonable. Finally the state must be financially and administratively competent to supply those rewards. These three in combination suggest that, in constructing an incentive system, the leadership of a country must be close enough to the peasantry to know what is important to its members, and be willing and able to shape its program around those aspirations.

To raise these issues is, however, to underline the difficulty which exists in promoting autonomous growth. Problems can arise with regard to any of these conditions. For example, a leadership or a political party drawn primarily either from an urban middle-class or urban working-class background might not possess close ties with the farming community. As a result, they would be handicapped in their efforts to either mobilize the countryside or even persuade the people in rural areas that the leadership's actions are appropriate. At the same time, the values of an urban political leadership might diverge from those of the agricultural population. It is plausible to hypothesize a situation in which material incentives and the use of the market might represent important aspects of the farm community's preferred way of life, but these same instruments might be anathema to a political leadership. Such discontinuities between the aspirations of the rural community and a society's leaders could well threaten the achievement of a voluntary structural transformation such as Thomas advocates. On one side the incentives constructed by the leadership might fail to result in the desired behavior by the peasants. On the other hand, failure to be responsive to the peasants' desires might result in a deep distrust on the part of the latter concerning the leadership's motives. In either case the cause of a voluntarist transformation would be undermined (see Mandle, 1981).

Problems such as those described here do not affirm the inevitable failure of efforts at autonomous growth, but the likelihood that problems like these will emerge serves to underscore the potential barriers which stand in the way of a successful strategy of socialist development.

To a considerable extent, the contrasting experiences in agriculture of the Soviet Union and the People's Republic of China can be understood in these terms. Upon assuming power, the Communist Party of China clearly had closer organizational ties to the countryside than did the Bolsheviks after the Russian Revolution. As a result of its many years of work in rural areas, the party possessed a strong structure in the countryside and was well represented by cadres. The Chinese party was thus able to discern and work with the peasants' aspirations. The opposite was the case with the Soviet party--a party largely composed of urban workers led by urban revolutionaries. This party possessed few organizational ties to the countryside and thus appreciated the self-defined interests of the farm community very little. With stress, these deficiencies could not help but tend to produce a deep estrangement between the urban and rural communities. The result of the different experiences of the two parties was that the transition to collectivization was far less traumatic in China than in the Soviet Union. In the Soviet case, collectivization was forcedly imposed on the countryside and was accomplished largely to the exclusion of voluntarist considerations. In China, there was a considerable degree of voluntary compliance by the peasants and virtually no use of violence (Lewis, 1968; Shue, 1980).

Even in China, however, the relationship between the ruling party and the people of the countryside has not been without its problems. The reforms undertaken since 1978 under the leadership of Deng Xiaoping have resulted in the dismantling of China's agricultural communes, and the use of markets to stimulate production. The reestablishing of China's peasantry represents a victory by the country's rural population as contrasted at least to the preferences of part of the Communist Party's leadership. If the use of force in the Soviet Union in collectivization is testimony to the weakness of the Soviet leadership's ties to the countryside, the continued adjustment on the part of the Chinese indicates that even where the ties are strong the problems which arise in transforming agriculture are not easily resolved.

This last issue--the fact that even the Chinese Party, with its wealth of experience in the rural areas, continues to experiment with its units of agricultural production--suggests that the appropriate form for socialist agriculture has yet to be developed. The difficulty in solving this issue stems from the fact that there is a need to reconcile three potentially conflicting goals within such a framework. The unit of production must at once contain within it an incentive system which results in the kind of careful, nuanced, and intensive work effort essential for successful agriculture. At the same time the structure of the production unit must accommodate the use of capital equipment and technologically advanced methods of production. Finally, work relations within these units must correspond to an agreed-upon definition of nonexploitation. It is easy enough to suggest the use of production forms which satisfy one or possibly two of these criteria, but in practice, it has been much more difficult to satisfy all three of these aspirations simultaneously.

The example of small-scale farming illustrates these tensions. If, in coming to power, a revolutionary leadership redistributes land in relatively small units to farmers, in most cases it would ensure the existence of a well-motivated labor force in the countryside. Work alienation would be absent. A family's income level would depend in such a situation on the intensity of the work effort of its members and a high level of motivation can be taken for granted. (This assumes, of course, that prices paid for outputs are sufficiently high to warrant the work effort.) Indeed the available evidence suggests that this is the case: small-scale farming typically results in relatively high levels of labor intensity.

It is still questionable, however, whether peasant agriculture is capable of supporting a modernization effort. Evidence that yields per acre are relatively high on small farms is not sufficient to establish this point. Intensity of factor use does not speak to the questions of technological dynamism over time and whether a small-scale peasantry can accommodate to persistent advances in technology. For his part, Thomas is skeptical that it can. He writes that modern agriculture requires units of production "which are larger than is generally available to peasants" (Thomas, 1974: 153).

One possible solution would be to allow successful farmers to increase the scale of their operations. By adding to their holdings, such farmers could be expected to continue the intensity of their work effort. A large unit of production might facilitate the introduction of modern inputs and thus contribute to productivity advances. The problems attendant to this solution are serious, however. In fact, the kind of "progressive farmer" strategy suggested here implies a tendency toward worsening of the rural income distribution, as wealth becomes concentrated in the hands of the successful farmers at the expense of the unsuccessful ones. Even more fundamentally, this strategy implies the need for wage labor as the units of production grow to levels where family labor is inadequate. In the context of a socialist development strategy, then, a progressive farmer strategy carries an obvious objection. It involves the creation of capitalist agriculture.

The antithesis of a progressive farmer strategy is the establishment of state farms. The argument on behalf of this approach is straightforward. Socialism means the public ownership of productive resources. A farm owned publicly is the embodiment, therefore, of socialism in the countryside.

Similarly, since there is no limit on the size of state farms, they are capable of efficiencies not otherwise achievable. Their ability to absorb large units of capital might allow them to be technologically dynamic and thus contribute to the development effort.

The weakness of the state farm approach, however, centers on the third variable of concern--worker motivation. In a state farm system, the form of compensation is wages, but while wages might be adequate to supply the kind of labor necessary in manufacturing, this is not clearly the case in agriculture. The nature of the required work effort is substantially different in agriculture than in manufacturing, especially assembly-line manufacturing. In agriculture, judgment is continuously required. Decisions must be made with regard to a vast array of questions ranging from crop selection and methods of cultivation at one pole, to seed placement and weeding at the other. To supervise all these judgments efficiently would involve a very heavy and costly overlay of management.

Far preferable to establishing such a supervisory role would be the ability to rely on the well-motivated and well-informed judgment of each of the participants in the state farm. However, for this to be feasible, two conditions would have to be satisfied. First, each of the individual workers would have to be a competent farmer, capable of making the decisions essential to sound agriculture. Second, each laborer would have to believe that there would be compensation for well-motivated and conscientious work. In a wage system, the connection between the quality of work and the level of compensation virtually disappears. Thus it is not obvious that wages produce the kind of work necessary in agriculture. If conscientious, year-round effort is to be forthcoming, it is necessary that such effort be rewarded.

For a state farm to work, wage rates alone are insufficient: they do not act as an adequate incentive to produce the behavior required to minimize errors of judgment or simple neglect. What is needed is a compensation system which connects work effort to compensation. A compensation system which involves a sharing of profits, and thus provides a motivation for efficient and attentive behavior, is more appropriate for agriculture than a wage system.

To suggest that individual participants in a state farm share in profits is to raise the possibility that the producer-cooperative form of production might be suitable for the task at hand. In cooperatives, profits are shared by members, and thus the connection between work effort and reward is retained. At the same time, cooperatives formed by combining individually owned holdings and placed under a unified management might be large enough to facilitate economies of scale and technological advance. Finally, by virtue of their membership provision, cooperatives can avoid creating alienating work relations. Policy is determined by the members, and thus self-governance can prevail. In this regard, problems of exploitation might arise only if the labor requirements of the cooperative were to exceed the supply of labor forthcoming from its membership. In such a situation, wage labor would have to be employed, raising the possibility of labor and management difficulties. However, it is generally presumed that this component of the labor force would be relatively small, and the bulk of the work performed would be carried out by members of the cooperative themselves.

It is possible that under a regime of voluntarism, producer cooperatives might fail to attract a large membership. To some extent, this will be determined by the incentives which are constructed by the government to encourage such membership. A farmer may wish to join a cooperative in order to secure production and marketing advantages and the higher level of income which is associated with them. Nevertheless, it is possible that substantial numbers of farmers might choose not to join. This reluctance might exist because the individuals fail to perceive the benefits of membership or because they value independence more than profits. To the extent that this is the case, cooperatives might grow at a rate slower than an economic optimum would require. But such foregone growth would have to be accepted as the price of voluntarism.

While the growth rate of the cooperative sector might prove to be a difficulty, an even more fundamental problem associated with cooperatives centers on their political implications. Fundamentally, producer cooperatives imply political decentralization. Cooperatives would break down or be rendered meaningless if a centralized political process were to impose its decisions regarding crop choice, output volume, or production methods. Nevertheless, this has been precisely the bias of contemporary socialism—to make decisions at the center in the form of an economic plan and require that the producing units abide by that plan. The use of cooperatives requires that there be a constraint on the authority of leaders at the center. To be sure, these leaders could attempt to influence the decisions made by the cooperatives, but ultimately that influence would only be indirect, working through incentive systems, and decision-making authority would rest finally in the hands of the members of the cooperative. In such a regime, political authority would be much reduced compared to that which leaders in contemporary socialist countries have come to expect. This conflict between the decentralizing bias associated with the use of cooperatives and the centralizing bias of present-day socialism in poor countries may account for the limited extent to which voluntary producer cooperatives have been employed in developing socialist societies to date.

Thus we arrive at a central problem of contemporary socialist theory. Socialist revolutions have occurred exclusively in poor nations which have had to look to agriculture as a source of development. The centrality of agriculture in the development process requires changed behavior and institutions in the countryside. In accomplishing such change, however, the use of coercion is both counterproductive and intrinsically undesirable. This leaves a political leadership with the necessity of shaping an environment in which farmers will find the means and the incentive to engage in technological change, while at the same time creating social relations of nonexploitation.

The problem of expanding the productive capacity of agriculture, then, will be dependent on whether socialist leaders are able to accommodate to the necessity of providing the farm community with both the opportunity and incentive to become effective producers. With those present, socialist development without coercion becomes feasible. However, to achieve that goal, members of the farm community will have to be provided with more respect and autonomy than typically has been the case in either socialist practice or theory.

BIBLIOGRAPHY

Cohen, Stephen F.
1973 Bukharin and the Bolshevik Revolution. A Political Biography 1888-1938. New York: Alfred A. Knopf.

Erlich, Alexander
1960 The Soviet Industrialization Debate 1924-1928. Cambridge, Mass.: Harvard University.

Gurley, John G.
1979 Economic Development: A Marxist View. In Kenneth P. Jameson and Charles K. Wilber, Directions in Economic Development. Notre Dame, Ind.: University of Notre Dame.

Lewis, M.
1968 Russian Peasants and Soviet Power. A Study of Collectivization. Evanston, Ill.: Northwestern University.

Mandle, Jay R.
1981 The Politics of Self-Reliant Development. Monthly Review 32 (11).

Marx, Karl
1906 Capital. New York: Modern Library.

Sawer, Marian
1977 Marxism and the Question of the Asiatic Mode of Production. The Hague: Martinus Nijhoff.

Shue, Vivienne
1980 Peasant China in Transition. The Dynamics of Development Toward Socialism. Berkeley, Calif.: University of California.

Thomas, Clive Y.
1974 Dependence and Transformation. The Economics of the Transition to Socialism. New York: Monthly Review.

4
Ethnic Leadership and Class Formation in Freetown, Sierra Leone

ALLEN M. HOWARD and DAVID E. SKINNER

The relationship between ethnicity and class has vexed scholars of Africa. In the 1960s, theorists of "modernization" and "national integration" often explained economic and political conflict in terms of the continuing influence of "primordial loyalties" and denied the existence of classes in Africa, whether past or present. Urban anthropologists helped to destroy the "primordial loyalties" concept by showing that ethnicity was situational, and that ethnic identities and institutions in cities were different than and not directly derived from the cultures and societies of the countryside. Historical research on the colonial era has shown that Africans created a variety of new associations (ethnic and otherwise), drawing selectively on social and cultural elements from the past (Mitchell, 1966).

In an effort to explain the upheavals of the independence and postindependence periods, scholars increasingly saw tribalism as a product of the colonial and national eras. European officials, it was argued, sought to divide their subjects ethnically, recruiting and rewarding some in order to better control them as a whole. Nationalist politicians manipulated tribal identities to build followerships, win elections, and secure offices and other resources (Sklar, 1967; Melson and Wolpe, 1970). The ideology of tribalism has not died with the achievement of independence. In the view of Archie Mafeje it has been "pedalled by both expatriate theorists and emergent African middle-class ideologists" who wish to obscure the "real nature of economic and power relations between Africans themselves, and between Africa and the capitalist world . . ." (1971: 261).

While tribalism is ideology, ethnicity cannot be dismissed as mere superstructure. For one thing, ethnicity has in part resulted from the interaction between capitalist and noncapitalist economies and social formations, an interaction that continues in the present. Colin Leys states that:

We would like to thank the following who made valuable comments on earlier versions of this chapter: Michael Adas, Samuel L. Baily, Raymond E. Dumett, Irving Leonard Markovits, Nelson Keith, Novella Keith, Michael Seidman, and Mary B. Skinner. Earlier versions of this chapter were presented at the African Studies Association, October 1980, and the Sierra Leone Studies Symposium at Birmingham University, July 1981.

The foundations of modern "tribalism" were laid when the various tribal modes and relations of production began to be displaced by capitalist ones, giving rise to new forms of insecurity, and obliging people to compete with each other on a national plane for work, land, and ultimately for education and other services seen as necessary for security. (1974: 199)

Ethnic groups were not simply the products of manipulation by colonialists or indigenous elites, but were formed by Africans who sought better ways to handle problems caused by their confrontation with the colonial power bloc of administrators and others (Saul, 1979: 353ff.). Since independence, ethnic community organization has continued to serve the needs of urban dwellers in dealing with the neocolonial power bloc. Furthermore, whatever their origins, ethnic identities have proven "capable of taking on a certain unpredictable life of their own" (Saul, 1979: 366).[1] Once people have adopted urban ethnic identities, they act on those identities in ways that leaders cannot control. Moreover, in the highly interactive urban milieu, people shift their loyalties from one ethnic group to another and may even alter their ethnic identities (Schildkrout, 1978: 264ff.; Harrell-Bond, Howard, and Skinner, 1978). Ethnicity is fluid. Its development and change must be analyzed within the larger economic and political context.

Freetown, the capital of Sierra Leone, is an excellent case for studying ethnicity and class over a period of nearly 200 years. From its origin in the late 1700s, Freetown was a base for the expansion of both commercial capitalism and British colonialism. Britain gradually spread its political influence during the nineteenth century and conquered the hinterland in the 1890s. Capitalism only slowly altered the indigenous noncapitalist economies.

Commercial capitalism existed comfortably with noncapitalist forms of production and exchange, and certain mixed forms evolved. Both peasants and slaves living in the interior produced food and other commodities for sale in Freetown and for export. Households in Freetown had some members engaged in nonwage labor for production of market goods while others worked for wages outside the unit. In the context of commercial capitalism and colonialism, a limited number of Africans developed into a commercial and professional bourgeoisie and gained a subordinate position in the power bloc, which was dominated by Europeans. Until the expansion of capitalism and colonialism in the late nineteenth century, however, only a small proportion of Freetown residents were full-time wage employees. Many Africans were artisans, petty traders, or casual workers who earned money but were also involved in noncapitalist forms of production and exchange; immigrants often retained close connections with the noncapitalist economies in the hinterland.

Ethnicity became a primary means by which immigrants to Freetown responded to capitalism and the colonial power bloc of administrators, merchants, and others. In defining ethnicity we are adopting the views of Cohen (1978) and Schultz (1984), who believe ethnicity is

"a _series_ of nesting dichotomizations of inclusiveness
and _exclusiveness_" (Cohen, 1978: 387). Situational
variability is undeniable, but the features upon which
these "nesting dichotomizations" are based reflect a
number of _potential_ identities which an actor may
assume. The orderly operation of society tends to
restrict the range of possible identities to which any
segment of the population may actually lay claim. This
range often changes with the passage of time. (Schultz,
1984: 46)[2]

In Freetown, people structured ethnicity principally
around communities which had institutions such as courts and
were led by headmen and elders. Immigrants created communities that were distinctly urban in organization and function,
although in doing so they drew on their political and cultural
heritage. People brought an ethnic consciousness based on
kinship, language, and cultural values. Such identities, which
had been fluid in the hinterland, were even more subject to
change in Freetown as people shifted their ethnic identities
according to circumstances (Harrell-Bond, Howard, and Skinner,
1978: 11-16). Ethnic communities became part of the economic
and social context of the city, and later immigrants built
new communities in response both to the existing groups, and
to the capitalist and colonial institutions.
Working-class organization has been slow to develop
because the great majority of urban dwellers have been cyclical migrants, casual workers, or petty traders, and thus were
not amenable to working-class consciousness. Full-time wage
workers have constituted a small percentage of the city's
population. Furthermore, governments have opposed, suppressed,
and coopted labor leaders. Ethnic identities and institutions
apparently also have hindered the development of working class
organization. Although there have been multiethnic unions and
labor manifestations, workers often have competed on an ethnic
basis for jobs. Most urban residents have expressed their
dissatisfactions with the economic and political order and
have made known their aspirations through demonstrations and
riots, the nationalist movement, and the activities of ethnic
and other urban organizations.
This chapter focuses on the roles of headmen and other
ethnic leaders in relationship to colonialism, capitalism,
and class formation.[3] These leaders--known by various
titles, including _alimami_ (from the Arabic, _al-Imam_), king,
prince, and tribal ruler--were recognized by their followers
as possessing special knowledge, skills, and resources relevant to the urban environment. Ethnic leaders--many of them
big men within the Freetown context, who often also had strong
ties with the societies of the hinterland--organized their
followers' activities in the noncapitalist and capitalist
spheres and created mixed forms of production and exchange.
They mediated between their people and the principal capitalist institutions, the colonial power bloc, and other ethnic
groups.
The mediating role of ethnic leaders could be ambiguous.
Although leaders pursued their own economic interests and
helped their followers to adapt to Freetown, colony officials
and businessmen used them as imperial agents and labor recruiters. After 1890, the government instructed leaders to

limit immigration and to control urban dwellers' activities, and in 1905 it formally recognized tribal rulers as colonial officials. Although the government placed demands on leaders, community members continually called for them to respond to popular needs, and rivalries led to the replacement of headmen and to fission of communities. During and after World War II, progressive ethnic leaders began to provide immigrants with additional social welfare and educational services. Through their connections with emerging nationalist parties, headmen and other notables also gave their communities a voice in urban politics. Since independence, however, the ruling parties have demanded that community leaders serve the interests of the party or national state, and a few community leaders have joined the power bloc. Thus, new possibilities of conflict within communities have developed, especially as the number of poor urban dwellers has increased greatly.

THE POWER BLOC AND THE ORGANIZATIONAL BOURGEOISIE

As Freetown grew during the nineteenth century, a power bloc gradually developed which had the ultimate legal authority in the city and provided the overall management of commercial and political relations with the hinterland. This power bloc consisted almost exclusively of European administrators and merchants, plus a few Africans. From the end of the nineteenth century, large-scale European firms took a dominant position in the Sierra Leone economy, and their managers became an important element within the power bloc. Only as independence neared did Africans--mainly those who held critical administrative posts or led political parties--gain an important place in the bloc. Given their political strength, and their role in establishing the postindependence neocolony, they were able to force the Europeans to bargain with them for a share of power.

From the early nineteenth century, a few Africans constituted a bourgeoisie whose position was based on wealth earned through commerce and ownership of land. Later in the century, the professions contributed to a further expansion of the bourgeoisie. For the most part, people whose family origins were in the interior did not join the bourgeoisie until after the Second World War, when the spread of "western" education and nationalist politics opened many jobs and business opportunities. Gradually, a multiethnic organizational bourgeoisie emerged. From the 1960s, the organizational bourgeoisie has dominated, to a considerable extent, the politics of the city and of Sierra Leone. Here we are following Markovits, who has written:

> I use the term organizational bourgeoisie to refer to a combined ruling group consisting of the top political leaders and bureaucrats, the traditional rulers and their descendants, and the leading members of the liberal professions and the rising business bourgeoisie [plus] top members of the military and police forces. . . . Over time, leading elements in this coalition change. Although the bureaucratic and political components have dominated until now, they have had to seek a social base. Increasingly . . . a developing commercial and business class provides that base. (1977: 208)[4]

It is this organizational bourgeoisie which has come to constitute the African element of the power bloc.

Increasingly, members of the bourgeoisie have acted to protect their educational, commercial, and political interests, to consolidate their position, and to pass it on to their children. Of course, a class cannot be defined only in terms of its own characteristics but should also be analyzed in relationship to other classes. Africanists have found this problematic because of the vertical ties (kin and other) between those in different strata, and because a proletariat in the European sense has been nonexistent or very small in size.[5] Certainly in Freetown, and in Sierra Leone generally, vertical ties have prevented class lines from being sharply drawn, at least until recently.

We will explore this issue in depth later; however, three factors are relevant here. First, because historically one ethnic group--the Krio--comprised the bourgeoisie, owned much of the land in Freetown, and held many important positions, other people commonly expressed their antagonism against them in ethnic terms and organized ethnically to gain a greater share of the resources available in the city.[6] Second, many immigrants remained linked with the noncapitalist economy and society, and existing vertical ties were carried to the city. Third, because ethnic leaders helped their followers to participate in the capitalist sphere and represented them vis-a-vis the colonial power bloc, vertical patron-client ties were built within the communities.

CAPITALIST AND NONCAPITALIST RELATIONS OF PRODUCTION AND EXCHANGE

Most Freetown ethnic communities developed in the nineteenth century and early twentieth century among people whose lives were shaped by noncapitalist relations of production and exchange in the hinterland. Certain ethnic groups grew up primarily around long-distance trade. Many of their leaders facilitated the movement of goods between the capitalist and noncapitalist spheres. Other groups provided laborers, for example on the docks and in construction, and their leaders recruited and organized work gangs. Thus, in a different way they also acted as intermediaries between their coethnics and the capitalist sphere. Even within the city itself, capitalist relations of production and exchange did not prevail among many urban dwellers, though to some degree they were involved in wage labor and had to purchase necessities.

In the noncapitalist sphere, land was not bought or sold. Kin groups or political authorities controlled access to land and gave others permission to use it. Noncapitalist relations included domestic-, peasant-, and slave-based production in which nonwage labor prevailed within the unit of production. Accumulation took place through production and trade, but also through other means, including redistributive circulation systems dominated by political authorities. Capitalist relations have involved the buying, renting, and selling of land; wage labor; and certain kinds of capital accumulation and investment that require market transactions of property. Social and political investments--such as the formation and maintenance of alliances--occurred within both

spheres. Such investments, in turn, generated further resources that were used both by the bourgeoisie to consolidate
their class position and by community leaders in the process
of ethnic group formation.

The main unit of production in the noncapitalist sphere
has been the household. Households have varied greatly in
size and composition and in their capacity to produce goods
for sale, enter social exchanges, and engage in trade. In the
hinterland, the basic production unit was the small, self-
sufficient household comprising kin (sanguineal and affinal)
and perhaps also a few non-kin (Dorjahn, 1977). Most migrants
to Freetown have come from such households. For heavy agricultural tasks, such units typically pooled their labor through
reciprocal arrangements. Youth also organized work groups
that went from place to place. In the past they were paid
with food or other goods, but more recently payment has been
in cash. Prior to the nineteenth century, most units did not
interact with the capitalist sphere and bought few if any
overseas imports; but after Freetown was founded an increasing
number began to produce things for consumption in the city or
for export.

At the opposite end of the spectrum were large households, headed by so-called "big men"; in the past, these units
often included many slaves and other non-kin dependents.[7]
In some cases slaves worked on plantations raising market
crops, and they were also important in food crop production
and trading activities. In the precolonial era, big men and
others of wealth, rank, and power were linked through marriage
and other networks, and constituted a dominant class. Many
leading families of the past have retained their position up
to the present, although colonialism brought opportunities
for some people of lower positions to rise (Howard, 1979;
Howard and Skinner, 1984).

Such units also existed in and immediately around
Freetown during the nineteenth century and into the twentieth.
Their members lived on the margin of the capitalist economy,
buying and selling goods but not dependent on wages. Households often had not only gardens but also access to plots of
land for growing staples (such plots were located in the
peninsula or the nearby hinterland). Households produced some
of their necessities and also purchased commodities manufactured by others and marketed in Freetown. Even when one or
two members worked for wages in the capitalist sphere, such
households preserved considerable self-sufficiency. In addition to the small units, there were largescale compounds that
were headed by immigrant big men who were involved in long-
distance trade, craft production, or Islamic education. They
did not pay members of their house- holds for their labor.
Many of them also held land in the interior that was worked
by kin, clients, or slaves.

However, the position of big men did not derive solely
from their control over material production and exchange, but
also came from their ability to draw on the indigenous ("traditional") and Islamic cultural sanctions of the hinterland
that had also permeated Freetown. The office of _alimami_ itself
had prestige, associated as it was in the minds of immigrants
with royal and Islamic authority. Titles and functions of
lesser officials within the communities were taken from the
indigenous and Islamic systems: _alikali_, _santigi_, and _kandeh_,

which also was the title of the headman in some communities (Skinner, 1978). Clerics and teachers who led the Freetown ethnic mosques and the Islamic schools held high status because they were educated at universities in the interior and had ties with famous scholars and holy men. Moreover, many of the notables in Freetown were scions of or had inter-married with families distinguished by their claims to king-ship or other high office or by their accomplishments in warfare, religion, or trade. The prestige associated with leadership of the Islamic institutions and ethnic communities did not diminish during the colonial period. Islam has grown stronger in the twentieth century as the numbers of adherents have increased and as it has adjusted to the new economic and political order. The institutionalization of headship in Freetown also gave the position added legitimacy, and its officeholders formed an association of headmen to increase its functions and to enhance its authority.

Until recently, the headmen and elders of most communi-ties were not part of the bourgeoisie in the capitalist sphere; even today many are not. As individuals and as community leaders they have had vital roles as intermediaries between the large body of Freetown inhabitants and the capi-talist sphere and colonial power bloc. In performing such roles, they gained opportunities to enhance their wealth, power, and status. This at least potentially put them at odds with their followers, but they reduced this conflict by re-distributing their wealth to community members and providing necessary services such as housing, jobs, schooling, and clinics. The leaders' activities to assist their communities were a major factor in shaping the development of ethnic rather than class-based organizations among the mass of migrants. Only since independence have there appeared marked contradictions between ethnic leaders who are part of the bourgeoisie and a rapidly expanding urban population who are surviving marginally by casual work within the capitalist sphere.

FREETOWN'S ECONOMIC AND SOCIAL FORMATIONS: THE BOURGEOISIE, PETTY BOURGEOISIE, WAGE WORKERS, AND CASUAL WORKERS

Freetown was founded in 1792 by the Sierra Leone Com-pany, which was led by abolitionists and businessmen intent on proving that the slave trade could be replaced by a thriv-ing legitimate commerce and that Christianity could compensate for the moral damage of the nefarious traffic in human beings. It led a shaky existence in its early years: its population was tiny and its links with the hinterland were tenuous. Over time it gained a firmer footing as the population grew, as Britain committed governmental and missionary support, as people in the town and hinterland forged political and econ-omic ties, and as African residents created a viable community life. A major turning point was 1807 when the British Parlia-ment unilaterally abolished the slave trade and established the Crown Colony of Sierra Leone to serve as a settlement for Africans liberated off slave ships. Gradually the port town became the premier entrepot serving a wide section of the coast, and its trade with the distant interior developed. Besides certain high-value exports, notably gold, traders based in Freetown and the nearby rivers handled bulky commodities--timber, peanuts, palm kernels, palm oil, hides, and other things--which were destined for industrial and consumer uses in Britain and elsewhere. Complementing this was an inward flow of manufactures. In addition, there arose a sizeable trade in foodstuffs, raw materials, and manufactures from the hinterland for the Freetown population, plus an inter-African export traffic, especially in kola. Much of Freetown's trade in exports and consumer items during the nineteenth century was with territories to the north and northeast which comprised the so-called Sierra Leone-Guinea system (Howard, 1976). The majority of the immigrants came from those areas.

After the British declared the Sierra Leone Protectorate over the interior in 1896, Freetown became the capital, whose administrative, commercial, and other functions were vastly more important than those of any other place in the region. The colonial administration was hierarchically organized. In the metropole, the Colonial Office and Parliament made general policy. In the colony, the governor was at the apex and below him were important central officials, then provincial and district officers, and finally the chiefdom authorities. Directives moved from the capital to the lesser centers, taxes in the opposite direction. A small number of officials controlled the state's coercive force and its legislative and judicial machinery, which could be used to benefit or harm the interests of one or another ethnic group or class. They were the dominant element in the colonial power bloc, but to an extent they shared power with the top managers of Europeans firms.

Prior to the 1930s, Sierra Leone exported only agricultural and tree crops, above all palm and kola. The railway carried a significant share of traffic to and from the protectorate, and it connected Freetown with the richest producing areas. Even when traders began to use lorries, Freetown remained the chief port. Virtually all the large foreign firms chose Freetown as their headquarters. Commerce also was organized hierarchically. From their Freetown offices, businesses controlled shops and warehouses located in the important trading centers. Credit flowed downward from the banks and major companies to the middle-level European and Syrian firms, and then to smaller and still smaller African businesses.

From the 1930s the modern Sierra Leone economy emerged, based on mineral exports--primarily iron and diamonds (Kaniki, 1973b; Laan, 1965). The actual mineral production took place away from Freetown, and most of the managerial operations also were located in Marampa (in the case of iron) and towns of the Eastern Province (in the case of diamond mining). Still, the principal firms (Sierra Leone Development Company for iron, and Sierra Leone Selection Trust for diamonds) maintained offices and political ties in Freetown, and also had connections with authorities in London. Both firms considered it essential to work closely with the colonial state in order to foster and preserve favorable relations of production and profits. Similarly, as independence neared, the two companies forged ties with Sierra Leonean political leaders and with members of the growing educated bourgeoisie, whom they employed or put on retainer. Such arrangements assisted foreigners in their often highly successful efforts to reap

profits.[8] While this situation has been especially marked
in the mining industries, it has also been true in the agricultural export, import, and import-substitution sectors of
the economy.

Members of Freetown's bourgeoisie--European, African,
and Syrian--have either owned the most prized residential
property or lived on the estates owned by missions, trading
firms, or the government (Fyfe, 1962: 144ff.; Laan, 1975).
More important, members of the commercial bourgeoisie have
been the owners and managers of the high-value property on
the waterfront and main business streets. Officials, merchants, and company agents have made major decisions on
investment in the infrastructure, and have been the largest
employers of wage laborers. Members of this stratum have
tended to interact socially and to set a standard for "fine"
behavior.

The petty bourgeoisie has included shopkeepers, large-
scale marketmen and women (who oftentimes supplied others),
owners of commercial vehicles (boats and, later, lorries),
owners of manufacturing workshops (such as furniture or
clothes), and some other small independent business people,
including, for example, the more prosperous laundresses.
Whereas until recently the bourgeoisie included few women
other than those whose position was mediated by men, women
have always been represented in the petty bourgeoisie and
lower classes (Howard, 1986). In the nineteenth century, many
people in this group were only partially involved in capitalist relations of production and exchange: though they lived
by selling goods and services and had to purchase materials
and domestic requirements, they did not pay wages to their
labor force, or at least not to those who were members of
their household. Over time, such businesspeople increasingly
became wage-paying employers. Many also were suppliers of
petty traders and producers. Ranking with them were those in
the middle levels of the service sector, namely clerks,
teachers, and others who were employed by the government or
by members of the bourgeoisie.

The petty bourgeoisie has also included self-employed
artisans who owned their means of production, sold their
goods for cash, and in some cases hired workers: tailors,
seamstresses, sandalmakers, goldsmiths, cloth dyers, and so
on. They gradually shaded off into a larger body of producers
who were actually dependent workers because others supplied
them with tools or materials, or controlled their sales.
Similarly, small-scale full-time traders ranged from those
who had sufficient capital to buy a stock of goods to those
who operated with consignments belonging to others and were
in effect employees paid through commissions. Some petty traders and commodity producers also spent time as wage laborers
and would move back and forth depending on the opportunities.

The full-time wage earning population gradually grew in
size, with important increases around the turn of the century,
after the First World War, during and after the Second World
War, and then in the national period. We do not wish to debate
whether (and when) elements among the wage workers constituted
a "true" proletariat, but note that shortly after the turn of
the century, workers on the docks and rails and in construction went on strike, and that there have been active labor
organizations ever since (Luke, 1985a, 1985b). Below such

wage workers were the lowest paid service sector personnel who included maintenance workers, domestic servants, and others similarly employed. At the bottom were day laborers and others who lived within the capitalist sector in that they lacked a subsistence base in the rural economy and needed cash to pay for food, rent, and other necessities. Many people at these lower levels attached themselves to the households of those who were better off.

Historically, the great majority of the laboring population in Freetown, and in the immigrant ethnic communities in particular, have not been full-time wage workers. Rather, they have participated in the noncapitalist or mixed forms of relations of production and exchange in the hinterland and in the city itself. During the nineteenth century, artisanal and trading households in Freetown, especially large-scale units, maintained a high degree of self-sufficiency because they retained noncapitalist forms of production and exchange while trading within the capitalist sphere, and because they were not subordinated to large merchant firms. Additionally, many short-term wage workers remained rooted in a noncapitalist sphere which was as yet little affected by capitalism. Until the last few decades, most rural residents have had access to land, and the fact that most land has not been capitalized helped to preserve the links between immigrants and kin in the countryside, despite other changes in the rural economy.

Over time, however, capitalism and colonialism have destabilized or actually destroyed the noncapitalist relations of production and exchange. This has had great impact on Freetown. Among other things it has resulted in the creation of what Bromley and Geary (1979) have aptly described as a casual labor force. First, the peasant production unit in the countryside has been weakened by loss of labor and by increased market vulnerability (for example, because of the low prices for crops produced). In recent decades, a number of factors have greatly intensified these changes in the peasant economy, including the widespread practice of inheriting land through senior sons and the attraction of the alluvial diamond mines (Kaniki, 1973b; Laan, 1965; Moseley, 1979). This has meant that increasing numbers of immigrants to the city have not been sustained by self-sufficient farm units.

Second, within Freetown, trading and artisanal households have lost their self-sufficiency as more members have engaged in wage labor (either directly or in one of the disguised forms) or as such units have become tied to firms which supply them with trade goods or raw materials. Third, self-employed traders and artisans, and their households, have become increasingly vulnerable to market forces such as competition from imports and the rising prices of food and other essentials. The self-sufficiency of large-scale households headed by big men has declined with the end of slave labor, the spread of wage labor, and the impact of the same forces that have made smaller households vulnerable.

THE EARLY COLONIAL PERIOD (1790s TO CIRCA 1830)

By 1830, Freetown had a population of some 8,000, the majority of whom were Repatriated Africans (Nova Scotians and Maroons) and Liberated Africans (freed slaves). The

Repatriated Africans arrived with a strong sense of identity and distinctive cultures that had been shaped in the Americas--many were Christians who spoke a dialect of English. Liberated Africans brought with them the cultures of the homelands from which they had been torn, and they too began to group together around common social practices and beliefs. Small numbers of immigrants from inland or down the coast also had settled and were forming communities (Fyfe, 1962: 31-120; Wilson, 1976: 361-408).

Except for timber trade in the adjacent rivers, commercial links with the nearby hinterland were poorly developed; a minor trade with the coast and far interior also existed. Once the colony was established, official expenditures for construction and other projects maintained the wages of a considerable number of Repatriated and Liberated Africans. The latter received subsistence, clothing, and tools after their release from the slave vessels.

While it may seem artificial to label the small European population of officials, Christian missionaries, and merchants a power bloc, many Repatriated Africans and immigrants certainly looked on them as such. This early period was turbulent as the Europeans in charge of the Colony sought to circumscribe the economic and political advancement of the African residents and to impose British forms of Christianity. Blacks protested limits on their rights to participate in government and to worship freely. They leveled acrimonious charges of administrative abuse, and some rebelled and abandoned the settlement.

Nonetheless, there were commercial and other opportunities, and an element among the Nova Scotians and Maroons soon formed a nascent bourgeoisie. Some had come from the Americas with marketable skills and a capitalist mentality. They and others who took advantage of opportunities in Sierra Leone became prosperous in trade, held governmental positions, or were highly skilled artisans who operated construction businesses (building ships, storehouses, and so on). They plowed their capital back into other businesses and into land and property for sale or rent (Fyfe, 1962: 100-103; Peterson, 1969: 86ff.). They advanced their interests through their social and economic investments, that is to say, through ensuring that their children obtained "western-style" education, by making prestigious marriages, and by acquiring property.

The great majority of people were petty traders and commodity producers, laborers, laundresses and suppliers of other services, farmers, fishermen, and--in the case of many who were newly liberated from slave ships--apprentices, servants, or (temporarily) wards of the colony. "Class" distinctions were indicated by housing: frame and stone houses ". . . were occupied chiefly by the older segments of the town's population . . . [who] set the standard to which the lower classes [living in mud and wattle or clapboard] aspired." (Peterson, 1969: 87)

Both the Nova Scotians and Maroons had a sense of group identity forged out of their American and Sierra Leonean experiences. In part, this identity grew from antagonism against their British sponsors who refused to grant them equality in government or as human beings, and against the new, recaptive population whom they viewed as upstarts and naked savages.

Eventually many of the Repatriated African families died out, but a remnant contributed to the development of the later Sierra Leonean (Krio) population, with its emphasis on Christianity and Victorian bourgeois values, attachment to England, and distinctiveness from the "aborigines."

Lacking their own material resources and struggling to survive, Liberated Africans freed from the slave ships naturally sought out those who spoke a similar language and had similar social practices. Administrators encouraged ethnic solidarity among liberated slaves by clustering in small settlements those who came from the same part of the coast. In these settlements they worked together in trade, farming, fishing, and other endeavors. This process of community building by those at the bottom of society became more marked in the following decades (Fyfe, 1962: 119-20).

Similarly, immigrants from the hinterland quickly formed communities. The Kroo provide an interesting example of how government intervention helped to consolidate people with a similar economic function into an ethnic group. With the increase in shipping and import-export trade, members of various Liberian "tribes" became dominant as dockworkers and shiphands. They were recruited partly because men from that area already had acquired a reputation as seamen during slave trading days. The collective name "Kroo"--a kind of "categorical" ethnic designation--existed before the first of them had come to Freetown. As their numbers and importance to the economy grew, the government in 1816 settled them in their own "Krootown" to the west of the city. Internally, the community was organized under headmen who led labor gangs. The heads or their affiliates recruited newcomers on the Liberian coast, often from their own village or a nearby area; generally employers paid wages to the headmen, who then in turn paid their subordinates. Individuals who stayed permanently in Freetown took up independent jobs, but for several decades much of the population of Krootown was temporary, returning home to a noncapitalist economy when their period of service was finished, and perhaps later joining another gang.

A rather different case was the Susu settlement located to the east of Freetown. It was led by Dala Modu Dumbuya--son of a prominent trader, landowner, and political leader from Sumbuya kingdom--who arrived in 1799 with about one hundred kin, clients, and other followers. Dala Modu came specifically to forge commercial and political ties with Freetown, and those under him were there to assist in that goal. In particular, he acted as a "landlord" (Mande: jatigi) who hosted caravans from the north, and he also aided the Sierra Leone Company agents in expeditions to the northern rivers. He became, in effect, the first headman of an ethnic community in Freetown, and was a bridge between the capitalist and noncapitalist spheres. In 1806, officials expelled the Susu community, alleging that they were slave dealers and that their Muslim practices were baneful. This was an early sign of an attitude of Christian chauvinism and exclusiveness held by many, if not all, authorities, missionaries, and Repatriated Africans--and later by a portion of the Liberated Africans and their Krio descendants. Dala Modu refused either to abandon Islam, as officials called upon him to do, or to sever ties with Freetown. Instead, he relocated his people in

Bullom, just across the Sierra Leone River, and not only continued to trade with the city but built strong business connections with a leading timber merchant and served as a political ally of the Colony in dealings with the hinterland.

In these respects, the Susu were the first example of how new immigrants who were not Christian shaped an ethnic identity and community within a Christian and capitalist environment dominated by Europeans and Christian Africans. Furthermore, it is important to stress that although both Kroo and Susu operated to some extent within the sphere of capitalist relations as laborers and traders, their internal social, economic, and political affairs were largely determined by patron-client and kin ties. Thus, community formation took place through a process by which leaders recruited members for an economic function; a sense of identity was forged not simply because of cultural similarity but out of awareness of a unique economic role and through direct patron-client and kin ties between leaders and followers.

THE MIDDLE COLONIAL PERIOD (CIRCA 1830-1870s)

The population of Freetown rose to about 15,000 by the 1870s. Liberated Africans and other residents of Freetown and the villages did much to transform commerce and the city itself. Their energetic pursuit of gain and their alliance-building helped to draw the city and its hinterland more closely together and to strengthen Freetown's role in overseas commerce. Export of palm oil, palm kernels, peanuts, and other commodities from the hinterland rose markedly; imports expanded comparably. Traffic in foodstuffs, raw materials, and manufactures for the city increased greatly, as did craft production within the center itself. Parliament ended subsidies for the support of Liberated Africans but continued naval and other subventions. For the most part colonial revenues were derived from taxes on commerce.

Increasingly, the social life of the city was structured by the ethnic communities: first the Liberated Africans, then the immigrants from the interior. People created institutions such as councils, churches, and mosques, which in turn were influenced by the interaction with government and missionary officials.

The Liberated Africans were divided into a number of ethnic groups. Largest was the Aku (Yoruba) which, despite efforts at unity, was split by religion and place of origin. Muslim Aku (plus some Hausa and others) organized three communities at Fourah Bay, Fula Town, and Aberdeen. The vastly more numerous Christian Aku, who lived in East Freetown and other suburbs, played an even more important role in social, political, and economic life. They formed the core of what later became the Krio community. Other Liberated African communities were internally divided by institutional affiliation (for example, churches), neighborhood, and struggles over leadership.

During this period, Liberated Africans and their descendants became merchants, educators, lawyers, colonial officials, religious functionaries, skilled craftspeople, and various types of traders. These occupations were within the capitalist sphere for the most part, although traders and some other businesspeople often used apprentices, wards, or other unpaid labor. Petty trade (and, occasionally, production) was the springboard into the bourgeoisie. A favorite device for initial acquisition of capital was the esusu association, whereby people from the same homeland regularly contributed small amounts of money and each in turn received the total collection. Liberated Africans also pooled their money to purchase quantities of goods auctioned off condemned slave ships. As traders rose, however, their businesses displayed more characteristics of the family firm.

Access to cheap labor--kin, servants, and apprentices--helped the developing bourgeoisie to consolidate their class position. For example, to the 1840s, colony authorities apprenticed many hundreds of newly freed Africans, mostly young people, to already settled Repatriated and Liberated Africans who used them as domestic servants, laborers, and business assistants. Some masters provided their servants and apprentices with education and even trading capital; eventually some moved into the bourgeoisie. Many remained in lowly positions, however, and there were frequent criticisms about the abuse of the so-called apprentice system (Fyfe, 1962: 106-7, 182-83; Howard, 1986).

The Church Missionary Society and the Wesleyan Missionary Society laid the base for a strong educational system in Freetown and the colony by opening Fourah Bay Institution (later Fourah Bay College, attached to Durham University) in 1827, by increasing the number of primary schools in the 1830s, and by founding secondary schools in the 1840s. The churches also sent selected students abroad for higher education. Individual missionaries and entrepreneurs also established institutions of learning at that time and during later periods. This system helped to retard the education of Muslims in "British" subjects, as there were no secular schools until the twentieth century. Western-style education not only provided many receptives and their children with the means of mobility, but also served to recruit them into the professional sector and into the lesser positions of clerk, teacher, and catechist, all roles needed for the European plan of "civilizing" West Africa through commerce and Christianity. With education went prized positions in the private and public sectors, and high social status. Before the end of this period, professionals of Liberated African background joined merchants in the bourgeoisie, and a few were drawn into the power bloc.

The missionaries also provided schooling in skilled trades, but much more training took place on the job; thus, Liberated Africans hired by the government or by merchants entered such full-time, salaried occupations as ship pilots, surveyors, and machinery (for example, crane) operators. Most of these people saw themselves as superior to the unskilled immigrants from the interior. Their religion, language, and kinship linked them with the more prestigious members of their community even though they often belonged to different churches and other associations. Such links helped to moderate class divisions among the Christian Sierra Leoneans and to preserve a base for the later development of a Krio identity.

From the late 1830s through the early 1850s, the division between the Christian and non-Christian communities was

sharpened by colonial government persecution of both the Muslim Aku and immigrant populations. This campaign included the
burning of mosques, restrictions on Muslim proselytization,
and trials of Muslim traders accused of slave dealing. In
part, Muslims formed ethnic communities to meet the challenge
of the Christian administrators, missionaries, and residents
of the city.

During this period, Freetown's trade with the far
interior increased greatly, and by the 1850s communities of
immigrants were becoming larger and better organized. These
communities became identified as Serakule, Mandingo, Susu,
and Fula, but each was diversified ethnically. For example,
the Mandingo group was composed of people who identified
themselves more discretely as Jakhanke, Bambara, Wasulunke,
Sangara, and others. Most of the headmen and elders were
either traders or Muslim religious specialists, and they
built the communities through the formation and use of networks that reached into the interior. This period saw much
network-building between big men of Freetown and the interior,
which allowed them to transfer resources from the noncapitalist to the capitalist sphere, and vice versa. This process
was integral to both ethnic group and class formation.

Within the emerging ethnic groups and within the Muslim
immigrant community as a whole there was a class order. The
superior class position of the headmen and elders was achieved
through their control of labor and other resources, their
commercial, religious, and political ties with the noncapitalist sphere, and their mediating position. They were linked
through kinship, alliances (including marriage), commerce,
and Islam to the slave-holding ruling class of northwestern
Sierra Leone and the interior. Some held land in the kingdoms
of the near hinterland, gained through so-called landlord-
stranger contracts with local authority holders and notables
who granted them use rights. Those lands were worked by kin
and slaves, and the food and other products were used to
support the urban compound or trading operations, such as the
hospitality furnished to heads of large caravans that reached
Freetown. Furthermore, through their alliances with big men
of the interior, the Freetown leaders were at least indirect
beneficiaries of the noncapitalist circulation systems that
were based on the extraction of products from women, junior
kin, clients, and slaves, as well as peasant subjects of the
rulers.

In Freetown the headmen and elders made connections with
merchants and government officials, and they obtained land on
which they erected large compounds for commercial operations,
manufacturing, and Islamic instruction. These urban activities, together with their offices and high status roles such
as _jatigi_ and _alfa_, enabled them to act as allies or patrons
to newcomers and to control the circulation of wealth within
the communities. They provided immigrants with housing and
backed them in trade and other occupations. Newcomers who had
connections with the interior, religious training, or capital
were able to form and then enlarge their own compounds.
Others lived within the households of the big men, where they
carried out auxiliary tasks such as transporting rice and
kola, tending cattle held for sale, or tying and dying cloth.
Some had their own small households and did tailoring, lea-
ther working, or petty trade, or were laborers and service

workers. These people looked to the community leaders for aid in obtaining the means of production, bride wealth, and other material things; for assistance in dealing with the police and other colony authorities; and for cultural needs centering around the mosques, <u>karanthe</u>, and annual holidays (Skinner, 1976: 511-20). Thus the ethnic groups were collections of big men plus their kin, dependents, and clients. They numbered from a few hundred to a few thousand at most. Typically, the communities split into factions based on competition for headship or other offices; they were not sharply divided along class lines because of the kinship and patron-client ties.

THE HIGH COLONIAL PERIOD TO THE END OF THE COLONIAL PERIOD (1870s-1949)

Between 1870 and 1949, the British conquered the interior and extended colonial rule over the protectorate, which, despite differences in its legal status, became integrated with and dominated by the colony. Freetown thus became the administrative headquarters of a greatly expanded territory and population, and its organizational role grew correspondingly. European, Lebanese, Syrian, and Indian firms set up operations in the administrative and commercial towns, effectively pushing Sierra Leoneans and other Africans out of the middle-level positions they had previously held.

As a result of upheavals associated with the spread of colonialism and capitalism, immigration from the hinterland increased substantially in the late nineteenth century, especially from the nearby Temne- and Limba-speaking areas to the north. By 1911, the population of the city had reached 34,000, and for the first time the Sierra Leonean-Krio population comprised less than 50 percent of Freetown's residents. The railway, spread of a money economy and other changes associated with colonialism stimulated a further increase in the population to 55,000 by 1931 (though the depression had probably already caused some exodus to the countryside by that year). The Second World War brought a rapid expansion because of the strategic importance of the port. It is estimated that the city's population reached between 64,000 and 70,000 by 1948.

Although there were periodic economic downturns, overall in the decades after the 1870s there was increasing demand for both skilled and unskilled workers to carry out Freetown's expanded commercial and administrative roles. Skilled employees were needed in construction, communications, commerce, shipping, and, of course, to fill many bureaucratic and educational posts. European import-export and merchandising firms, old and new, established branches throughout Sierra Leone, managed from their main offices in Freetown. The railway, colonial administration, banks, and other agencies similarly had Freetown headquarters requiring sizeable staffs which organized and supervised work done elsewhere in Sierra Leone. This expansion was one of the factors which caused the Christian and Muslim educational systems to grow, requiring more teachers and administrators and also opening up opportunities for many people who had been excluded previously. The number of Muslim schools in Freetown increased

from one to six between 1891 and 1903, and many of the sons
and daughters of the Muslim elite were afforded English
instruction in either the Christian or Muslim schools. They
began to join the ranks of the clerks, bureaucrats, and other
white collar employees, although most of the new positions
requiring western-style education still went to Christian
Krios.

At the lower end of the economic structure, head por-
terage and casual labor were required for the construction of
streets, houses, wharves, and warehouses, and for the recoal-
ing of steamers and the transshipment of palm kernels, peanuts, kola, bales of cloth, hardware, and many other bulky
commodities. Most of these laborers remained cyclical or
seasonal migrants, but a growing number became long-term or
permanent residents. This was reflected in the occupational
statistics for indigenous people (immigrants from the hinterland or descendants of immigrants) recorded in the 1931
census. A majority (over 59 percent) were unemployed, unskilled, or low-skilled workers; nearly 41 percent were
skilled or semiskilled; and only .014 percent were professionals. In the first category, more than four out of ten were
listed as unemployed, and about an equal number were either
casual laborers or street peddlers. Presumably, a significant
portion would return to the countryside. In the category of
the skilled and semiskilled were craftspeople, seamen, petty
traders, commercial and government workers (clerks), teachers,
clerics, and soldiers.

During the last quarter of the nineteenth century, the
number of Europeans grew. They expressed a more virulent
racism toward Africans, especially toward bourgeois Sierra
Leoneans, whose accomplishments they disparaged. Government,
missions, and business firms discriminated racially in filling
upper-level posts, and Europeans formed such institutions as
members only clubs and the "Hill Station" residential area.
The Sierra Leone bourgeoisie fought back politically and
culturally, particularly through the press, which became a
vehicle for the development of a Krio identity and a means
for reaching the petty bourgeoisie and laborers, many of whom
were threatened by the competition of interior people or
migrants.

Both Christian and Muslim Krio communities were economically and socially stratified. The Christian (and later the
Muslim) Krio bourgeoisie became well defined by commercial
activities, landownership, rental property, higher governmental and educational positions, and professional qualifications. Those with the greatest wealth and status were in many
respects as bourgeois as their European counterparts, and
they differentiated themselves from poorer Krios even though
they shared many cultural characteristics. While Krio culture
retained strong elements of the various cultures brought by
Liberated Africans (for example, Yoruba practices such as
awujo), bourgeois Krio culture was a new entity, defined
through a dialectical interaction with English culture. Krio
ethnic identity, as expressed by the bourgeoisie in poetry,
newspaper articles, and genteel social practices, was forged
in the colonial context. Racial pride was a way of asserting
the position of this class in the face of the slurs and
discriminatory practices of whites. Furthermore, many of the
concrete issues from the 1870s through the 1920s--from the

days of the Native Pastorate controversy to the National
Congress of British West Africa--involved efforts of the Krio
bourgeoisie to protect or advance their position within the
capitalist sphere or power bloc: to win legislative seats,
gain administrative jobs, combat Lebanese business incursion,
and stem the flow of immigrants from the interior (Porter,
1963; Spitzer, 1974).

Around the turn of the century, ethnic lines between
Krios and other Africans hardened. Prior to that time, many
Sierra Leoneans had traded in the rivers near Freetown, where
they often formed commercial and marital alliances with indigenous people. Furthermore, Freetown residents often adopted
interior people into their households and families. The ethnic
boundary was permeable. Apparently, however, although such
interaction did not cease, the economic and political changes
of the late nineteenth and early twentieth centuries rigidi-
fied ethnic distinctions and gave rise to a more strongly
self-conscious Krio identity. This identity was shaped particularly by members of the bourgeoisie. In addition, starting
in 1896, the British administration made the Sierra Leoneans'
unique status as British subjects applicable to the protectorate as well as the colony, and legally differentiated them
from the indigenous population. The Hut Tax war of 1898 led
to the deaths of many Sierra Leoneans and drove others from
their shops in the river towns, at least temporarily. This
heightened the apprehension of those living in Freetown, who
felt threatened by a "flood" of "aborigines." (An article of
1887 in a Sierra Leonean-edited newspaper likened them to the
"plague of locusts that once troubled the Egyptians": see
Harrell-Bond, Howard, and Skinner, 1978: 125-27.) Job competition between immigrants and Krios brought about flare-ups
of interethnic violence. Syrians took over important sectors
of trade after colonial rule was established, supplanting
Sierra Leoneans. Krios of all classes reacted defensively
and, at times, hostilely to immigrants and Syrians. The Krio
petty bourgeoisie increasingly turned to salaried occupations,
while the bourgeoisie sought to consolidate themselves in the
professions and middle-level salaried jobs through secondary
and higher education (Kaniki, 1973a; White, 1982). This
afforded some Krios a share in the power bloc and strengthened
the position of Krios as a group vis-a-vis people from the
hinterland, who perceived them as dominating many aspects of
urban life.

Immigrants arriving in ever-greater numbers augmented
old ethnic communities and formed new ones. The leaders of
the communities helped the poor to meet the problems of
living in a city where capitalism prevailed and one ethnic
group predominated. Most importantly, they acted as interpreters in both the literal and the broader cultural senses
and as representatives of their communities to the colonial
government. These roles positioned the headmen as the primary
mediators with the power bloc. Community leaders also provided
a structure for social life, most notably by settling disputes
in their courts. To a degree, they also helped people to
secure housing, jobs, western education, and--toward the end
of the period--other social services. Leaders varied greatly
in their effectiveness; those who were politically and
economically weak were severely limited in what they could
accomplish for their members.

The colonial government saw the importance of recognizing both headmen and ethnic institutions. Officials sought
means to communicate with and control the immigrant population. This process, which started during the 1870s, began to
be institutionalized in 1890 with the circulation of a list
of duties of alimamis and in 1891 with the founding of a
government-sponsored Muslim school (madrasa). The headman
system was incorporated into the colonial administration in
1905 through legislation that recognized and defined a role
for tribal rulers. (Harrell-Bond, Howard, and Skinner, 1978:
105-56ff., appendices B and C). Between 1908 and 1940 the
number of headmen sanctioned by the government increased from
five to fourteen, as each ethnic community agitated for representation. This was a reflection of the growing significance
of the non-Krio population and of ethnic identity. Thus, by
formal recognition, the colonial government reenforced the
efforts of headmen and communities to strengthen ethnic
institutions and identities.

The internal structure of the newer ethnic communities
formed by the Temne, Limba, Mende, and others from the protectorate was different in certain key respects from the older
Mande and Fula communities. Whereas the early trading communities were small and tightly knit through networks dominated
by big men, communities such as the Temne were much larger
and more unstable in membership. Although the kinds of networks which typified the Mandingo, for example, were not
altogether lacking, such networks did not closely link most
members of the larger communities who were dispersed throughout the city, nor did their leaders have the material resources and high standing in the traditional-Islamic society
to dominate the communities. By the end of this period, however, a complex internal structure had developed in some
communities, with neighborhood santigis or other officials
organizing those who lived around them.

By serving as labor recruiters and interpreters for
government and businesses, and by operating official courts,
headmen and elders acquired influence and a certain amount of
wealth and power. Some ethnic officials abused their positions. In particular, those who acted as labor recruiters
were able to demand a "dash" or a share of wages. Within
communities there was pressure from below, and rivals sometimes succeeded in removing corrupt or authoritarian leaders.
Officials also disciplined some leaders accused of impropri-
ety. The government, however, also expected headmen to act as
colonial administrators and to oversee and report on their
people, which created the potential for cooptation. Recognizing this dilemma, headmen and elders resisted being fully
incorporated into the colonial structure and maintained
considerable institutional autonomy (Harrell-Bond, Howard,
and Skinner, 1978: 85-104ff.).

The immigrant ethnic communities were economically
stratified, but class divisions were not marked. Throughout
most of this period, leaders in the smaller, commercially
oriented communities continued to derive much of their wealth
from estates in the hinterland, support of kin and other
dependents, or trade and other activities that involved the
noncapitalist sphere. Most traders did not accumulate large
amounts of capital, and those who were most successful did
not make major investments in the capitalist sphere, but

rather continued to operate businesses that had noncapitalist characteristics. The leaders of the larger communities typically were not prosperous traders and did not acquire wealth sufficient to differentiate them greatly from their followers. Acting as labor suppliers, for example, did not secure their position, nor could they tap significant resources flowing within their communities because of the poverty of most of the members. Though some leaders owned urban land and housing, they used it more to accommodate kin and other supporters than to profit through rental. Moreover, virtually all headmen and elders remained socially and culturally close to their followers because they lived in physical proximity to them, interacted with them regularly, shared in the major annual religious and other cultural events, and were not separated by the acquisition of western education to the exclusion of Islamic or indigenous culture.

Immigrants who were clerks, semiskilled laborers, or other full-time employees often became dependent on wages, though they lived in households where other members traded or engaged in crafts. Day laborers, too, were concerned with work conditions and wages since they bought food, clothing, and other things. There thus existed a potential for both full- and part-time workers to strike or take other job actions, alone or in concert with Krio coworkers. In 1919 and again in 1926, cross-ethnic strikes did in fact occur, and headmen took a role in the latter strike. The solidarity between Krio and other workers was short-lived in both cases, however (Wyse, 1981). The 1919 strike quickly turned into a general populist protest and riot, and government repression of strikers was harsh. Furthermore, job competition continued to generate interethnic rivalry, even violence, with headmen and other community leaders involved.

The strikes of 1919 and 1926 had shown that some wage workers were willing to organize for action, but because most urban dwellers remained peripheral to the capitalist sphere, the potential for a sustained, broadly based workers' movement was limited. The nearest Sierra Leone came to such a movement was just before the Second World War, when a movement was sparked by the activities of the West African Youth League (Sierra Leone branch) led by I. T. A. Wallace-Johnson.

Wallace-Johnson, born in Sierra Leone in 1894 of poor Krio parents, was a strong Pan-Africanist and nationalist who had stayed for a short time in the Soviet Union. During the 1920s and 1930s, he had close contact with Africans and Europeans who were Marxists and Marxist-influenced. He was knowledgeable about Marxism and generally oriented toward its principles. In some of his writings and speeches, and in certain political actions during the late 1930s, he appeared to be following Marxist ideological or organizational principles. He understood, however, that Krio conservatism, the lack of a proletarian base, and government opposition would prevent revolutionary change. While the West African Youth League in Sierra Leone had a brief militant phase from 1938 to 1939, it encountered severe government repression. During the war, Wallace-Johnson and some key associates were imprisoned and became demoralized. The Youth League did not survive the war as a militant movement, and Wallace-Johnson emerged from prison without a radical base. He did not take up his former efforts to unite the Krio progressives and the enlightened leaders of the various interior peoples with lower class activists, and he became a rather conservative advocate of Krio rights.[9]

Access to English-language education allowed more members of ethnic communities to achieve salaried positions in the European-dominated capitalist and colonial order, and a few moved into the better paying salaried jobs and even into the bourgeoisie. During the 1930s and 1940s, the first awakening of nationalist and radical anticolonial politics also provided opportunities for a new kind of leader, who often worked in cooperation with the more progressive Krios. J. T. Reffell, a Bassa leader and later headman, was an official of the West African Youth League. Kandeh Bure, a Temne school teacher and later headman, formed a youth group that openly challenged the Temne elders; in the 1950s, he became active in national politics and helped to form the Sierra Leone People's Party. Many who later became community elders had by the Second World War gained wage-earning skilled labor jobs or civil service posts, were clerks or teachers, or had begun to move into trade in the capitalist sphere. Thus, community leadership positions could be obtained by younger people who had acquired modern urban jobs and sources of status, and were responsive to the needs of the rapidly growing body of semiskilled and casual workers. This helped to channel urban forms of conflict into the ethnic structure and away from political movements based on working-class interests. Such leaders were especially influential when they also acquired traditional-Islamic sources of status or teamed with western educated scions of the earlier community leaders.

THE NATIONALIST AND POST-INDEPENDENCE PERIOD (1950-1980s)

During this period, Freetown changed from being the capital of a colony to the capital of a neocolonial state. It retained its economic and administrative domination over the hinterland. Foreigners continued to hold a preeminent position in the economy, concentrated in mining, import-export, and the increasingly important construction and import substitution industries (oil refining, brewing, and basic consumer goods). New opportunities arose for Africans to gain wealth through business and the professions, and the non-Krio bourgeoisie grew in numbers and prominence. As Freetown's population increased, non-Krio leaders played a more powerful role in city politics. A few progressive Krio, some ethnic leaders in Freetown, and a newly emerged group of western-educated leaders from the protectorate joined to force the British to relinquish political authority. The African organizational bourgeoisie--Krio and non-Krio--came to play a major role in the power bloc, and in part served as intermediaries between the world and Sierra Leonean economies.

The population of Freetown increased from about 130,000 at independence in 1963 to well over 300,000 fifteen years later. Although there is no precise statistical information on the demographics of this increase, data from other African cities, the 1963 Freetown census, and field surveys suggest that while immigration accounted for over half of the new residents, births in the city may have been nearly equally as important (Harvey, 1968). Newborns and migrants swelled the size of the ethnic communities. For example, the Temne population in 1963 was just over 30,000, while in the 1975 Temne headman election there were almost 30,000 votes cast, primarily by adult males (Harrell-Bond, Howard, and Skinner, 1978: 34, 295). Similarly, it was estimated that the Fula population rose from more than 6,000 to about 30,000 during the same period. While salaried positions increased substantially, petty producers and traders, casual workers, and unemployed constituted most of the urban youth and adult population.

Nationalist- and independence-era politics lacked a Marxist-Leninist or even a democratic socialist movement. With the decline of the Youth League and the retirement of Wallace-Johnson from radical politics, no other left-wing political or social movement developed to organize the lower classes. The 1939 labor crisis had revealed that thousands of workers and others were responsive to Wallace-Johnson's radical anticolonial, prolabor appeal. Furthermore, in the 1940s, union organizers gained some successs. However, no broadly based workers' movement emerged, many labor leaders were coopted by the government and employers, and those militant workers who did exist failed to radicalize the national movement.[10] Nationalism and reformism--in other words, anticolonialist and Pan-Africanist ideologies, coupled with a call for Africanization--were taken up by progressive leaders. The important activists included Albert Margai (a Mende barrister), Siaka Stevens (a Limba trade union leader), Constance A. Cummings-John (a Krio politician and feminist), and Kande Bureh. Late in 1951, they and others joined to form the Sierra Leone People's Party (SLPP), which became the first African-led government in 1957 and the ruling party in 1960, when the country gained independence. In 1961, dissidents within the SLPP plus other politicians founded the All People's Congress (APC), which later became the dominant party in Sierra Leone (Cartwright, 1970: 55-181; Cummings-John and Denzer, forthcoming).

Among the more prominent nationalist and reformist leaders, none was a Marxist or even a democratic socialist. They had people-oriented ideas and policies but lacked any conception of or program for proletarian consciousness-raising or nationalization of the economy. Two of the founders of the SLPP subsequently became heads of the national government. Their policies demonstrated no tendency toward socialism, but rather were consistent with the development of a neocolonial national bourgeoisie. Albert Margai, prime minister from 1964 to 1967, pursued procapitalist, acquisitive goals. Siaka Stevens, head of state from 1968 to 1985, was hostile to any program of socialism and to the development of militant trade unionism. In 1955, trade unionists attacked Stevens because he failed to support the goals of workers, and in 1981 they strongly criticized his administration. He also had a long career of cooperation with multinational corporations and acquisition of personal wealth (Cartwright, 1970, 1978; Allen, 1978; West Africa, Aug. 10, 24, 31; Sept. 7, 14, 21, 28, 1981).[11]

Leaders of the political parties--along with some higher-ranking civil servants, military officers, and police; company managers; professionals; wealthier business people;

and headmen and traditional authorities--became the organizational bourgeoisie and members of the power bloc. Thus, they helped to manage the neocolonial economy in Sierra Leone. Incomes from salaries, business profits, rental properties, speculation, or corruption allowed many to live luxuriously. They invested in additional property, bought expensive consumer goods (Mercedes Benz autos, stereo systems, color televisions, furniture), sent their children to private schools in West Africa or overseas, took expensive vacations, and transferred funds to foreign bank accounts or even invested abroad. In short, they behaved in ways consistent with their class position and often did not favor policies that would benefit the majority of Sierra Leoneans.

The Krio bourgeoisie continued to predominate in certain sectors of the civil service and advanced education (especially at elite secondary schools and in the colleges and university) and in higher Christian church positions, law, medicine, accounting, advertising, media, and management of businesses, particularly in the multinational firms (sharing such posts with Europeans, North Americans, and Syrians). During the national period, however, bureaucratic, educational, and other professional positions increased greatly in number, and most were filled by members of other ethnic communities. As the immigrant proportion of Freetown's population grew, as the franchise was expanded, and as the cultural character of the city became predominantly Muslim and indigenous, leaders obtained higher government and corporate positions because of their influence and power within the ethnic structure. Foreign businesses recognized the political and other advantages in hiring or allying with such people. Some headmen and ethnic leaders became part of the bourgeoisie through their wealth, education, or jobs. Conversely, as ethnic and national structures became more completely integrated, people who had achieved high positions outside their communities could use their wealth and influence to win the headship. Overall, as the big men of the ethnic communities gained more influence within national economic and political institutions, they expanded or created patron-client networks and promoted the interests of their kin, friends, and associates.

Community leaders had a particularly important role in the processes of ethnic representation, political organization, and class formation. In 1956, the property qualifications for voting in municipal elections were reduced, and women were given the franchise. Whereas only 544 people voted in 1954 for the Freetown Municipal Council, 9,900 elected a much more broadly representative Council in 1957: two Muslim Krios, five Christian Krios, two Temne, one Fula, one Limba (son of a former headman), and one Bassa (J. T. Reffell, the headman). Also in 1957, Kande Bureh, the Temne headman, was appointed minister of works and housing in the SLPP government. From the late 1950s, Freetown headmen often used their ethnic community base to become active in party politics, and party affiliation became an important factor in headmen elections. It is during this period that some ethnic headmen became shapers of the national political system, as well as intermediaries between their followers and government or business.

During the postcolonial period many of the headmen became integrated into the national bourgeoisie, yet they retained strong ties with ruling houses or other notable families in the interior and kept use of their own family lands. All of the headmen were active either in Christian or Muslim organizations and most were senior officials of their churches or mosques. Most had formal education; in 1976 eleven of them were literate (five in English, five in Arabic, and one in both English and French). They had access to both urban and rural resources, and wealth acquired in the capitalist sector was invested to develop plantations. Eleven of the headmen in 1976 had extensive farms in rural areas, and nine were important holders of rental or business property in the Western Area (Freetown and the former colony). The Temne head, King David Kamara, had substantial lands through his paternal relations and connections with a ruling house of Kaffu Bullom chiefdom, and he also owned considerable property in Freetown. A. M. Pujeh, the Mende head who was descended from an important Muslim political family, became an APC member of Parliament from Kenema West and gained the management of a petroleum distribution concession in Sierra Leone. Others had important governmental positions before being elected to their headship. Robert Chanyour (Sherbro headman) was a civil servant in the ministry of public works for thirty-six years and retired as senior inspector of works, after which he owned a construction company. The Kroo head, John Wales, was active in many community organizations and also rose to the post of assistant commissioner of police in Freetown. Kandeh Ibrahim Conteh was educated both in English and Islamic studies and spent more than twenty years as an administrator in Susu organizations before being elected headman in 1975. He was a large property owner in town.

Still, it should be stressed that most ethnic headmen, elders, and clerics remained on the periphery of the bourgeoisie. They did not participate in extreme forms of conspicuous consumption, although they certainly attended to the education of their own children. Often, they channelled much of their income back into their communities, and they retained close relations with the lower classes there. This continues to be an important reason why class contradictions have not significantly divided ethnic communities. The ethnic leaders--most of whom have lived in neighborhoods composed of artisans, laborers, petty traders and commodity producers, other casual workers, and the unemployed--have operated an economic redistribution system that has helped to mitigate the degrading social and economic conditions of urban life: poverty, lack of amenities, crime, and social dislocation. Not only have they provided money for mosques, churches, schools, clinics, and "fetes," they have found their followers jobs and housing. In addition, they have run courts which have reduced both intra- and interethnic tensions. The activities of the headmen and the ethnic communities--such as the construction of mosques, churches and schools; the display of floats; the feasts and celebrations at religious holidays; the gatherings of the women's ja'ama associations; and other social or religious affairs--generally have given their lower class followers a sense of identity and well-being. Ethnic identity has compensated for feelings of social and economic inferiority and dislocation experienced by many of the urban poor.

The continued vitality and importance of the headmen and ethnic institutions have been demonstrated in a number of ways. Urban dwellers accord great respect to headmen and other notables within the various communities, viewing the more important of them as equal in stature to national politicians. The headmen's courts have not lost their popularity or value in the eyes of the communities, who turn to them to resolve disputes and to obtain justice in an inexpensive and understandable manner. An effort by the National Reformation Council or NRC (military government) to eliminate the ethnic structure faltered. In 1967, the NRC abolished the system of headmen, ethnic officials, and courts, considering it part of the corrupt political process and a waste of national resources. However, the large increase in the size of Freetown's immigrant population, the persistence of illegal ethnic courts and governments, and the difficulty of organizing the disparate population through conventional municipal government or party institutions caused the APC government under the leadership of President Stevens to reestablish the office of headship on January 1, 1969, and headmen elections resumed (Harrell-Bond, Howard, and Skinner, 1978: 267ff.). The number of ethnic groups rose to sixteen by 1975. Groups with as few as 200 members wanted to be represented in the urban political structure, hoping to share in whatever resources might become available thereby.

Nevertheless, the contradictions have been serious. Since the 1890s headmen have had to deal with the efforts of the government to coopt them and the temptations to accumulate wealth at their people's expense. For example, the Freetown police have long sought the cooperation of headmen in monitoring immigrants and apprehending suspected criminals. Government departments and private firms have remunerated headmen directly for supplying laborers or have allowed them to collect fees from workers. Tribal courts became adjuncts of the colonial administration, yet headmen and elders were subject to little supervision and often abused their positions by collecting excessive fees and making preferential decisions. In 1975, the government began to use the community officials to collect taxes, which enabled them to pocket tax monies while discrediting them as tax agents.

These administrative contradictions, however, are not as fundamental as the political contradictions. From around 1957, the SLPP, United People's Party, and People's National Party initiated the practices of interfering in headman elections and of using headmen as party adjuncts, who would help to win municipal council and Parliamentary seats. Disloyalty to the ruling party became a basis for dismissal from headship (Harrell-Bond, Howard, and Skinner, 1978: 201, 249ff.). The APC has made even stronger efforts to draw headmen into party politics. Three headmen—K. D. Kamara (Temne), A. M. Pujeh (Mende), and J. T. Reffell (Bassa)—have had considerable influence within the APC, and that has given the party direct links with the ethnic political machinery. Other headmen and their lieutenants have been made to feel that cooperation with the dominant party was necessary, and they have helped deliver votes to the APC and control the urban population. These political obligations may cause the urban poor to view the ethnic leaders as part of the "downpressing" power bloc and may in the future generate actions to replace particular ethnic leaders or to form populist ethnic or transethnic organizations. [12]

CONCLUSION

The Freetown case suggests that an analysis of ethnicity and class requires examination of five interrelated historical processes:

1. the impact of capitalism on the noncapitalist economies;

2. the composition and policies of the colonial (and national or neocolonial) power bloc;

3. the ability of particular African communities to forge an identity, assert their cultural symbols, and gain a position of relative dominance, which then conditions the behavior of later migrants and the subsequent formation of communities;

4. the class position of ethnic leaders and their capacity to satisfy or control followers by drawing on resources in the capitalist and noncapitalist economies and by creating mixed forms of economic relations; and

5. the capacity of workers and others to organize on class lines and the broader appeal of the programs and ideologies they develop.

Colin Leys (1974) correctly argues that the impact of capitalism on noncapitalist relations of production and exchange has given rise to new forms of insecurity and competition, and hence to a modern form of tribalism. The impact of capitalism, however, has varied greatly from territory to territory. In some African territories the presence of European settlers, private ownership of land, or large-scale investment in mining and manufacturing led to the radical alteration of the relations of production and exchange at an early stage in the colonial era. These influences have given rise to a sizeable landless urban population and a proletariat. In Sierra Leone and in Freetown itself capitalism transformed the noncapitalist economy slowly and incompletely. Until the 1930s, only commercial capitalism existed in Sierra Leone. Patterns of ethnic and class formation were deeply affected by the fact that most residents were cyclical migrants, petty traders, and producers, or were otherwise only partially involved in the capitalist economy. Furthermore, since the 1930s, the great majority of new residents have been casual workers or unemployed. On the one hand, headmen and other leaders of the immigrant communities have gained power and influence by aiding their followers in moving from the noncapitalist to the capitalist economies and by providing assistance in dealing with the urban environment. On the other hand, there was only a small proletariat. Broad working-class movements were difficult to organize; workers' manifestations were episodic, often explosive, and tended to be a catalyst

for populist actions. Although there have been leftist trade
unionists who have espoused a class analysis, there has not
been a strong expression of working-class consciousness, as
distinct from nationalist or populist consciousness. Sustained
union organization has been confined to certain sectors of
the work force, for example teachers, railway and dock workers, and some areas of the civil service.

Ethnicity in Africa has also been shaped by the interaction between urban dwellers and the power bloc of administrators and others who have set state policy. Typically,
colonial governments sought to control the growth of cities,
establish artificial councils for managing urban affairs, and
suppress or coopt urban leaders, although eventually they
were obliged to come to terms with the organizations that
Africans created. The Sierra Leone government--never possessed
of a bounteous treasury or elaborate administrative machinery
--found it advantageous to use headmen and other ethnic leaders as emissaries, promoters of trade, recruiters of labor,
and monitors of the burgeoning urban population. Because some
urban big men had links with big men and commercial and
political networks in the hinterland, they provided a bridge
between those networks and the colonial government. The
colonial government formally recognized and rewarded headmen,
which enhanced their role as mediators between their people
and the colonial power bloc, and encouraged immigrants to
form new communities. During the national period, governments
often had a similar need to manage urban populations through
ethnic leaders. A new politicization of ethnicity occurred
because leaders were able to deliver voters to the ballot box
and make gains for themselves and their followers through
ties with political parties. In some countries the competition
among national political parties intensified cleavages within
ethnic communities and provided a framework for cross-ethnic
alliances (Schildkrout, 1978: 206ff.). This happened to a
degree in the formation of the Sierra Leone People's Party
and the rise of the All People's Congress.

The relationship between the power bloc, ethnicity, and
class has been further complicated because during the colonial
era Europeans treated Africans as racial inferiors and deni-
grated their cultures. Throughout the continent, Africans
responded in a variety of ways, including the development of
nationalist, Pan-Africanist, and Pan-Islamic ideologies and
movements, as well as by asserting narrower loyalties. In
Freetown, racial confrontation was a major stimulus to the
development of a Krio identity by bourgeois Sierra Leoneans,
and they emphasized cultural similarities with lower class
Sierra Leoneans to protect their socioeconomic and political
positions. Furthermore, nationalist and anti-imperial ideologies have provided the basis for appeals by bourgeois politicians for solidarity across class lines. This strategy has
often undermined efforts to organize labor actions.

In certain African cities, one ethnic group has held a
prominent position because it originally occupied the area,
was favored by the colonial authorities, or had access to
resources needed in the urban environment. In such situations,
this has added a special dimension to the competition between
ethnic groups. In Freetown, the Krio had such a position.
Paradoxically, Krios were among the architects of Pan African-
ism and Sierra Leone nationalism, but because Krios owned

much of the land in the city, had a high degree of literacy in English, and controlled certain institutions, the non-Krio perceived the urban environment in ethnic terms. The fact that the Krio bourgeoisie had a peripheral position in the power bloc also stimulated ethnic leaders to organize in an attempt to challenge the supposed Krio dominance. The sequence of migration, community building, and ethnic movement into certain occupations furthered this tendency toward ethnic confrontation, as later immigrants organized themselves ethnically to compete for jobs and influence. Scholars have pointed to similar phenomena in other African cities. However, the importance of the actual historical sequence in relationship to the rise of transethnic labor movements has not always been sufficiently examined (Gutkind, Cohen, and Copans, 1978: 15-27; Hughes and Cohen, 1978: 31-55).

In Freetown, headmen and elders have faced two kinds of contradiction. Politically, they often have been caught between the demands of their people and the demands of the colonial and later national governments. Their roles as representatives of their communities and as mediators between their people and the dominant institutions have conflicted with their roles as government administrators and party agents and activists. Secondly, in class terms, their high position in the noncapitalist and (more recently) capitalist spheres, and their ability to accumulate wealth could separate them from their followers. Until recently, headmen resolved both contradictions by emphasizing their legitimacy in traditional and Islamic terms, by redistributing resources through the ethnic organizations while eschewing conspicuous consumption of luxuries, and by remaining accessible to their people on a daily basis through the courts, receptions, and festivals. Furthermore, ethnic leaders have resisted being coopted by the colonial and national governments to the point where they would lose their credibility, yet they have participated in the postcolonial political system and have been able to channel goods and services to their followers.

These contradictions may intensify, however. As more of the ethnic leaders move into the bourgeoisie and the ruling party establishment, they may not be able to manipulate ethnic identity with the success they have had in the past. As Freetown increases in population, as the capitalist sphere grows more pervasive, and as the sociopolitical conditions become more complex, the headmen and elders may be faced with problems they cannot solve and with people they cannot influence. Considerable evidence has accumulated in recent years suggesting that the ethnic and economic situation in Freetown is changing to a great extent and consequently that ethnic leaders are becoming less relevant. Surveys conducted during the 1970s indicate that the densely populated neighborhoods of inner Freetown are composed of ethnically mixed households. In these households the owner or landlord often deals with problems of an interpersonal nature, and if he or she cannot resolve them, people go to a neighborhood court composed of representatives of more than one ethnic group (Harrell-Bond, Howard, and Skinner, 1978: 320-41).

In addition, new types of communities have formed on the outskirts of Freetown. One type has been squatter settlements largely composed of youth, especially males. Inhabitants of certain settlements pursue a common occupation, are self-governing, and seek to be self sufficient. Furthermore, youths have created associations outside the ethnic communities to pursue both work and leisure activities. For example, the settlement known as Firestone, one of several organized around ode-lay and other masquerades, reportedly numbered 90 members in 1978, with 3,000 masquerade supporters. The society had a sacred shrine, officers, and rules of conduct; its members espoused an eclectic, internationalist culture that included smoking marijuana and dancing to reggae music, but they also creatively reinterpreted older Freetown urban cultural forms and raised considerable money to support their masquerades and other functions. Although authorities have attempted to limit the dancing and other activities of such societies, individual politicians and the APC itself have become patrons in order to exert control and direction and gain followership (Nunley, 1982; Nunley, forthcoming a and b). The linkages between such groups and the formal leadership of the ethnic communities are unclear, but it appears that youth settlements and dance societies are quite separate from preexisting ethnic organizations. This may indicate that Freetown has become such a large, socially and culturally diversified urban agglomeration that the existing ethnic structures cannot serve the interests of all the residents, particularly the casually employed and unemployed youth.

Another important development is the resurgence of militant trade unionism in opposition to government policies, which may indicate the potential for a working-class movement autonomous of the bourgeoisie. These activities have been organized by better-off salaried and wage workers who want to protect and improve their standard of living, but who also have a specific critique of the APC government's economic program and an agenda for reorientation. In 1981 the Sierra Leone Labour Congress (SLLC) promoted a general strike, and spoke out in its principal memorandum against inflation, rising unemployment, falling productivity, smuggling, corruption, and mismanagement. Sierra Leone's economic dependency was pointedly addressed by the SLLC, which protested the conditions which the International Monetary Fund had placed on a debt restructuring package, including currency devaluation, reduction of subsidies for food and transport, and encouragement of foreign investment. The memorandum had wide appeal among the underclass, as it addressed their basic needs and grievances. The cost of rice became a key issue during the strike, and the government quickly responded by lowering prices. It also declared a state of emergency and detained many trade unionists. Government repression and cooptation of union leaders have prevented sustained militancy (West Africa, 1981: August 10, 24, 31; Sept. 7, 14, 21, 28; Luke, 1985b: 650-54).

As economic conditions worsen, the much larger body of poor wage workers, casual laborers, and unemployed may force their demands upon the government. As in the past, the government could look to the ethnic leadership to help control this situation, but the headmen and elders would probably lack sufficient resources and might exhaust the reservoir of loyalty that has helped to maintain ethnic cohesion under difficult conditions in the past. The saliency of ethnicity may decline over time, but it could also take new forms. Leaders from within ethnic communities may build cross-ethnic movements of a populist nature, with a radical, secular nationalist, or Islamic ideology.[13]

NOTES

1. John Saul, building on the work of Ernesto Laclau, states:

> What, we may now ask, are the ways in which interpella-
> tions and ideologies (including ethnicity) structured
> around the centre-periphery contradiction will be
> "articulated in the ideological discourses of antagonis-
> tic classes." Such an approach would seem to give some
> promise of clarifying the conditions under which ethni-
> city (like Third World nationalism) can give expression
> to the potentially anti-imperialist features hypothe-
> sized for it earlier, and also the conditions under
> which it will play a less savoury role. (Saul, 1979: 363)

With regard to the part that ideology plays, Ken Post points out that there is no simple way of expressing determination and contradictions in colonial and postcolonial systems, and that four general points concerning the process of determina-tion should be kept it mind.

> First, just as social formations as totalities are
> centered round economic practice, so determination on
> its first level takes its main thrust from primary
> (economic) contradictions. Nevertheless, second, there
> is always some form of "concentration" between primary
> structures and political practice; economics are deter-
> minant "in the last instance," but, in the words of
> Althusser, "From the first moment to the last, the
> lonely hour of the last instance never comes." Third,
> since determination must involve a variety of non-
> economic [ideological] structures and their contradic-
> tions, it is likely that these will vary in significance
> at different points in time. Fourth, determination may
> not concentrate economics in one direction: since it is
> a complex process involving contradictions with opposing
> moments, a variety of determinations may produce a
> variety of results. (Post, 1978: 51-52)

2. A survey of the current literature and theoretical problems pertaining to ethnicity is found in Cohen (1978).
3. Complete documentation for the history of headmen in Freetown may be found in Harrell-Bond, Howard, and Skinner (1978). See also Banton (1957).
4. Richard Sklar has presented an excellent description and analysis of what he calls the "managerial bourgeoisie":

> . . . it would be useful to devise an apt term for the
> dominant classes of those underdeveloped countries that
> maintain market economies. Any such term or category
> should reflect the coexistence of a newly developing and
> dependent private enterprise sector with a preponderant
> yet protective public sector. In this circumstance . . .
> businessmen, bureaucrats, leading politicians, and

members of the learned professions constitute a new ruling class. I suggest the term 'managerial bourgeoisie'
to designate this class. . . . [This] reflects the
apparent disposition of bourgeois elements in newly
developing countries to manage the production and
distribution of wealth rather than to create new wealth-
producing enterprises. (Sklar, 1975: 198-99)

Sklar's concept is quite close to Markovits', but we prefer
the latter because it includes the traditional rulers and
their descendants and because it refers to the tendency for
those who accumulate wealth as administrators and professionals to invest it in the industrial-commercial sector.

5. Markovits (1977) and Sklar (1979) provide comprehensive discussions of the problems pertaining to the analysis
of class in Africa.

6. Krio here refers to, first, the descendants of the
Repatriated and Liberated Africans, plus others who assimilated to them, and, second, the unique culture they developed
in Sierra Leone (Fyfe, 1962; Porter, 1963; Peterson, 1969;
Spitzer, 1974; Skinner and Harrell-Bond, 1977; Wyse, 1982).

7. The term "big man" is a direct translation of terms
used in Sierra Leone languages, for example, in Temne, wuni
bana. Some women also became wealthy and influential, and
they were "big persons" in their own right. For a more
comprehensive discussion, see Howard (1979) and Howard and
Skinner (1984).

8. Hoogvelt and Tinker have analyzed the relationship
between Delco and the colonial and national governments of
Sierra Leone, including the question of the corporate cooptation of African elites. Furthermore, they have examined the
transfer of earnings from the country, concluding that, "It
appears that no less than 82.75 per cent of the total economic
benefits generated by the Sierra Leone [iron ore] mines found
its way back into the coffers of British capitalism." (1978:
73).

9. For the biography of Wallace-Johnson and his political activities in the WAYL and other organizations, see
Denzer (1977); Denzer (1982); Spitzer and Denzer (1973);
Spitzer (1974: 210-16, especially n. 85, p. 210); Cartwright
(1978: 60, 101).

10. Allen states:

In Sierra Leone, despite basic similarities to other
West African states at the end of the war, we do not
find any radicalizing effect of workers on the nationalist movement, which remained in the hands of the
educated protectorate elite and the Creole leadership.
Sierra Leone had had a much earlier provision of bargaining machinery and co-optation of union leaders than
elsewhere. Under the direction of the Labour Officer,
Edgar Perry, Wages Boards and Joint Industrial Councils
were established from 1946, and union recognition by
employers secured, leading to a series of early wage
increases in major industries. Union leaders, apart from
enjoying an assured status until then confined to the
elite, were protected from their rivals by prohibitions
on the formation of competing unions. Patronage was also
provided, in that union leaders were able to nominate at

least half of the vacancies filled through the Labour
Exchange, which all major employers were obliged to use.
As a result the turnover of leaders was very low and
there were only five strikes from 1946 to 1950. Indeed
there were few strikes of any size, and little other
proof of industrial militancy, until the 1955 strike and
riots in Freetown. . . . The 1955 strike arose, however,
not from any radical influence but from the combination
of sharp increases in food prices resulting from the
diamond boom of the early 1950s, and the attempt by
government and employers to abuse the bargaining machinery and avoid restoring real wages. The riots and loot-
ing that broke out reflected the unpopularity of Lebanese
store owners and the scarcity of goods. The stoning of
ministers' houses was due to their involvement in denying wage increases or in the hoarding of foodstuffs.
Such roles were the direct or indirect result of the
SLPP's integration into colonial government. There is,
however, no evidence that the rioters' hostility arose
from any "Fanonist" consciousness of this integration,
as opposed to its resulting from simple objection to the
actions themselves. (1978: 206-7)

11. In several important publications on the history and
functions of trade unionism in Sierra Leone, Dr. David
Fashole Luke has presented evidence that substantially sup-
ports the thesis of this chapter. Historically, militant
trade unionism and class consciousness have been vitiated
through programs of the colonial and national governments
which undermined radical leadership and coopted moderate
leadership into the national bourgeoisie. Dr. Siaka Stevens
is a prime example of this process (Luke, 1985a: 441ff.;
1985b: 650ff.; 1985c).
12. The contradiction between national and ethnic politics was demonstrated by the way in which Temne headmen were
selected in the 1980s. After the death in 1983 of King David
Kamara, who had been elected to the office, the vice president
of Sierra Leone, S. I. Koroma, appointed Alhaji Abu Sankoh as
acting headman. In 1985, when Dr. Siaka Stevens decided to
step down from the national presidency, S. I. Koroma considered himself to be the leading candidate. However, he did
not have the support of Dr. Stevens or the Freetown bourgeoisie. A sign of Koroma's weakness was evident when Dr.
Stevens replaced Alhaji Sankoh, who was a Koroma supporter,
with Mohammed Kamara, who was not. Subsequently, Mr. Koroma
was informed that he would not be the APC candidate for the
presidency, and Major-General J. S. Momoh was selected by
party officials to run for president. He was elected in a
national referendum in November of 1985 (West Africa, 2
December, 1985: 2513). The position of Temne headman was
manipulated for partisan purposes, and the members of the
Temne community in Freetown were not allowed to vote for the
leader of their choice.
13. In this chapter, we have not dealt with social and
cultural organizations that have cross-ethnic membership and
affect class formation. One of the authors, David E. Skinner,
is currently engaged in a study of the relationship of ethnicity, Islamic organization, and politics in the Gambia, Ghana,
Senegal, and Sierra Leone. Although some Islamic organizations

have been established by ethnic communities, many others have nonethnic or transethnic characteristics and may form a basis for national and transnational movements (Skinner, 1983).

BIBLIOGRAPHY

Allen, Christopher
1978   Sierra Leone. In John Dunn, ed., West African States: Failure and Promise. A Study in Comparative Politics. Cambridge: Cambridge University.
Banton, Michael
1957   West African City: A Study of Tribal Life in Freetown. London: Oxford University.
Bromley, Ray, and Chris Gerry, eds.
1979   Casual Work and Poverty in Third World Cities. New York: John Wiley and Sons.
Cartwright, John R.
1970   Politics in Sierra Leone 1947-1967. Toronto and Buffalo: University of Toronto.
1978   Political Leadership in Sierra Leone. Toronto and Buffalo: University of Toronto.
Cohen, Ronald R.
1978   Ethnicity: Problem and Focus in Anthropology. Annual Review of Anthropology 7: 379-403.
Cummings-John, C. A., and L. Denzer
forthcoming The Autobiography of Constance A. Cummings-John.
Denzer, La Ray
1977   I. T. A. Wallace-Johnson and the West African Youth League: A Case Study in West African Nationalism. Unpublished Ph.D. thesis, University of Birmingham, England.
1982   Wallace-Johnson and the Sierra Leone Labor Crisis of 1939. The African Studies Review 25: 159-83.
Dorjahn, Vernon R.
1977   Temne Household Size and Composition: Rural Changes over Time and Rural-Urban Differences. Ethnology 16: 105-27.
Fyfe, Christopher
1962   A History of Sierra Leone. London: Oxford University.
Gutkind, Peter C. W., Robin Cohen, and Jean Copans, eds.
1978   Introduction. African Labor History. Beverly Hills, Calif.: Sage.
Harrell-Bond, Barbara E., Allen M. Howard, and David E. Skinner
1978   Community Leadership and the Transformation of Freetown 1801-1976. The Hague: Mouton.
Harvey, Milton
1968   Implications of Migration to Freetown: A Study of the Relationship between Migrants, Housing and Occupation. Civilization 8: 247-68.
Hoogvelt, Ankie M. M., and Anthony Tinker
1978   The Role of Colonial and Post-Colonial States in Imperialism. A Case Study of the Sierra Leone Development Company. The Journal of Modern African Studies 16: 67-79.

Howard, Allen M.
1976 The Relevance of Spatial Analysis for African Economic
      History. The Sierra Leone-Guinea System. The Journal
      of African History 17: 365-88.
1979 Production, Exchange, and Society in Northern Coastal
      Sierra Leone during the 19th Century. In V. R.
      Dorjahn and B. L. Isaac, eds., Essays on the Economic
      Anthropology of Liberia and Sierra Leone. Philadelphia:
      Institute for Liberian Studies.
1986 Work, Gender, and Class in Freetown, 1831. Paper pre-
      sented at the Social History Seminar, Rutgers Univer-
      sity (April, 1986).
Howard, Allen M., and David E. Skinner
1984 Network Building and Political Power in Northwestern
      Sierra Leone, 1800-1865. Africa 54: 2-28.
Hughes, Arnold, and Robin Cohen
1978 An Emerging Nigerian Working Class: The Lagos Exper-
      ience 1897-1939. In Peter C. W. Gutkind, Robin Cohen,
      and Jean Copans, eds., African Labor History. Beverly
      Hills, Calif.: Sage.
Kaniki, M. H. Y.
1973a Attitudes and Reactions Toward the Lebanese in Sierra
      Leone During the Colonial Period. Canadian Journal of
      African Studies 7: 97-113.
1973b Economic Changes in Sierra Leone during the 1930s.
      Transafrican Journal of History 3: 72-95.
Leys, Colin
1974 Underdevelopment in Kenya. The Political Economy of
      Neocolonialism 1964-1971. Berkeley and Los Angeles:
      University of California.
Luke, David Fashole
1985a The Development of Modern Trade Unionism in Sierra
      Leone, Part I. The International Journal of African
      Historical Studies 18: 425-54.
1985b The Development of Modern Trade Unionism in Sierra
      Leone, Part II. The International Journal of African
      Historical Studies 18: 625-55.
1985c Dock Workers of the Port of Freetown: A Case Study of
      African Working-Class Ambivalence. Canadian Journal
      of African Studies 19: 547-67.
Mafege, Archie
1971 The Ideology of "Tribalism." The Journal of Modern
      African Studies 9: 253-61.
Markovits, Irving L.
1977 Power and Class in Africa. An Introduction to Change
      and Conflict in African Politics. Englewood Cliffs,
      N.J.: Prentice Hall.
Melson, Robert, and Howard Wolpe
1970 Modernization and the Politics of Communalism: A Theo-
      retical Approach. American Political Science Review
      64: 1112-30.
Mitchell, J. Clyde
1966 Theoretical Orientations in African Urban Studies. In
      M. Banton, ed., The Social Anthropology of Complex
      Societies. London: Tavistock Publications.
Moseley, Kay
1979 Land, Labour and Migration: The Safroko Limba Case.
      Africana Research Bulletin 8: 14-44.

Nunley, John
1982 Images and Printed Words in Freetown Masquerades.
      African Arts 4: 42–46, 92.
  forthcoming a Art and Politics in Urban Africa. Champaign-
      Urbana, Ill.: University of Illinois.
  forthcoming b Urban Ode-Lay Masquerades of Sierra Leone
      (Take it to the Streets).
Peterson, John
1969 Province of Freedom. A History of Sierra Leone 1787–
      1870. Evanston, Ill.: Northwestern University.
Porter, Arthur T.
1963 Creoledom: A Study of the Development of Freetown
      Society. London: Oxford University.
Post, Ken
1978 Arise Ye Starvelings. The Hague: Martin Nijhoff.
Saul, John S.
1979 The Dialectics of Class and Tribe. Race and Class 20:
      347–72.
Schildkrout, Enid
1978 People of the Zongo. The Transformations of Ethnic
      Identities in Ghana. Cambridge: Cambridge University.
Schultz, Emily A.
1984 From Pagan to Pullo: Ethnic Identity Change in North-
      ern Cameroon. Africa 54: 46–64.
Skinner, David E.
1976 Islam and Education in the Colony and Hinterland of
      Sierra Leone (1750–1914). Canadian Journal of African
      Studies 10: 499–520.
1978 Mande Settlement and the Development of Islamic Insti-
      tutions in Sierra Leone. The International Journal of
      African Historical Studies 11: 32–62.
1983 Islamic Education and Missionary Work in the Gambia,
      Ghana and Sierra Leone during the 20th Century.
      Bulletin on Islam and Christian-Muslim Relations in
      Africa 1: 5–24.
Skinner, David E. and Barbara E. Harrell-Bond
1977 Misunderstandings Arising from the Use of the Term
      "Creole" in the Literature of Sierra Leone. Africa
      47: 305–19.
Sklar, Richard L.
1967 Political Science and National Integration--A Radical
      Approach. Journal of Modern African Studies 5: 1–11.
1975 Corporate Power in an African State. The Political
      Impact of Multinational Mining Companies in Zambia.
      Berkeley and Los Angeles: University of California.
1979 The Nature of Class Domination in Africa. Journal of
      Modern African Studies 17: 531–52.
Spitzer, Leo
1974 The Creoles of Sierra Leone: Responses to Colonialism
      1870–1945. Madison, Wis.: University of Wisconsin.
Spitzer, Leo, and La Ray Denzer
1973 I. T. A. Wallace-Johnson and the West African Youth
      League. International Journal of African Historical
      Studies 6: 413–52, 565–601.
van der Laan, H. L.
1965 The Sierra Leone Diamonds. London: Oxford University.
1975 The Lebanese Traders in Sierra Leone. The Hague:
      Mouton.

Walker, James W. St. G.
  1976 The Black Loyalists. The Search for a Promised Land in
        Nova Scotia and Sierra Leone 1783-1870. London:
        Longman and Dalhousie University.
White, E. Francis
  1982 Women, Work, and Ethnicity: The Sierra Leone Case. In
        E. G. Bay, ed., Women and Work in Africa. Boulder,
        Colo.: Westview.
Wilson, Ellen G.
  1976 The Loyal Blacks. New York: G. P. Putnam's Sons.
Wyse, Akintola J. G.
  1981 The 1926 Railway Strike and Anglo-Krio Relations: An
        Interpretation.   International   Journal   of   African
        Historical Studies 14: 93-123.
  1982 The Sierra Leone Krios: A Reappraisal from the Pers-
        pective of the African Diaspora. In Joseph E. Harris,
        ed., Global Dimensions of the African Diaspora.
        Washington, D.C.: Howard University.

5

Political Change and the Catholic Church in Brazil and Nicaragua

THOMAS BAMAT

The Catholic Church has played a central role in the exercise of social domination in Latin America's history. The cross and the sword (Catholicism and colonization) were complementary elements in a single historical process. After Latin America's independence from Spain and Portugal, Catholicism survived first as the official religion of the state in many countries and then--in a context of growing secularization and ideological pluralism--as a principal source of legitimation for the exercise of state power.

Today we are witnessing a significant transformation in the role of the Catholic Church. The Latin American bishops in their Medellin, Colombia (1968) and Puebla, Mexico (1979) conferences took strong stands on social justice and declared a "preferential option for the poor." Church-state conflicts over national policies and human rights violations have grown in numerous countries. Radical sectors of the Church are developing a systematic "liberation theology" and have fostered its growth in faith communities of peasants, workers, and the urban poor. Christian participation in movements for reform and even revolution is significant. Growing numbers of lay workers, nuns, and priests have become victims of repression and organized state terror; two bishops, at least one hundred priests and religious workers, and thousands of lay people have been murdered (see Lernoux, 1980).

This process has not gone unnoticed nor been considered insignificant by the United States and local governments. At the end of the 1960s, the transformation of the Church was examined in the Rockefeller Report and in a well-known Rand study for the U.S. State Department (Einaudi et al., 1969). More recently, concrete strategies have been developed for dealing with the Church. The 1975 "Banzer Plan" and the 1980 "Santa Fe document" prepared by advisors to President Reagan for the Council for Interamerican Security propose systematic attacks against liberation theology and more progressive sectors of the Church; "divide and conquer" tactics at the level of the hierarchy; and the intimidation or expulsion of foreign Church personnel (see LADOC, 1975; Bouchey et al., 1980).

Much of what is popularly written about changes in the Church, while recognizing some of its limits and the existence of divisions within the institution, tends to oversimplify and even sensationalize. Riding (1981: 3) has called the changing role of the Church the most important single variable affecting the resurgence of revolutionary struggles in Latin America, and the metamorphosis of the Church "the most important political development in Latin America since the Cuban revolution." Marzani (1982: 27-28) has affirmed in sweeping global terms that "the Church has decided that the capitalist system is slowly sinking and has no intention of going down with it."

The best sociological and historical analyses today readily recognize the limits on the institution's role in social and political change.[1] Houtart (1979: 236) suggests that the institutional Church in Latin America is taking not a revolutionary but rather a social democratic (or Christian democratic) position, and that in a struggle for socialism the popular classes are unlikely to get more than occasional support from it. Smith (1975: 24-25) discusses the complex "ambiguities and tensions operating within and across norm-ative, structural and behavioral levels in the Church" which prevent the emergence of more forthright radical positions. Among such factors are the universal scope of Church member-ship and the existence of internal theological, ideological, and pastoral differences; the Church's hierarchical and many-faceted organizational nature; the role of the Vatican and the importance of tradition; foreign financial and personnel dependence, and the general need to survive and prosper as an institution. He has discussed such factors in some concrete detail in examining the Church's defense of human rights in five specific Latin American countries (1979), and in analyz-ing the political role of the Chilean Catholic Church from 1920 to 1980 (1982).

In this chapter I review the issue of social domination in contemporary Latin America, and the roles the Church can play and is playing in opposition to authoritarian regimes and in the creation of elements for a potential, popular hegemony-in-gestation. Focusing on Brazil (particularly since 1964) and Nicaragua (particularly since the early 1970s), I argue that the moral discourse and denunciations of the institutional Church are important in delegitimizing some authoritarian regimes, but that the development of organiza-tional abilities, leadership, and critical consciousness among grassroots Christians is far more important in terms of the prospects for an alternative "historical project," that is, some form of socialist future in Latin America.

NONHEGEMONIC DOMINATION IN LATIN AMERICA

The domination exercised by foreign capital and local classes via the state in Latin America—and in most of the Third World—is a domination that is chronically weak in hegemony.[2] That is to say, there tends to be an inadequate distribution of material goods and an absence of the symbolic interpellations necessary for creating and sustaining nation-al unity around the forces that exercise state power in these social formations. In the absence of a broad base of support, class domination is exercised quite overtly by force and the threat of force.

The factors that have contributed to this situation in-clude local poverty, long periods of foreign control over economic development, the exacerbation of socioeconomic inequalities by capitalism, and ethnic or racial divisions, among other elements. The historical development of nonhegemonic patterns of domination varies, however, over time and from one country to another.

In this chapter I examine Brazil and Nicaragua principally because of their current importance in Latin America and the progressive role played by key sectors of the Church in both countries. It is worth noting, however, that these countries are good examples of two very different general patterns of economic development, political domination, and popular resistance in modern Latin American history.

As outlined by Cardoso and Faletto (1978), the first of these two patterns (involving Argentina, Chile, and Uruguay as well as Brazil) saw the national bourgeoisie play a leading political role--at least for a time--in a process of national consolidation that crossed class lines, and in the subordinate integration of the local economy into the international system. In the latter pattern (Peru, Bolivia, the Central American "banana republics" and others), foreign investment in export enclaves and direct foreign links with precapitalist latifundia helped block national integration and even the temporary establishment of class domination with strong hegemonic pretensions. Such factors had important effects on the development of popular movements for change in each of the countries. I will review these patterns of domination and resistance before taking up the role of the Church directly.

The Brazilian Pattern

The key elements in the Brazilian pattern of postwar development, domination and resistance, have been sketched succinctly by Cotler (1979: 259-62). After World War II, Brazilian industrial sector growth and mounting class conflicts led to the displacement of an old oligarchic-imperialist power alliance. It was replaced temporarily by a coalition led by the national bourgeoisie, which assimilated the middle and working classes through top-down corporatist organization. The populist alliances during the 1945-1964 period that Bruneau (1982: 57) calls a "somewhat unusual democratic experience," simultaneously promoted capital accumulation in industry--including the public sector--and growing distribution of material goods and services to the popular and middle strata of the cities. The political organizations of Brazil's popular classes (to the extent they did develop) were incorporated into the system, and tended to support the basic class orientation of the state. They experienced little autonomous development and made no attempt to promote an anticapitalist alternative.

When the contradictions inherent in Brazil's populist pattern of growth resulted in balance of payments and balance of trade problems, fiscal deficits, and mounting inflation in the late 1950s and early 1960s, class conflict sharpened again and the populist formula came apart. The local bourgeoisie and foreign capital (which by then had come to control a number of leading economic sectors) mobilized middle-class support and resolved their crisis through a military coup and the formation of a new dominant alliance.

The 1964 Brazilian coup established "order" to create the conditions necessary for reconstituting and expanding capitalist production. The militarization of the State was to bring the elimination of civil liberties and brutal systematic repression; but popular mobilization and the state's direct attack on the popular classes forced the state to openly reveal its class-based, dependent, and coercive nature.

The situation since 1964 has been analyzed by numerous writers and from a variety of perspectives. Evans (1979) has provided the most thorough examination of what he calls a "triple alliance" between transnational, state, and private local capital in the country's process of accumulation and economic growth--one which saw an average annual growth in GDP (Gross Domestic Product) of 10 percent between 1968 and 1974. Comblin (1977) has explored most extensively the "National Security" ideology employed by the military regime to justify its repressive rule.

Nevertheless, even if the economic boom and messianic anticommunist doctrines provided some cohesion and legitimacy for a time--principally among capitalists, the military, and the middle sectors of society--the situation has changed again. Economic growth slowed, a staggering foreign debt developed, and inflation began to plague Brazil. Income distribution after 1964 benefited primarily the top 5 percent of the population.[3] Government policy in rural areas concentrated holdings and forced many people off the land. Repression was extreme and corruption rampant. Divisions emerged within the military itself. And broad sectors of civil society began to mobilize and clamor for a return to democracy. The labor movement in Sao Paulo was particularly militant (see Green, 1979), and the Church's role in questioning the regime's legitimacy and supporting various opposition groups became more significant.

In the mid-1970s, Brazil entered a period of controlled political liberalization or <u>abertura</u> (opening). It passed through the establishment of a system of multiple political parties (1980), a new congress and governors (1982), and finally the indirect election of a civilian president and vice-president in 1985. A major step in the return to civilian government was the November 1986 direct election of a national assembly charged with drafting a new constitution for the country.

Brazil's "New Republic," despite the political spaces and freedoms it provides for popular organizations and political parties, is nonetheless an elitist and restricted democracy. Its economic policies (such as the "Plan Cruzado" of February 1986, which included price freezes, a new currency, and emphasis on a growing economy) are reformist measures that do not really address endemic problems like the increasing concentration of income and land, severe inequality, and rampant hunger. Socioeconomic and political domination has not so much been modified as rearticulated.

The Nicaraguan Pattern

In Nicaragua the pattern of development, domination, and resistance has been different, of course, and there have been radical changes since the 1979 overthrow of Anastasio Somoza.

During most of this century, Nicaragua shared the basic
traits of agricultural and mineral enclave economies like
Peru, Bolivia, and Guatemala.   In such countries the local
dominant classes were more thoroughly subordinated to the
interests of foreign corporations and governments.   Industrialization was slow to develop.   The extension and deepening
of the local market was more limited than in Brazil or the
Southern Cone.   Local bourgeoisies failed to establish a
similar class hegemony, or to create a national identity and
broad alliances around development policies.   In these Latin
American enclave countries, as Cotler notes, popular mobilization brought together peasants, workers, and middle sectors in movements that were simultaneously anti-oligarchic
and anti-imperialist.   These popular national movements
tended to be more independent from bourgeois direction than
was the case in Brazil, and aimed at the elimination of
foreign capital, which constituted their capitalist core.
Popular movements thus tended to assume an "anti-capitalist
posture" (1979: 265-66).

In the early twentieth century Nicaragua had been a
"banana republic" with no bananas; wood and mining were the
principal foreign interests.   The U.S. Marines were there to
help maintain control between 1912 and 1932.   Then in 1937,
the Somoza clan and the U.S.-trained Guardia Nacional took
the reins of power and imposed an order that was to last for
more than four decades.

In the 1960s and 1970s Nicaragua and the Central American
countries experienced some important growth and economic di-
versification.   The working and middle classes expanded. There
was industrialization and export growth (cotton, coffee, bananas, and livestock in Nicaragua), but this heightened social
inequalities and brought growing immiseration for many.   Central America's dominant classes made little or no effort to
construct ideological and organizational dominance.   Lacking
political support but armed to the teeth, they relied on
violent repression and systematic terror to control the
popular classes.

There was no populist, class-conciliating social pact in
Nicaragua comparable to that in the history of Brazil or Argentina.   In the absence of legal opposition, mass parties,
business unionism, and populist ideologies, the demands of
the poor became national and political.   The popular organizations that emerged through Central America in the 1970s also
tended to be broad-based and multifaceted movements rather
than traditional political parties, and they engaged in fron-
tal confrontations with the forces of domination (Torres-
Rivas, 1981: 54-56).

By the middle of the 1970s, the Somozas and the military
had gained control of some 60 percent of the national economy.
Class relations were overshadowed or suppressed in much of
the economy by "forcible appropriation sanctioned by political
and military power."   Corruption and extortion were rampant
and the terrorism of the National Guard was used when other
practices proved inadequate (Jung, 1979: 69-71).

Opposition to the Somoza regime was somewhat unique when
compared to other Central American countries, because opposition to the regime in Nicaragua came from big bourgeois as
well as popular sectors.   The small but significant Conservative Party was able to control and channel popular resistance

to the Somozas in the 1940s. That party and the non-Somoza
big bourgeoisie played a vacillating role after 1950, and
neither was in a good position to provide national leadership
to opposition forces thereafter. From the aftermath of the
Managua earthquake in the early 1970s until Somoza's overthrow
in 1979, it is nonetheless true that a bourgeois-dominated
opposition force was one of the two basic forces struggling
to overthrow Somoza. According to Jung (1979: 81-86) it was
not until 1977-1978 that the radical and soon-to-be-victo-
rious Sandinista National Liberation Front--itself encompas-
sing three distinct tendencies--was able to take definitive
political and military initiatives and assume clear leadership
of the overall struggle.

The domination exercised by the Somozas and the Guardia
Nacional in Nicaragua was undermined in the 1970s by socioeconomic factors including unprecedented levels of corruption,
a growing foreign debt financed by increased taxes on both
production and consumption, rising inflation, a decline in
the real income of wage-earners and ultimately--as armed conflict increased--the total stagnation of the economy. In
international political terms, the regional policies of the
Somozas and ruthless repression helped weaken their support
in the United States (Jung, 1979).

All this takes nothing away from the Sandinistas. As
Torres-Rivas puts it:

> in Nicaragua they put together--for the first time in
> Latin America and in an original form--guerrilla warfare
> in the countryside, insurrectional forms of urban
> struggle, the general strike, work among peasants, work
> in neighborhoods and factories. This effort included
> winning over an important fraction of the smaller bour-
> geoisie and intellectuals, until the Sandinista National
> Liberation Front (FSLN) was surrounded by a ring of mass
> political organizations which gave an extraordinary
> strength to its military actions. (1981: 57)

Since the revolutionary victory in 1979, there have been
sweeping changes in the pattern of development and in the
exercise of political power in Nicaragua. The Somoza holdings
have been nationalized and the Guardia Nacional has been replaced by a popular army and militia. Much of the country's
illiteracy has been eradicated. There are new popular organizations and new expressions of democracy and popular culture.
Resistance today comes not from the poor but from the bourgeoisie, landowners, and sectors of the petty bourgeoisie;
from the "contras" replete with remnants of the Guardia Nacional; and, of course, from the U.S. government. The country
lives with a war economy, a compulsory draft, and severe
economic shortages. A strict national state of emergency,
declared in October 1985, remains in effect; and the threat
of counterrevolution, while diminished somewhat, remains real.

In all this history, the role of the Nicaraguan Catholic
Church has been important. The Archbishop of Managua played
a significant role in delegitimizing Somoza's rule, and
publicly recognized the peoples' right to collective armed
resistance in 1978. Grass-roots Christian participation in
the revolution was unparalleled in Latin American history.
However, since 1979, the divisions within the Catholic Church

concerning the process of revolutionary change have been extreme, too, and the archbishop--now a cardinal--became the
principal figure of opposition to the Sandinistas. It is to
the Church and its role in both recent Brazilian and Nicaraguan history that we turn next.[4]

THE CHURCH IN BRAZIL

Brazil is the largest "Catholic country" in the world
and its Catholic Church is widely recognized as the most
progressive in Latin America. Its bishops have been out-
spoken on human rights, and highly critical of many national
policies. Among the rural and urban poor, "Basic Christian
Communities" number as many as 80,000. The Church has suffered persecution; but it is a divided Church, in which the
bishops, clergy, and religious and laypersons truly committed
to fundamental social change encounter resistance. Marcio
Moreira-Alves' (1974: 239-44) estimates of a decade ago that
perhaps 5 percent of the bishops favored "socialism" and
another 10 to 15 percent favored basic "social transformations" are too low today, but such sectors remain a powerful
minority even in a Church as progressive as that of Brazil.

To examine the historical roots of the social and political changes in the Latin American Catholic Church as a
whole over the past twenty years would take us far afield.
Suffice it to say here that, throughout the entire region,
the Church has been strongly affected since the early 1960s
by a number of factors. These include the normative changes
sanctioned and promulgated by the Second Vatican Council;
recent papal positions on social questions; the growth of
broad-based movements for radical change and the failed
efforts of imperialism to stem the tide (from counterinsur-
gency programs to the Alliance for Progress); the influx of
foreign missioners in Latin America; the development of
liberation theology as a method of Christian reflection that
seriously examines social conditions from the perspective of
the poor; and growing repression against the poor and Church
personnel themselves.

Bruneau (1982: 69-75) has pinpointed three factors he
believes were particularly important in changing the Brazilian
Catholic Church during the 1970s:

1. a growing realization by Church leaders that they had
   lost political clout, and had far less influence among
   Catholics than they had assumed;

2. a growing appreciation of the devastating social implications of the "Brazilian economic model"; and

3. repressive actions directly affecting Church leaders
   or personnel.

The combination of these, he argues, helped consolidate a new
"model of influence" that focussed on the poor and the
oppressed and led to a "reorientation and mobilization of the
remaining resources of the Church to assist in the liberation
of the people" (1982: 75).

In this section, as in the subsequent discussion of the Church in Nicaragua, I will trace the evolution of the Church's recent social and political commitments; review the major developments at three levels: the Church hierarchy, specialized social programs, and grassroots pastoral work; and mention both government reactions and internal Church tensions.

The Evolution of Church-State Conflict in Brazil

In the years immediately preceding the 1964 military coup, an elite minority within the Catholic Church was active in the social ferment that pervaded the country as a whole. This elite worked on regional development programs, rural cooperatives and unionization, and literacy programs. A small nucleus of bishops, particularly in the impoverished Northeast, already were developing the kind of commitments that came to characterize a broad segment of the hierarchy. Perhaps the most important organization of the pre-coup period was the MEB (Grass-roots Education Movement), a key figure in which was Paulo Freire. It concentrated on literacy training and peasant self-help. After the coup in April 1964, most of the organizations of the Catholic Left were suppressed; the MEB survived, but only at the cost of sacrificing its radical populist orientation (see De Kadt, 1970).

During the first six years after the coup, the Church was relatively slow to react to the dictatorship. Smith (1979: 162-63) and Bruneau (1974) note that most bishops hoped the regime would bring stability for development, and that repression was not pronounced in the years 1964-1968. However, Antoine (1973: 267) argues that there was a successful military strategy in this period to "win over [the] center group to their side, thus neutralizing the revolutionary capabilities of the Church."

The situation changed in the late 1960s, at any rate. Government repression increased sharply in 1968 and most remaining democratic rights were suppressed in Brazil. The grassroots "Basic Christian Communities" and lay-directed social programs grew. In May 1970 the National Conference of Bishops issued its first public critique of the government, focussing on the use of torture and the lack of fair trials, and calling both for more "social participation" and government respect for "legitimate criticism" (Smith, 1979: 163-64).

Church-state conflict became sharper in 1975-1976 with the assassination of journalist Vladimir Herzog in Sao Paulo; the murders of Frs. Rodolfo Lunkenbein and Jao Bosco Penide Burnier in Amazonia for defending the Indians' rights and victims of torture; and the kidnapping, beating and abuse of the Bishop of Nova Iguacu (see Bruneau, 1982: 74-76). The conflict steadily gained momentum thereafter.

As the political abertura developed, the Church became a strong supporter of direct elections and the establishment of a broadly participatory democracy. It was also a prime mover of popular demonstrations against repressive military rule. Now, with the creation of the "New Republic" in 1985, the Church must redefine its relation to the state and to politics, resist government efforts to legitimize itself by "coopting" the Church, and reestablish the nature of its pastoral work among the poor (see Perani, 1985).

With this brief historical sketch in mind, let us examine the key developments at the level of the hierarchy, the Church's specialized social programs, and the grass-roots pastoral efforts.

The Hierarchy

However progressive and exceptional it may be, the Brazilian hierarchy of over 350 bishops is by no means monolithic in ideology and orientation. There are reactionaries as well as socialists among it, but the bishops' collective documents since the mid-1970s provide a useful avenue for understanding at least the state of episcopal consensus on political issues and the appropriate role of the Church.

At least since 1976 the bishops have made decisive denunciations of the military government, and Pope John Paul II's visit to Brazil in 1980 gave added weight to their critiques. In addition to condemning political murders and attacking policies that "absolutize national security," the bishops argued "that the present model of Brazilian development is characterized by injustice and promotes institutionalized violence" (Smith, 1979: 166). They took progressive positions in key documents like "Christian Requirements of a Political Order" (February 1977), "Aids for a Social Policy" (August 1979), "The Church and Land Problems" (February 1980), "Christian Reflection on the Current Political Situation" (August 1981), and "Urban Land and Pastoral Action" (February 1982). They failed to go beyond an abstract stance in favor of greater "participation" and equality, however, to question capitalism directly as a system.

"Christian Requirements of a Political Order" affirmed the primacy of a moral order over the political one, and insisted on the Church's right and need to apply ethical principles to politics and society. It upheld the state's obligation to promote the common good and follow the rule of law, and the Church's obligation to defend the poor in particular. It stressed the need for democratic rights like habeas corpus, independent trade unions, political parties, communication free from arbitrary censorship and peoples' right to choose freely those in positions of political authority. "Aids for a Social Policy" treated the military regime's controlled political opening as a means to defuse and coopt opposition forces while consolidating the socioeconomic model, and argued that the population's needs should be "the only basis for a redistributive model" (see Bruneau, 1982: 77-80).

"Christian Reflection on the Current Political Situation" (Conferencia Nacional dos Bispos do Brasil, 1981) reaffirmed many of the themes of the earlier documents and announced the Church's strong support for "participation" and "the establishment and consolidation of democracy." Noting that Brazil has one of the highest rates of inequality between upper- and lower-income groups, it also defined democracy broadly as including better education and a higher standard of living for the poor, as well as full participation in public decisionmaking. Political democracy, the bishops stated, is "a form and a prerequisite, whose content and destination is social democracy."

In April 1984, during the congressional debate on an amendment to reestablish direct elections for the presidency in 1985, the General Assembly of the Bishops' Conference voted 218 out of 243 to send a telegram in support of the amendment, though it failed to receive the necessary congressional support (Bruneau, 1985: 278).

Since the inauguration of the "New Republic," the land issue--treated in episcopal documents in 1980 and 1982--has become more central. In October 1985 the new president of the country, Jose Sarney, promulgated a National Agrarian Reform Plan, but a year later there still had been no expropriations, only violent conflicts and at least a hundred murders, including that of Fr. Josimo Moraes Tavares, a land reform leader. The nearly fifty bishops who participated in the National Encounter of Base Christian Communities in July 1986 issued a document reaffirming their commitment to landless peasants, and recognizing the legitimacy of peaceful takeovers of unused lands (ALAI, 1986:24).

There is currently grave concern over the development of national economic policies and over the nature of the new constitution. The latter elicited a pastoral letter from the Bishops' Conference in April 1986, which insisted that the current political moment must be seen within a long historical struggle to overcome an "elitist society" and create economic and social, and not just political democracy. The letter also emphasized the importance of ensuring the broadest possible forms of popular participation in the elaboration of the constitution and in the exercise of Brazilian democracy (Conferencia Nacional des Bispos do Brasil, 1986: 3-5).

Specialized Social Programs and Organizations

The hierarchy has not limited itself to declarations, it has authorized and supported the work of numerous national and local organizations that defend the rights of the oppressed. The most important of these have been the Justice and Peace Commissions, the Pastoral Land Commission, and the CIMI (Native Missionary Council).

The Justice and Peace Commissions were founded in 1972 to conduct studies of socioeconomic needs and assist prisoners and their families. They exist both at the national level and in a number of dioceses, and work in different ways to promote human rights. None, however, matches the dynamism of the Commission in Sao Paulo. It has initiated programs concerning civil, social, and economic rights; published works on government repression and social inequality; prepared lists of "disappeared" persons; provided emergency relief to prisoners and their families; offered legal and social services to workers; and assisted other dioceses to establish similar Justice and Peace Commissions (Smith, 1979: 164-65).

The Pastoral Land Commission began functioning nationally in 1977, and has consistently called attention to the economic problems and human suffering inherent in government land policies, as well as promoting agrarian reform. It does studies on land conflicts, assesses reform programs, publicizes cases of injustice, encourages judicial assistance by diocesan groups, and engages in educational campaigns aimed at peasants and pastoral agents. Smaller commissions work along the same lines in many dioceses.

In 1982, the Land Commission and the Bishops' Conference were among the sponsors of the National Agrarian Reform Campaign. Since President Sarney took office in 1985, the Land Commission has worked untiringly to help pressure the new government to enact extensive land reform (see Novaes, 1985).

The CIMI, founded in 1972, overlaps with the work of the Land Commission but concentrates on defending the rights of Brazil's 150,000 to 200,000 unassimilated indigenous peoples. It informs Church personnel on the situation of the Indians, helps coordinate defense strategies among various tribal groups, and intervenes with the government to seek amendments in legislation or call for the implementation of existing laws. There have been serious conflicts between CIMI and the government National Indian Foundation, FUNAI (which tends to subordinate the interests of the indigenous nations to the march of economic "progress" and the exploitation of the Amazon area), and numerous attacks on CIMI and Church personnel working with Brazil's Indians (Bruneau, 1982: 86-89).

Grass-roots Pastoral Efforts: The CEBs

While the Bishops' pronouncements and the work of organizations like the Justice and Peace Commissions, the Land Commission, and the CIMI constituted important challenges particularly to the military regime, and undermined government claims to legitimacy especially among sectors of the Catholic faithful, it is the development of "Basic Christian Communities" (CEBs) among the peasants and in working-class and marginalized urban neighborhoods that constitutes the most serious challenge to Brazil's reigning system of social and political domination. This is because CEBs foster a sense of human dignity, a critical social consciousness, and popular democratic values among the people. CEBs help them to appropriate and produce new expressions of their faith and uncover its radical potential, and have provided organizational and leadership skills to the oppressed as they work for social change.

CEBs have developed in many Latin American countries in the past ten to fifteen years, but nowhere as extensively as in Brazil, where they number perhaps 80,000. CEBs are interpersonal and relatively homogeneous faith communities, and usually form in impoverished rural and urban areas. They meet regularly to read the Bible, and often reflect on social reality or discuss the implications and challenges for Christian faith. Leadership is ideally exercised by laypersons, while priests or nuns function as advisors. The Sacraments (Baptism, the Eucharist, and so on) and mutual assistance play an important part in their community life. Many of the CEBs are committed to social change, though political commitment is less common. While there is a considerable diversity from one CEB to another, many can be characterized as constituting "a privileged meeting place for [an oppressed and believing] people trying to familiarize itself with its situation of misery and exploitation; to fight against that situation and to give account of its faith in a liberating God" (Gutierrez, 1981: 112-15; see also Marins, 1976).

Libanio (1981) explains the genesis of the CEBs in Brazil in terms of general psychosocial phenomena like alienation and a search for community, but also in terms of the pre-1964 Brazilian lay movements and popular education efforts like the Barra do Pirai catechist experience, the "Movimiento Natal," and the aforementioned Grassroots Education Movement (MEB). He also refers to Church involvement in the political effervescence that preceded the Brazilian coup, and to the effects of the repression exercised by the military thereafter:

> This, then, was the social context in which the "comunidades de base" were born. The Church became involved with the projects of the popular classes and was present in their midst. During the dark years of repression, the Church was virtually the only possible space in which anyone could work on behalf of the poor. There the popular classes found a place in which to exist, to think, to pray, to discover themselves, to plan and to dream. (1981: 6)

It is important to note--as does Bruneau (1982: 127-30) --that the CEBs are an integral part of the Catholic Church, and tend to be legitimized and actively supported by the Catholic hierarchy in Brazil, though not everywhere. They respond to the shortage of clergy in Latin America and are a relatively effective way of reaching large numbers of people with the Christian message. They resonate with current theological emphases on service among the poor, the formation of community, and lay ministries. While serious tensions can develop between these communities and hierarchical levels of the Church--as we will see in looking at Nicaragua--the CEBs are not independently developing sects.

Many of the CEBs are important in the dynamics of domination and liberation, for a number of reasons. For one thing, they help the common people of the popular classes to appreciate their own human dignity and subjectivity. They provide instances in which the oppressed can reappropriate and produce religious symbols--as opposed to merely consuming them--and realize some of the radical implications of the Gospel (see Maduro, 1982b). They help allow the poor to examine and question the social relations and even the structural roots of domination, while strengthening a religious motivation to struggle for greater justice and equality. They involve people in organizing themselves and participating in efforts to resolve very concrete problems like housing, land tenure, and basic services. They help train grass-roots leaders. Finally, because of relationships to other popular organizations through overlapping memberships and forms of collaboration, at least some of the CEBs have spillover effects on organizations and social movements like neighborhood associations, rural and industrial unions, and even political organizations. An important example of the latter is the influence of their emphasis on collective, democratic forms of leadership, and broad-based organizational participation (Bruneau, 1982: 131; Maria Helena Moreira-Alves, 1981: 20-21).

It must be stressed that the CEBs are a very recent development in Brazil and have lost some of their former vitality during the current transition to civilian rule, as other organizations have begun to compete openly for membership and leaders among the poor. Some of the most recent evaluations of CEBs have questioned the extent of their political dimensions, or have indicated that their leadership is often less grass-roots in nature than previously asserted. Others stress that a considerable degree of direction by pastoral agents or middle-class intellectuals will be essential to the political development of the CEBs, and have critiqued what they see as highly romantic populist tendencies among many Church workers (see Mainwaring, 1984). While it would be misleading to lionize the role of the CEBs in present or future struggles for social change, their significance and potential cannot be ignored.

Aggression against the Church

In the face of the Church's growing opposition to the Brazilian military regime in the 1970s and early 1980s, the forces of domination responded with a vengeance. Where possible, the regime and its supporters sought to exploit internal divisions within the Church itself. A good example of this was the widespread coverage the government-controlled media afforded to Archbishop Sigaud's 1977 accusations that two of his fellow bishops, Pedro Casaldaliga and Tomaz Balduino, were communists (see Smith, 1979: 167).

The forms of aggression were numerous and diverse, however. While they are certainly limited when compared to the repression carried out against peasants, workers, and political leaders since 1968, these attacks were nonetheless significant. The following categories and examples from the years 1968-1978 give some indication of their nature (CEDI, 1979):

1. Public verbal and written attacks by government ministers, top military officers, members of congress, and the press on bishops, priests, or the Church in general.

2. Some fifty invasions of churches, offices, residences, activity centers, and meetings.

3. Government censorship of O Sao Paulo, the weekly newspaper of the Sao Paulo Archdiocese, even after nationwide censorship was lifted; the suspension and closing of Church radio stations; and instructions to the press not to publish any declaration by or news of Archbishop Helder Camara of Recife.

4. Government prohibition of a variety of meetings and pastoral efforts, and of the use of two catechisms considered "threats to national security."

5. Falsifications of letters and Church publications.

6. Some seventy-five summons to Church personnel to make sworn statements of one kind or another.

7. Over ten abductions of bishops, priests, or other Church personnel.

8. The arrest of nine bishops, eighty-four priests, thirteen seminarians, and six nuns during the ten-year period.

9. Some thirty-five registered cases of torture against Church personnel.

10. Some twenty recorded indictments against more than 140 Church personnel, including 2 bishops.

11. The expulsion of nine priests, and threats of expulsion against many more.

11. The assassination of at least three priests, the violent death of a small number of other pastoral agents, and at least eighteen death threats.

The actions of the Church and the attacks against it gained it new sympathizers. The confrontations between the Church and the military regime also tended to forge greater internal unity within the Church, and to move the hierarchy into a progressive consensus.

What will happen to this essentially progressive unity in the emerging "New Republic"--given greater legal freedoms, the multiplication of popular organizations, competing political tendencies, divisions within the Church and the desire of some of the leadership to concentrate now on more strictly "spiritual" tasks--remains to be seen. Some predict a significant retreat from social and political commitments, though most Church leaders have remained strong thus far on the land reform issue and on the rights of the poor (see Perani, 1985; Ribeiro de Oliveira, 1986; Bacchetta, 1986).

The Brazilian hierarchy's emphasis on social justice, and the relative harmony between it and the CEBs, are at any rate in sharp contrast to what has developed in Nicaragua since the 1979 overthrow of Anastasio Somoza.

THE CHURCH IN NICARAGUA

The Nicaraguan people are very religious, although their beliefs and practices tend to be more Catholic and less culturally diverse than those in Brazil. Nicaragua's Catholic Church, for its part, has been considerably more traditional than that of Brazil. While there were anticlerical attacks against the church by liberals in the 1890s, church-state relations in Nicaragua were peaceful for most of the twentieth century. Not even the formal separation of church and state in 1939 caused many ripples.

Sectors of the church in Brazil took social questions seriously as early as the 1930s, but there were no apparent changes of a similar nature in Nicaragua until well into the decade of the 1960s. The church's emerging tendency to identify with the poor thereafter and to assume a more prophetic social stance roughly coincided with the heightening of opposition to Somoza. What had been a very traditional church, then, was ironically to assume an unprecedented role as a significant force in a popular struggle for national liberation.

The widespread participation of Christians in the insurrection against Somoza, their support for and involvement in
the Sandinista movement, and the presence of Catholic priests
in key government posts after 1979, stand in marked contrast
to other revolutionary experiences in this century. As Dodson
and Montgomery point out (1982: 163), however, there are
various aspects of the "uniqueness of Nicaragua" that need to
be understood. Among them are active Sandinista encouragement of Christian participation in the struggle, the way in
which repression converted churches into a focal point of
popular resistance, and the distinct positions assumed at
different levels of the Church. The Catholic hierarchy, in
particular, supported the overthrow of Somoza but was never
pro-Sandinista. Both before and after 1979 it has taken
positions that are not revolutionary but rather are similar
to those of the "bourgeois opposition" (see also Berryman,
1982).

The Evolution of the Church's Role

The first indications of a break in the decades of
social peace between church and state in Nicaragua can be
traced to the mid- and late 1960s, as liberation theology
and the 1968 Medellin Bishops' Conference were making themselves felt throughout Latin America. The first attempts at
forming Basic Christian Communities (CEBs) in Nicaragua came
in that period. In 1968, seven Nicaraguan clergy issued a
declaration calling for a halt to repression, freedom for
political prisoners, and a more equitable economic order. In
that same year, newly-appointed Archbishop Obando y Bravo of
Managua sold the Mercedes Benz automobile offered him by
Somoza, and gave the money to the poor (Dodson and Montgomery,
1982: 163-64).
Despite developing strains with the regime, it was not
until the aftermath of the devastating 1972 earthquake that
the Church's opposition role became pronounced. Indeed, the
earthquake and the Somoza regime's subsequent manipulation
and appropriation of relief supplies marked an important
turning point in the nation's overall political history. In
the years between 1972 and Somoza's overthrow, Church developments ranged from public episcopal and clerical criticisms of
human rights abuses, to the radicalization of rural and urban
CEBs, to active participation by Christians in popular organizations, guerrilla warfare, and the final insurrection (see
Berryman, 1984).
Immediately following the Sandinista victory in 1979 (as
well as during the years immediately preceding it) divisions
within the Catholic Church were overshadowed by common and
broad opposition to Somoza's rule. Internal divisions and
the Catholic bishops' obvious distrust of the Sandinistas
came into the open, however, in 1980. The revolutionary
government's decision to expand the newly formed state council
by fourteen seats--most going to pro-Sandinista organizations
--brought sharp reaction from the bourgeoisie and the "private
sector." Shortly thereafter, the national clergy association's (ACLEN) representative himself withdrew from the state
council (though he was replaced by a priest who supported the
revolutionary process). Controversy erupted concerning the

role of several priests holding high government offices when the bishops asked them to step down and return to pastoral duties. Finally, the Sandinistas issued their official declaration on religion in October of that year--guaranteeing full respect for religious beliefs and practices--only to be answered with sarcasm and innuendo by the hierarchy (Berryman, 1982: 10-14). Since 1980, there has been an increase in intrachurch tensions and in the number of incidents marking church-state conflict.

Supporters of the revolution include several highly visible Catholic priests in top government positions, including the foreign minister, the minister of culture, and the minister of education. Many other priests and Catholic lay people hold high-ranking jobs in the government and popular organizations. There are Church organizations such as the Central-American Historical Institute and the Center for Agrarian Promotion and Education (CEPA), as well as ecumenical centers like the Antonio Valdivieso Center and several Protestant organizations promoting the revolution. More important in the long run are the pastoral agents in the CEBs and the grass-roots communities of believers who support the process, who participated in the national literacy crusade, and who are ready to defend Nicaragua against counterrevolution at all costs.

In the opposition are the majority of the hierarchy and the diocesan clergy, a minority of the religious clergy, and petty-bourgeois Church groups publicly raising fears about the coming of totalitarianism. Many of the Catholic faithful in the middle sectors and even the peasantry are there as well. Not only religious policy, but the economic, social and military successes or failures of the government, and the role of external factors such as the United States and the Vatican, will have important effects on the ultimate resolution of their allegiances (see Berryman, 1984).

With this brief historical sketch in mind, let us examine the key developments at the level of the hierarchy, the Church's specialized programs, and grassroots pastoral efforts.

The Hierarchy

The Nicaraguan hierarchy of ten bishops is far smaller than its Brazilian counterpart, and it has been far more conservative in recent history. It has also exhibited less administrative independence than the Brazilians. Indeed, particularly since the Sandinista victory, the Nicaraguan bishops have been very much influenced by the Latin American Bishops Conference's (CELAM) conservative Archbishop Lopez Trujillo, and by Vatican authorities--though the latter have often been a moderating force (see, for example, Batsch, 1981).

The bishops' role in helping to delegitimize Somoza in the 1970s and legitimize the opposition--even armed opposition --cannot be ignored. As Dodson and Montgomery (1982: 164-74) point out, Archbishop Obando y Bravo in particular supported student protests against repression, criticized the regime in front of Somoza at a public mass in 1973 (only to have National Guardsmen disconnect the loudspeakers), and served as mediator between the government and the Sandinistas after the latter seized officials at a 1974 Christmas party--an episode that gave the Sandinistas greater visibility and popular support. The hierarchy defended the right to electoral abstention in the 1970s, and issued significant pastoral letters in that decade. "Renewing Christian Hope" (January 1977) strongly criticized the Somoza regime's human rights violations in the countryside and aggression against the Church itself. It called for guarantees to life and work, a return to civil rights, proper trials for common and "political" crimes, and "freedom to promote a more just and equitable order" (LADOC, 1977).

The bishops' statement of June 2, 1979--less than two months before the Sandinista victory--condemned "assassinations and every violation of human rights," and demanded respect for ethical norms in combat. It argued, following the papal encyclical "Populorum Progressio," that a revolutionary uprising was morally and juridically legitimate when " . . . manifest, longstanding tyranny does great damage to fundamental personal rights and dangerous harm to the common good of the country." As Jerez (1980: 15) puts it, the bishops became "the first National Conference of Catholic Bishops ever to have declared a revolutionary insurrection with leftist leanings to be legitimate." However, the document's basic political thrust seems to have been toward negotiated settlement rather than revolution. Insisting on the need for pluralism and new foundations for the nation's destiny, the document specifically asked that Nicaraguans "supersede all party factions, every ideological difference and particular interest" to achieve unity (LADOC, 1979a).

After the U.S.-sponsored efforts at mediation broke down, the National Guard disintegrated and the Sandinista-led opposition suddenly took state power in July 1979, the bishops wavered vis-a-vis the new government. Two weeks after the victory they expressed mostly misgivings and stressed the importance of spiritual values (LADOC, 1979b). Four months after the victory, they published a pastoral letter firmly supporting the main thrust of the revolutionary process. While eschewing "blind enthusiasm" for any revolution, stressing the need for Christian freedom and pluralism, and mentioning certain "abuses," this pastoral letter affirmed socialism rooted in popular power and participation, going as far as showing its Christian coherence. It recognized the positive social potential of class struggle, as opposed to hatred against persons and, at another level, it recognized the importance of the Christian communities in helping discern the Church's commitments and future directions (Episcopado Nicaraguense, 1979).

The "honeymoon" ended in 1980. The pastoral letter of November 1979 remains a high-water mark and an exception to the overall stance of the hierarchy vis-a-vis both the revolutionary government and the Church at the grass roots. Since then, most of the bishops have been thoroughly defensive about their societal influence, institutional interests, and authority; closely aligned with the bourgeois opposition; and highly critical of the Sandinistas.

A series of conflicts involving the Church hierarchy and the government have erupted since 1980. As mentioned above, the Sandinistas' October 1980 communique on religious freedom

received a hostile response from the bishops, as did government efforts to foster changes in some traditional religious
celebrations. In 1981, the bishops protested government
action to end Archbishop Obando y Bravo's monopoly control
over a televised weekly Mass, and to "rotate" parishes so
that more progressive clergy could be heard.

In 1982, a conflict broke out regarding the expulsion of
two priests and three nuns from the country (an action later
reversed by the government, which blamed middle-level
officials). A pastoral letter charged the government with
serious violations of human rights in moving the Miskito
Indians from their homes near the conflict-ridden Honduran
border, and provoked a sharp government reply. There was
tension, too, following the printing of a controversial papal
letter to the Nicaraguan bishops on Church unity and the
"popular Church." Radio Catolica was closed for a month for
transmitting "distorted" information, and its director, Fr.
Carballo, became the center of a controversial public
scandal.[5]

In 1983, the situation worsened. The Pope's visit
heightened the Nicaraguan bishops' opposition to the revolution. It supported Obando y Bravo, the conservative archbishop, while bitterly disappointing the more popular and
progressive sectors of the Church, and it added to internal
polarization. In August, the Nicaraguan hierarchy attacked
the new military draft and called on young people to refuse
to serve.

In 1984 the bishops issued a confrontational pastoral
letter on "Reconciliation" in which they indicted the Sandinistas and their project, virtually ignored the prominent
U.S. role in counterrevolutionary action, and called on the
government to begin a dialogue with all sectors of society,
including those who had taken up arms against it--a position
identical to that of the opposition CDN (Cordinadora Demo-
cratica Nicaraguense)--as a condition for its participation
in the November 1984 elections (Williams, 1985; Dodson,
1986). Ten priests were expelled from the country in July.
Church-state relations reached their lowest point ever in
1984-1985.

The year 1986 has been marked by bitter controversy
surrounding the direct or indirect support of now Cardinal
Obando y Bravo and Bishop Pablo Vega, vice-president of the
Episcopal Conference, for U.S. policy against Nicaragua. It
has also been marked by government closure of Radio Catolica,
its refusal to permit Fr. Carballo to reenter the country
after a trip abroad, and the July deportation from Nicaragua
of Bishop Vega for his open defense of counterrevolutionary
efforts. Official dialogue between church and state was
reestablished at the end of September, however. As the year
ended there were signs that Church-state tensions might
indeed be lessening (Melendez, 1986).

The hierarchy's battles have not only been with the
government. A related series of controversies has developed
between the bishops and supporters of the revolution within
the Church. The most widely publicized is the dispute over
whether the priests in government--symbolically as well as
technically important--should remain in their posts or step
down. The controversy erupted in May 1980 and was at least
temporarily resolved in July of 1981 when a compromise,

apparently supported by the Vatican, allowed the priests to remain in their positions on condition of refraining from priestly functions (Berryman, 1982: 12-17; Batsch, 1981). Nevertheless, during his 1983 visit, the Pope publicly reproached the Minister of Culture, Ernesto Cardenal, for holding that post. Education Minister Fernando Cardenal was forced to resign from the Jesuits in 1984, and pressures have continued against Foreign Minister Miguel D'Escoto.

Another series of conflicts has involved measures by the Catholic hierarchy to bring grass-roots organizations like the CEBs into line and to weaken the efforts of clergy, religious women, and laity supporting the revolution. The bishops have insisted on their authority as the basis of Church unity--a principle upheld in the Pope's June 1982 letter to them--and have warned of the danger of grassroots communities becoming a "parallel Church." A number of progressive priests and nuns have been transferred from previous work locations, too, despite popular protests and demonstrations (see Reiter, 1981; Goff, 1982).

It is important to note that neither the Nicaraguan government nor most progressives in the Church seek to exacerbate these conflicts. Serious divisions in the Church strengthen the hand of imperialism and counterrevolution. The Sandinistas have undoubtedly made some errors of judge-ment--as, for example, in their heavy-handed use of the official press and some undue harassment of Church personnel --but they have also reaffirmed their basic commitment to religious liberty and have consistently requested dialogue with the bishops.

After intermittent contacts between Church and state officials during 1985 and most of 1986, seven of the ten members of Nicaragua's Episcopal Conference, as well as the new papal representative Paolo Giglio, participated in Sep-tember's renewal of dialogue. Nicaraguan President Ortega and Cardinal Obando y Bravo met for the first time in almost two years, and monthly sessions between government and Church officials are currently aimed at a plan to normalize rela-tions and reach a "global agreement."

The Vatican itself seems more open to the Sandinistas, perhaps because it now perceives them as solidly in power. John Paul II and Cardinal Secretary of State Casaroli met cordially in Rome with Nicaraguan Vice-President Ramirez in June 1986, and Mons. Giglio, who arrived in Managua shortly thereafter, appears strongly committed to dialogue rather than confrontation with the government (Melendez, 1986).

Specialized Social Programs and Organizations

Compared to Brazil, the Nicaraguan Church has had little in the way of specialized programs or organizations. Nicara-gua has witnessed cursillo and charismatic movements, as well as catechetical and lay leadership programs, but there is little history of Church organizations directed specifically to issues of social justice. Smaller size, a more conserva-tive tradition, and the nature of the struggle against Somoza in the 1970s may help explain some of this. What is more, however, most of the specialized programs and organizations that do exist today are not--in contrast to those in Brazil--

officially sanctioned by the hierarchy. Three bear mention
here: the Jesuits' CEPA (Center for Agrarian Promotion and
Education), their Central American Historical Institute, and
the ecumenical but predominantly Catholic Antonio Valdivieso
Center.

As Dodson and Montgomery (1982: 170) explain, CEPA began
in 1969 with the Catholic hierarchy's support. Originally a
self-help program to train peasants in agricultural techniques, enable them to meet their everyday needs, and better
understand their faith and its implications, it came to focus
on helping peasants organize to defend their rights and interests. Many Christians in CEPA became highly politicized and
anti-Somocista. Some (including several priests) joined the
Sandinistas' Association of Rural Workers when it was founded
in 1977. Some Christians became armed Sandinista combatants.
As CEPA radicalized, the bishops sought to restrict its activities. When the restrictions became too confining, CEPA cut
its ties to the hierarchy, and continued to do socially and
politically committed religious work as an independent
Christian organization.

The Jesuits' Central American Historical Institute and
the Antonio Valdivieso Center--the latter established shortly
after Somoza's overthrow--have both sought to document the
history of Christian involvement in the struggle against
Somoza and promote Christian participation in the revolutionary process. The Institute publishes a newsletter on Nicaragua for international audiences and the Center devotes much
attention to publications and workshops for CEBs and Christian leaders within Nicaragua (Dodson and Montgomery, 1982:
177-78). The bishops have made it clear that neither the
Institute nor the Center has their official approval or
recommendation (Berryman, 1982: 15).

Grass-roots Pastoral Developments

A similar lack of harmony characterizes the relation
between the hierarchy and many grass-roots Christian communities in Nicaragua. Again, this is in marked contrast to
the Brazilian pattern, where the hierarchy is more supportive
of such efforts and organizations. In both countries it is
at this level that changes affecting Catholicism and politics
have been most significant.

A diversity of pastoral efforts linking faith reflection
to an examination of social reality were initiated at the
grass-roots level in Nicaragua in the 1960s and early 1970s.
They led to the creation of both formal CEBs and more spontaneous small communities of Christians with greater autonomy
from the hierarchy and the institutional Church. New pastoral approaches were used in Managua, in the central moun-
tains, in Esteli, on the Atlantic coast, and elsewhere.
Ernesto Cardenal began the famous lay community of Solentiname. Fr. Jose de la Jara and others began their work in
Managua's 14 de Septiembre neighborhood. The student community in Managua's poor Riguero neighborhood, which produced
Sandinista leaders such as Luis Carrion, was founded. In
rural areas like the state of Zelaya, which have an acute
scarcity of clergy, the training of lay "Delegates of the
Word" was a key to CEB growth; and CEPA's work contributed to

CEB development in the countryside (Dodson and Montgomery, 1982: 164, 170-72, 179; Batsch, 1982; Berryman, 1982: 2; Reiter, 1981: 45-46).

Particularly in the 1970s there was a growing politicization and radicalization of Christians at the grassroots and as well as growing links between them and the Sandinistas. By no means were all communities experiencing, the phenomenon, but Nicaraguan Catholics "became a dynamic force within the liberation movement, both ideologically and organizationally." They joined the other mass organizations like street defense committees and peasant, women's, and student bodies, as "mainstays" of the revolutionary movement (Reiter, 1981: 45-46).

During the insurrection of 1979 and the preparations for it, Christian communities and pastoral agents played specific support roles. They accumulated supplies, and stored water and medicine. They taught first aid and helped coordinate relief efforts. They hid people sought by the National Guard, and organized communication links and transportation services with and for the Sandinistas. Throughout this process they engaged in serious and painful reflections on the meaning of religious principles: the importance of prayer in their everyday life was heightened dramatically (Jerez, 1980: 15; Dodson and Montgomery, 1982: 173).

After the victory, many grass-roots Christian communities, dozens of clergy and thousands of Catholic high-school and college students participated wholeheartedly in the national literacy campaign (directed by Jesuit Fr. Fernando Cardenal) and the tasks of national reconstruction. The positive contributions of Christian faith to promoting "honesty, austerity, selflessness... and a restraint in the use of power" have not been lost on the Sandinista leadership (Jerez, 1980: 16). The absence of authorized executions following victory, the unanimous refusal of the Council of State to legalize capital punishment, and the relatively good treatment of prisoners, have also been attributed, at least in part, to the pervasiveness of Christian values in this revolutionary process.

Explicitly Christian organizational support of the revolution is nonetheless less extensive today than it was under Somoza, when repressive rule closed many avenues of social and political expression and gave parishes and Christian communities exceptional functions. There is still considerable interaction between Church and Sandinista organizations, but the latter also compete--even if indirectly--for the time and energies of grass-roots leaders. Religious practices have diminished in certain communities compared to the religious fervor of 1979-1980, and some Delegates of the Word have left their ministries (though not their faith) to join Sandinista organizations (Dodson and Montgomery, 1982: 178). In a period of external military aggression as well as popular political and cultural development, the Church's role is now principally religious and motivational (see Marchetti, 1982: 45).

The Basic Christian Communities in Nicaragua remain an influential minority phenomenon within the Church, and a small but very significant part of the social base of the revolution. Indeed, the "church of the poor," following the demoralizing experience of the 1983 papal visit and the authoritarian, conservative role played by Obando y Bravo, has expressed a new vigor since mid-1985. Some speak of an "evangelical insurrection" sparked by Foreign Minister Fr. Miguel D'Escoto's thirty-day fast, in July and August of that year, for peace, life, and an end to counterrevolutionary terrorism.

During the fast, six thousand representatives of the basic communities from all over Nicaragua met in the city of Leon with the plea, "Christ, Lord of Life, strengthen our hope in the face of aggression." Days of prayer and fasting multiplied throughout the country, involving not only organized Christians but also broad sectors of the poor and even government officials, including President Ortega. Cardinal Arns of Sao Paulo, Brazil, publicly expressed his support for what he called D'Escoto's "prophetic gesture to alert the world's conscience to the grave situation experienced by the people of your country," and Bishop Casaldaliga accompanied D'Escoto and the others in official representation of twenty-three members of the Brazilian hierarchy.

In September 1985, in the context of this continuing gospel "insurrection," Brazilian theologians Leonardo Boff, Clodovis Boff, and Frei Betto visited Nicaragua in solidarity, as did Nobel Peace laureate Adolfo Perez Esquivel.

Since 1985, the so-called "church of the poor" has assumed new initiative and vitality--organizing vigils, processions, liturgies, and making more extensive use of oral communication through the radio. These actions maintain their political dimension but employ religious rather than political language and symbols, and actively merge with traditional religiosity.

The most dramatic event to date in this resurgence of grassroots religious support of the process and against the counterrevolution was a 325 kilometer procession from Matagalpa to Managua in February of 1986. It is estimated that 100,000 people participated in at least some moment of this two-week Way of the Cross, including ten victims of the contra war who covered the length of the march in their wheelchairs. Fifteen thousand people, including some 30 percent of the country's priests, participated in the closing ceremony in the capital (IHCA, 1986).

Popular Religion

The tradition of popular religious protests against injustice in Nicaraguan history had already found new expression during the 1970s struggle against Somoza. In their own testimonies, the Christian poor frequently affirm how faith and prayer gave them courage, solidarity, and hope, and how the sense of God's presence energized their commitment to resist and struggle for victory.

Since 1979, popular religion has been expressed in a variety of celebrations and feasts in Nicaragua and in the mystical understanding of new life as both gift and accomplishment. In the "Misa Campesina" (Peasants' Mass), the people sing:

You are risen/in every arm that is raised
To defend the people/from the exploiter's
    dominion. . . .
You are three times Holy/You are three times Just,
Liberate us from the yoke/give us freedom

Popular religion is not without its alienating elements and expressions, but in contact with new theological currents and a revolutionary social practice, it has been a creative and vital force for liberation and life in Nicaragua (Irarrazaval, 1981).

The very strength of religious symbols in Nicaraguan culture and the revolutionary process has been important in determining their widespread use in political and ideological conflict. Since 1979, for example, the bourgeois press itself has done everything possible to depict the revolution as anti-Christian and to discredit those Christians who support it (see, for example, Marchetti, 1982: 46-47). In efforts to construct a national and popular socialist hegemony in Nicaragua, as well as in the attempt to forge a bourgeois counterrevolution, Christian symbols play an important role.

Aggression against Sectors of the Church

The bourgeois opposition and its press, in conjunction with the majority of the bishops, have decried Sandinista interference with religious practice as well as government and progovernment attacks on both Protestant and Catholic church personnel in Nicaragua. They denounce "calumnies" and violence as steps in a high-priority government project aimed at "the destruction of true Christianity and its replacement by a cult to the state and Marxist revolution" (Belli, 1982: 26). Such charges are distorted and self-serving, but there is a pronounced ideological struggle, and indeed there have been incidents in which individuals have even menaced certain bishops.

What has changed since 1979 are the sectors of the Church that have felt the brunt of government and progovernment hostility, and the nature of the attacks themselves. Under Somoza's rule in the 1970s there was censorship of some Church broadcasts and publications. The National Guard harassed and detained Church personnel (Holland, 1981: 109), especially Delegates of the Word from the rural Basic Christian Communities. Ernesto Cardenal's Christian community in Solentiname was bombed from the air and burned. Today it is the conservative bishops who feel such hostility most keenly, though the nature and extent of such attacks hardly compare with what occurred under the military regime in Brazil, and their class content is very different.

CONCLUDING NOTES

In this chapter I have reviewed the contemporary patterns of social domination and struggles for liberation in Brazil and Nicaragua, and examined the Catholic Church's multifaceted role vis-a-vis the state and politics. In concluding, I will comment first on some similarities and

differences in Church ideology and practice in the two
countries, and then on the nature of the Church and its
overall political role in Latin America.

Similarities

The Catholic Church has of course undergone significant
changes on a global scale in the past twenty years. At all
levels, it now tends to speak of a connection between religious faith and the promotion of social well-being, justice,
human rights, and personal dignity. In Latin America, the
Church has developed a more national and regional character.
It is more critical of those who wield socioeconomic and
political power, and of their policies. It has affirmed a
special commitment to the poor and has developed new organizational forms, the most important of which is the Basic
Christian Community (CEB). These broad institutional transformations have marked the Church in both Brazil and Nicaragua.

At different levels and in different ways, the Church
has been an important force for change in Brazil and
Nicaragua. In the 1970s, the bishops of both countries
became strong public critics of repressive dictatorial
regimes and widespread violations of human rights. In both
countries, grass-roots communities of rural and urban Catholics emerged, and forged a variety of links with broader
popular movements. In neither country, however, has the
Church or sectors of it assumed a vanguard role in popular
struggle, nor has the Church itself, particularly at the
level of the hierarchy, been the key factor in bringing about
concrete social reforms or political change.

Repressive right-wing rule in both countries seems to
have fostered greater unity in the Church as well as more
progressive political positions. In Brazil, direct attacks
on the Church by the military regime and its supporters
heightened internal cohesion in the 1970s and led to sharpened critiques of government policies. In Nicaragua,
Somoza's reign of terror provoked broad condemnation by the
Church, and at least overshadowed important internal
divergences. Repression also contributed to a belated but
significant justification of armed insurrection by the Nicaraguan hierarchy. However, popular, left-wing government in
Nicaragua has been associated not with greater Church unity
but with growing internal tensions. While overall unity is
far stronger in Brazil than in Nicaragua, the transition to
civilian rule seems to highlight tensions between conservative, moderately progressive, and more radical sectors of the
Church, in the effort to establish the appropriate sociopolitical roles for the institution and for grass-roots Christians under the "New Republic."

Finally, in Brazil and Nicaragua both, the most dynamic,
radical changes in the Church have come at the base. The
methodology of liberation theology has become a powerful
instrument of the poor and oppressed, as they affirm their
human dignity and struggle for a more equitable social
order. Popular religiosity has found expressions consistent
with the reality of suffering and the hope of liberation.

Contrasts

The principal differences between the Catholic Churches of these two countries today should be evident. The political and theological stances of Brazil's bishops are, on the whole, very progressive. while those of Nicaragua have become, on the whole, very conservative. The most important social programs and organizations of the Church are directly linked to and strongly supported by the bishops in Brazil, but are unaffiliated to and largely repudiated by the bishops in Nicaragua. The same pattern characterizes the relationships between the Basic Christian Communities and the bishops.

Distinct social structures and histories have certainly been significant in producing such contrasts. One could speculate that the progressive and cohesive Catholic Church of Brazil would experience much greater strains if--as in Nicaragua--the left became clearly ascendant or if socialists held power. It is already experiencing some strains with the onset of liberal democracy. Be that as it may, the Church in Brazil--despite its size and diversity--is far more progressive and unified today than the Church in Nicaragua, and it remains so despite centralizing, authoritarian positions in the Vatican, the latter's naming of more traditional bishops, and a relative strengthening of the conservatives within the national hierarchy.

The Church in Latin America is obviously not monolithic, either within or across national boundaries: its political roles and their effects vary widely. While that is important to recognize, it is not the only valid assertion one can make. In closing, some comments seem to be in order about the hierarchy on the one hand and the Church at the grass roots on the other, as well as about Church divisions and unity, and struggles for socialism.

Hierarchies, Grassroots, Christians and Liberation

On the whole (though there are many striking exceptions) the Catholic hierarchy in Latin America is more conservative than the Church personnel in specialized social programs and organizations or the pastoral agents at work among the rural and urban poor. This is not so much a question of class origins or good or bad intentions, but a function of the objective places that the bishops occupy in the social and ecclesial structure. On the one hand, the hierarchy tends to be more removed from the common people and their everyday lives, sufferings, and struggles. On the other, it is they who are charged especially with maintaining and strengthening the Church as a complex social organization and with protecting and promoting its broad material and social interests.

Popular political struggle presents a particular threat to the institutional Church. The Church's maximum material and symbolic power appears to depend on maintaining and expanding a diverse and multiclass membership. The bishops in particular seek to serve and be heard by people of all social classes. They specialize in abstract and often ambiguous moral discourse. They criticize human rights abuses, and support certain reforms and broad, democratic rights; but they seek reconciliation instead of social division, and generally prefer not to take sides in class conflicts or party politics.

Socialist regimes constitute a related but different concern, given the history of the Church in Eastern Europe or Cuba. The hierarchy and others fear a loss of property and income, an undermining of their own moral authority and influence in society (including the Catholic school system), restrictions on institutional and individual rights, atheism as a state ideology—in short, the social margination of the Church.

I am talking, of course, about common denominators and broad social parameters. Concerns about class conflict, the maintenance of allegiance and support from diverse social classes, and good relations with the state have not prevented Latin America's bishops from stating a "preferential option for the poor" or strongly criticizing authoritarian regimes—though such positions can also be interpreted as historically new "strategies of influence" (Bruneau, 1982) with their own inherent limits. Likewise, concerns about socialist regimes marginating at least sectors of the Church do not necessarily dictate a confrontational stance like that which the Nicaraguan hierarchy adopted after 1980. One could certainly argue, even from the perspective of narrow self-interest, that the bishops would be wise to assume a more conciliatory stance toward the Sandinistas—and some in the Vatican now seem to be doing just that.

Church personnel at work in specialized social programs, and particularly pastoral agents living and working among the poor today, have a greater propensity to identify with the popular classes, to perceive the social structures that perpetuate their subjugation, and to favor more radical social change. For both pastoral agents and—more importantly—the poor themselves, liberation theology has provided new, coherent links between practical experience, social analysis, Biblical understanding, prayer, reflection, and action for justice.

It is at the grass-roots level, among peasants, workers, and slum dwellers that radical Christianity takes root and becomes a part of popular movements for change. Despite certain setbacks or limits, and continued "clericalism," Basic Christian Communities and other organizations can foster a sense of personal dignity and critical consciousness among the people, as well as leadership skills and organizational abilities. The emphasis on the need of the oppressed to recognize and resolve their own problems and the democratic structure of the CEBs has, in some cases, buttressed the Latin American Left's own growing recognition of the importance of popular education and broad participation in struggles for change, and dampened the tendency toward misguided vanguardism and manipulation.

Throughout Latin America, to one extent or another, the Catholic Church is divided. It is traversed by the region's social and class divisions, though it expresses them in ways specific to itself as church and in distinct modes in each national and historical context. At the same time, however, the Church has an internal unity. Despite strains as severe as those between the hierarchy and the "church of the poor" in Nicaragua, more radical sectors and organizations operate as part of the institution, and not as separate sects. The

Church's social programs and grass-roots communities must live with certain restrictions, but they also have much greater leverage in influencing the hierarchy than they would without such unity. Furthermore, repression directed at members of Basic Christian Communities and at Church personnel engaged in social justice work has often moved the hierarchy to stronger stands against dictatorial and authoritarian regimes.

The Catholic Church, then, is an important force for change in today's Latin America. It has contributed to the delegitimation of many authoritarian regimes and tends to speak for broad democratic rights. It has helped rechannel popular religiosity toward social issues. It fosters critical consciousness and diverse forms of organization among the exploited and oppressed classes. However, the Church is an ambiguous, multifaceted force which has particular difficulties coming to terms with popular political struggles and with socialism.

One must remember, finally, that the prospects for an "alternative historical project" for socialism in Latin America depend on much more than a simple lack of support for authoritarian regimes, ideological changes, and popular mobilization. They also depend on more than good political leadership. At both the international and national levels, economic, political, cultural, and military conditions must be right. Successful social revolutions are still rare historical occurrences. Despite growing social contradictions, some political breakthroughs, and the development of important changes in the Catholic Church, the historical structures of domination in Latin America remain strong.

NOTES

1. Among those analyses are works by Bruneau (1974, 1982), Levine (1979, 1981) and Maduro (1982a). I am particularly indebted to Otto Maduro, and thankful for his very helpful comments on the first draft of this chapter.

2. The fullest development of the concept of hegemony is found, of course, in the writings of Antonio Gramsci.

3. The percentage of income pertaining to the top 5 percent of the economically active population in Brazil grew from 28 percent in 1960, to 35 percent in 1970, to 39 percent in 1976. The percentage pertaining to the next 15 percent of the population remained fairly steady, but there was a relative decline for the remaining 80 percent. The poorest 50 percent of the economically active population went from 18 percent in 1960, to 15 percent in 1970, to 12 percent in 1976. (Preliminary data from INPEZ/IPEA, published in Jornal do Brasil (Oct. 22, 1978) and cited in CEDI, 1979).

4. While diverse Protestant and evangelical communities are numerous and rapidly growing in both Brazil and Nicaragua (some 10 percent of the population affiliated to one or another), the discussion here is limited to the Catholic Church alone for reasons of parsimony.

5. For a very one-sided version of these events, interpreting them simply as attacks on the Church, its bishops, and religious freedom, see Belli, 1982.

BIBLIOGRAPHY

ALAI (Agencia Latinoamericana de Informacion)
1986   Erase una vez una reforma agraria. Servicio mensual
       de Informacion y Documentacion (October): 23-24.
Antoine, Charles
1973   Church and Power in Brazil. Maryknoll, N.Y.:Orbis
Bacchetta, Vittorio
1986   Obispos del Brasil acrecientan su participacion en
       escena politica. Noticias Aliadas (October 9): 3-4.
Batsch, Christophe
1981   Nicaragua: Les deux voies de l'Eglise dans la
       revolution. Le Monde Diplomatique (October): 22.
Belli, Humberto
1982   Una Iglesia en Peligro: Reportaje sobre la Situacion
       de la Iglesia Nicaraguense. (Segunda version corregida
       y aumentada; personal copy of mimeo).
Berryman, Phillip
1982   Christians and Sandinistas: Ideological Conflict over
       the Role of Religion in the New Nicaragua. Paper
       presented at the Tenth National Meeting of the Latin
       American Studies Association, Washington, D.C. (March).
1984   The Religious Roots of Rebellion. Maryknoll, N.Y.:
       Orbis.
Bouchey, L. Francis, Roger W. Fontaine, David C. Jordan,
Gordon Sumner, and Lewis Tambs (The Committee of Santa Fe),
eds.
1980   A New Inter-American Policy for the Eighties.
       Washington, D.C.: Council for Inter-American Security.
Bruneau, Thomas C.
1974   The Political Transformation of the Brazilian Catholic
       Church. London and New York: Cambridge University.
1982   The Church in Brazil: The Politics of Religion.
       Austin: University of Texas.
1985   Church and Politics in Brazil: The Genesis of
       Change. Journal of Latin American Studies 17
       (November): 271-93.
Cardoso, Fernando Henrique, and Enzo Faletto
1978   Dependency and Development. Berkeley and Los Angeles:
       University of California.
CEDI (Centro Ecumenico de Documentacao e Informacao)
1979   Repression against the Church in Brazil 1968-78.
       Washington, D.C.: LADOC "Keyhole" no. 18.
Comblin, Jose
1977   A ideologie de seguranca nacional: poder militar na
       America Latina.   Rio de Janeiro: Civilizacao
       Brasileira.
Conferencia Nacional dos Bispos do Brasil
1981   Christian Reflection on the Current Political
       Situation. Latinamerica Press (September 17, 24): 3ff.
1986   Por uma Nova Ordem Constitucional (April).
Cotler, Julio
1979   State and Regime: Comparative Notes on the Southern
       Cone and the "Enclave" Societies. In David Collier,
       ed., The New Authoritarianism in Latin America.
       Princeton, N.J.: Princeton University.
De Kadt, Emanuel
1970   Catholic Radicals in Brazil. London and New York:
       Oxford University.

Dodson, Michael
  1986 The Politics of Religion in Revolutionary Nicaragua.
        The Annals of the American Academy 483 (January):
        36-49.
Dodson, Michael and T. S. Montgomery
  1982 The Churches in the Nicaraguan Revolution. In Thomas
        W. Walker, ed., Nicaragua in Revolution. New York:
        Praeger.
Einaudi, Luigi, R. Maullin, A. Stepan, and M. Fleet
  1969 Latin American Institutional Development: The Chang-
        ing Catholic Church. Santa Monica, Calif.: Rand
        Corporation.
Episcopado Nicaraguense
  1979 Compromiso Cristiano para una Nicaragua Nueva. Mana-
        gua, Nicaragua (November 17).
Evans, Peter
  1979 Dependent Development: The Alliance of Multinational,
        State and Local Capital in Brazil. Princeton, N.J.:
        Princeton University.
Goff, James E.
  1982 Nicaraguans Protest Manipulation of Religion. Latin-
        america Press 14, 33 (September 16): 1ff.
Green, Jim
  1979 Liberalization on Trial: The Workers' Movement. NACLA
        Report XIII, 3 (May-June): 15-25
Gutierrez, Gustavo
  1981 The Irruption of the Poor in Latin America and the
        Christian Communities of the Common People. In Sergio
        Torres and John Eagleson, eds., The Challenge of Basic
        Christian Communities. Maryknoll, N.Y.: Orbis.
Holland, Clifton, L., ed.
  1981 World Christianity IV: Central America and the Carib-
        bean. Monrovia, Calif.: MARC
Houtart, Francois
  1979 Religion et lutte des classes en Amerique Latine.
        Social Compass XXVI, (2-3): 195-236.
IHCA (Instituto Historico Centroamericano)
  1986 La Iglesia de los Pobres en Nicaragua. Envio (April):
        1-18.
Irarrazaval, Diego
  1981 Nicaragua: una Sorprendente Religiosidad. Paginas VI
        (March): 5-10
Jerez, S. J. Cesar
  1980 The Church in Central America: Faith, hope and love
        in a suffering Church. London: Catholic Institute for
        International Relations.
Jung, Harald
  1979 Behind the Nicaraguan Revolution. New Left Review
        117: 69-89.
LADOC (Latin America Documentation. USCC, Washington, D.C.)
  1975 The Bolivian Government Plan Against the Church.
        LADOC 59 (June): 1-3.
  1977 Nicaraguan Bishops: Renewing Christian Hope. LADOC
        VII, 5 (May-June): 1-5.
  1979a 1979 Message to the People from the Nicaraguan Bi-
        shops. LADOC X, 2 (November-December): 15-19.
  1979b Nicaraguan Bishops Speak to Catholics and All Nicara-
        guans. LADOC X, 2 (November-December): 20-23.

Lernoux, Penny
1980 <u>Cry of the People</u>. Garden City, N.Y.: Doubleday.
Levine, Daniel H.
1981 <u>Religion and Politics in Latin America: The Catholic Church in Venezuela and Colombia</u>. Princeton, N.J.: <u>Princeton University</u>.
Levine, Daniel H., ed.
1979 <u>Churches and Politics in Latin America: Recent Trends on the Subcontinent</u>. Beverly Hills, Calif.: Sage.
Libanio, J. G.
1981 Experiences with the Base Ecclesial Communities in Brazil. <u>LADOC</u> XII, 2 (November-December): 1-20.
Maduro, Otto
1982a <u>Religion and Social Conflicts</u>. Maryknoll, N.Y.: Orbis.
1982b Is Religion Revolutionary? Keynote Address to the Massachusetts Sociological Association. Amherst, Mass. (November).
Mainwaring, Scott
1984 The Catholic Church, Popular Education and Political Change in Brazil. <u>Journal of Interamerican Studies and World Affairs</u> 26, 1 (February): 97-124.
Marchetti, Peter
1982 Church and Revolution in Nicaragua. <u>Monthly Review</u> 34, 3 (July-August): 43-55 (Reprint of interview in <u>Working Papers</u>, March-April, 1982).
Marins, Jose
1976 Basic Christian Communities in Latin America. Washington, D.C.: <u>LADOC</u> Keyhole Series (14): 1-7.
Marzani, Carl
1982 The Vatican as a Left Ally? <u>Monthly Review</u> 34, 3 (July-August): 1-42.
Melendez, Guillermo
1986 Nicaragua: Iglesia y Estado reanudan dialogo. <u>Noticias Aliadas</u> (October 23): 1-2
Moreira-Alves, Marcio
1974 <u>L'Eglise et la Politique au Bresil</u>. Paris: Editions du Cerf.
Moreira-Alves, Maria Helena
1981 Grassroot Organizations, Trade Unions and the Church: Challenge to the Controlled <u>Abertura</u> in Brazil. Paper delivered at the annual meeting of the American Political Science Association. New York (September 3-6).
Novaes, Regina R.
1985 Igreja Catolica, Reforma Agraria e Nova Republica. <u>Religiao e Sociedade</u> 12, 3 (December): 54-62.
Perani, Claudio
1985 Rumos da Igreja No Brasil. <u>Cadernos do CEAS</u> 100 (November- December): 66-73.
Reiter, Jackie
1981 Nicaragua: A Church Divided. <u>NACLA Report</u> (May-June): 45-47.
Ribeiro de Oliveira, Pedro A.
1986 A Igreja Catolica e a transicao brasileira para a democracia. <u>Comunicacoes do ISER</u> 5, 19 (May): 37-40.
Riding, Alan
1981 The Cross and the Sword in Latin America. <u>New York Review of Books</u> (May 28): 3ff.

Smith, Brian
1975   Religion and Social Change: Classical Theories and
        New Formulations in the Context of Recent Developments
        in Latin America. Latin America Research Review X, 2
        (Summer): 3-34.
1979   Churches and Human Rights in Latin America: Recent
        Trends on the Subcontinent. In Daniel H. Levine, ed.,
        Churches and Politics in Latin America.   Beverly
        Hills, Calif.: Sage.
1982   The Church and Politics in Chile: Challenges to Modern
        Catholicism. Princeton, N.J.: Princeton University.
Torres-Rivas, Edelberto
1981   Seven Keys to Understanding the Central American
        Crisis. Contemporary Marxism 3 (Summer): 49-61.
Williams, Philip J.
1985   The Catholic Hierarchy in the Nicaraguan Revolution.
        Journal of Latin American Studies 17 (November):
        341-69.

6
Ideological Dimensions of Peasant Persistence in Western Kenya

STEVEN L. JOHNSON

Kenya is often referred to as a model of capitalist development in sub-Saharan Africa.[1] Commodity production and
circulation are widespread. An African bourgeoisie has
appeared in certain areas of the country (Kitching, 1980), as
have both an urban proletariat and a rural labor force comprised of landless and submarginal farmers (Stichter, 1982).
These facts lead Gavin Kitching (1980: 4) to argue that there
is only one mode of production operative in Kenya, namely
capitalism.

This conclusion needs to be carefully scrutinized,
however, for not all peasant producers in Kenya have been
similarly incorporated into this system, either as laborers
or suppliers of agricultural products. For example, data
from Migori Division in western Kenya (see Fig. 6.1) suggest
that peasants in this region of the country have not been
fully captured by the capitalist system. They are primarily
involved in subsistence-oriented agricultural production.
Commodity production is not central to their lives, and their
ties to commodity markets are weak when compared to those
existing in other regions of the country. There is no evidence of an African bourgeoisie which is accumulating either
land or control over productive technology. Wage labor is
common, but a class of landless rural laborers does not
exist. Relations of production are often mediated by kinship
ties and generalized exchange rather than ownership and
control of access to the forces of production. These data
suggest that another mode of production is operative in
western Kenya which articulates with capitalism within the
overall structure of the Kenyan economy. This articulation
of differing modes of production underlies the persistence
(and power) of the peasantry in Kenya.

The persistence of a social formation within which capitalist and noncapitalist modes of production articulate with
one another can be accounted for in two ways. Many argue
that this formation is created and preserved by the forces of
international capitalism to serve its own ends. For example,
a peasantry can feed its sons and daughters who are employed
in the cities, thus reducing the cost of labor for employers
(Wolpe, 1972). The promotion of peasant agriculture, too,
can impede the development of an indigenous class of capitalist farmers, thus maintaining the monopoly of international
capital over large-scale commodity production and circulation

(Cowen, 1981a). The argument, in essence, is that the transition to capitalism has been blocked by international capital.

Other theorists argue that peasant persistence is related to the fact that the peasantry is uncaptured, and thus powerful (Hyden, 1980a). This power is rooted in peasant control over the forces of production, and, consequently, in their ability to reproduce themselves without full-scale participation in the wider, capitalist system. Individual producers are normally involved in both the capitalist and noncapitalist systems since the two interpenetrate one another (Long and Richardson, 1978: 186-87), but if pressured too much by the state (on behalf of capital) they can disengage and still meet their basic needs through subsistence production and reciprocal exchange with neighbors and kin. Peasants are seen to be active (not passive) participants in the shaping of the social formation within which they live. This latter interpretation of the persistence of noncapitalist modes of production more nearly fits the data from western Kenya.

However, while the material dimension of peasant power and persistence is important, there is an ideological dimension which must be considered as well if we are to fully understand the articulation existing in this area of the country. There are cultural forces which militate against the appearance of a fully developed capitalist mode of production and an indigenous class of capitalist farmers. Key values related to kinship (Parkin, 1978), personal prestige (Johnson, 1983) and autonomy from the market (Kongstad and Monsted, 1980: 160) ensure that, while differentiation may exist among these peasant producers, relationships between people will not become impersonal. As long as these values are important, commoditization of the forces of production and the establishment of capitalist relations of production will be circumscribed.

Capitalism has directly affected the lives of most Kenyans, but it would be misleading to say that capitalism is the only mode of production operative in Kenya. An examination of microlevel data from western Kenya reveals another mode of production which is similar in certain respects to the lineage modes described in West and Central Africa (Dupre and Rey, 1973; Meillassoux, 1978). The persistence of this noncapitalist mode of production is based, in large part, on the material power of the peasantry, but there are ideological dimensions to this persistence which will be explored in depth in the following discussion.

PRODUCTION AND CIRCULATION IN WESTERN KENYA

Before moving to a discussion of the role of ideology in peasant persistence, it is necessary to summarize the data gathered in Migori Division during 1976-1977. These data provide us with an understanding of the distinctive character of the social formation in this region of western Kenya.[2]

Land

Within Wasweta I Sub-Location of Migori Division, land is a crucial force of production which is required by peasants so that they can produce crops for both subsistence and the market. Capitalist and noncapitalist modes of production can be distinguished from one another based on the manner in which peasants obtain access to land for productive activities. Within the capitalist mode of production operating here, land is a commodity, and access to it is gained through purchases and rentals. Within the noncapitalist mode of production, access to land is granted to relatives and neighbors, usually by senior clan (dhoot) members, as part of a system of generalized reciprocity in evidence in the region. In this latter system, land is not treated as a commodity.

Land in Wasweta I has been surveyed, and title deeds written. Not all the deeds have been collected by landowners because of their cost, but all the land is now privately owned. This privately owned land is distributed unevenly, with holdings ranging in size from 0.4 hectare to 63.9 hectares (Johnson, 1980a). Most larger holdings belong to the elders of a single dhoot who inherited their land from the area's first colonial chief.

As a consequence of this pattern of land distribution, immigrants, submarginal farmers, and (less frequently) marginal farmers will approach larger landowners in order to gain access to land for productive activities. Both the controllers of large tracts of land and those wishing access to this land must determine which set of relations (capitalist or noncapitalist) they will utilize in the transfer. Some will use both systems simultaneously (for example, the landowner who sells some of his land, rents out another portion, and donates yet another segment to a son-in-law or neighbor).

Transfers in which land is treated as a commodity have grown more common in recent years. This is now an important method used to gain access to land, particularly by the large number of immigrants who have moved to Wasweta I to avoid overcrowding in other parts of western Kenya. Forty percent of the small holders in the research area purchased their land, and 10 percent rented land from their neighbors.[3]

More often, however, peasants gain access to land without purchasing or renting it. This is particularly true for those who already own land, and who have lived in the area for most of their lives, surrounded by kin. Often land will be donated to kin or neighbors free of charge. Exchange is occurring, but it can best be understood under the rubric of generalized reciprocity (Sahlins, 1965). In other instances, land may be exchanged for a certain number of days of labor. This is similar to a payment of rent, but differs to the extent that the two parties are involved in other instances of reciprocal exchange. Half of the peasants in Wasweta I have been granted access to land in this manner, and 43 percent have themselves donated land to others.

Land transactions are common here due to an influx of immigrants and an uneven distribution of land among the peasants who already reside in Wasweta I. Private ownership of land is now the norm, but access to land comes in two ways: one associated with capitalist relations of production, the other with noncapitalist relations.

The Means of Production

The agricultural cycle in Wasweta I Sub-Location has five stages: clearing, plowing, planting, weeding, and harvesting. During clearing, the means of production consist of the machete (panga) and the bush knife. Once cleared, land must be prepared for planting. To accomplish this, most peasants utilize single-bottomed plows drawn by two or four oxen. Occasionally a producer will rely only on hoes during field preparation, but this is extremely rare these days. Nearly as rare is the use of tractor-hire services. Planting normally occurs along with the last cycle of plowing. Few tools are required, but seed must be obtained from the previous season's harvest, other homesteads, or the market. The means of production required during weeding and harvesting consist of hoes, knives, sticks, and baskets.

The means of production are distributed more evenly in Wasweta I than is the land, but differential control of these resources still exists among the peasantry. This means that submarginal and marginal peasants (along with newly arrived immigrant families) must again approach their more prosperous neighbors in order to gain access to the means required for production. This is especially true with respect to ox-plow teams and seed. As was the case with land, this can be accomplished in two ways.

One method used to gain access to the means of production can be associated with a capitalist mode of production, for the means are reduced to commodities which can be purchased or rented. For example, hoes, knives and other small tools are nearly always purchased and can cost up to 25 Kenyan shillings (Ksh) each (or U.S. $3.00). Less often, peasants will purchase seed (particularly beans and hybrid maize) at local markets, or from licensed agents of Kenya's Maize and Produce Board.[4] Ox-plow teams can also be purchased, but only by the wealthiest peasants.[5]

Those peasants who are unable to purchase an ox-plow team will sometimes hire their neighbors to plow for them, an option chosen by 22.5 percent of sampled homesteads during the short rains of 1976.[6] Peasants will also exchange their labor for the use of an ox-plow team. This strategy was employed by 20 percent of the sampled farmers during 1976 as a means of gaining access to these teams. Owners enlist drivers to operate their plow teams, and in return drivers can use the teams to prepare their own fields. Normally drivers will work two to three days for owners in return for one day's use of the plow in their own fields. The other means of production are rarely rented by the peasantry in this manner.

A second method used to gain access to the means of production does not reduce these means to commodities. Instead, access is gained free of charge from one's relatives or neighbors. This method is often used by peasants to gain access to seed. It is less commonly employed to gain access to ox-plow teams, hoes, or bush knives.

The importance of kinship obligations and generalized reciprocity suggest an association with a noncapitalist mode of production which is operative in Wasweta I Sub-Location. Peasants participate less frequently in this mode when mobilizing the means of production than they do when mobilizing land.

Labor

Households in Wasweta I act as separate production units, even though a certain number of submarginal small holders are dependent on their neighbors for access to land and the means of production (Johnson, 1979b). The ultimate source of labor for these production units is the homestead itself, since family labor is cheapest to employ and easiest to mobilize. For some phases of production, however, peasants find it necessary to mobilize labor from outside the household. They can either hire laborers, or establish reciprocal exchange relations (Johnson, 1980b). The laborers who are mobilized will often be landowners themselves, and may be kin, friends, or neighbors.

Wage labor in agriculture first appeared in this area of Kenya in the late 1950s and early 1960s. Local residents say it was introduced by Abaluhya immigrants from Western Province. The introduction of wage labor occurred later in this region of Kenya than it did in other, less remote areas of the country.[7] This may be partly due to the fact that South Nyanza was not as fully encorporated into the system of migrant labor established during the colonial period as were these other regions (Stichter, 1982).

Individuals are hired to do all types of piecework, from clearing to harvesting. Groups are also hired, but they tend to engage only in weeding. These labor teams are comprised of people who represent churches, lineages, and ethnic groups; women predominate in most groups.

In Wasweta I, however, laborers are more often mobilized who do not demand wages for their work. These may be relatives or neighbors who ask only that they, themselves, be assisted at some point in the future. The reciprocal relations established can be either generalized or balanced, depending upon the strength of the bond existing between the peasants involved. These reciprocal exchanges of labor between households are usually mediated by women. They can occur at each stage of production, but are most common during harvest.

Less common these days are forms of reciprocal labor exchange which involve the mobilization of work teams. There are two types of nonwage labor teams, both of which have a festive character to them. One is called saga, and is a group called together by a single individual who has a task which must be performed rapidly. The other is called rika. This is a group of young men who travel from one homestead to another performing various tasks at each. Both saga and rika are rare today, though some peasants continue to utilize saga occasionally.

Wage labor is associated with a capitalist mode of production, and its presence in Wasweta I Sub-Location suggests that capitalism is operative in that region of Kenya. The issue is complicated, however, by the fact that classes of owners and workers are difficult to discern. Workers often own both land and the means of production. In fact, the largest landowners (or members of their families) may occasionally engage in piecework.

The situation becomes even more complicated when we realize that most labor is mobilized from among one's kin and neighbors through a system of reciprocal exchange. Instead of seeing agricultural laborers working for landowners, we see women and their sisters, daughters, or friends helping each other during weeding and harvesting. It is not absolutely necessary for these households to participate in the system of wage labor in order to reproduce themselves as viable social units.

Circulation

Goods circulate in Wasweta I either as commodities in a market system or as gifts and donations in a nonmarket exchange system. As was seen with respect to the forces of production, peasants will involve themselves in both systems (sometimes simultaneously).

Three marketing structures exist in this area of Kenya:

1. a local, biweekly market for agricultural products in which peasant households buy and sell their products;

2. a national market for agricultural products operated by licensed agents of the Maize and Produce Board who buy peasant produce; and

3. a market for goods and services controlled by private merchants from whom peasants buy.

Because peasants produce primarily for household consumption here, they have a degree of autonomy from these structures which is not shared by Kenyan small holders engaged in non-food cash crop production.

The major crop grown in this region of Kenya is maize. Maize is a staple here, as it is in many other areas of the country. Sixty percent of the peasant households interviewed sold maize either in the local or national markets, but they sold only 7 to 8 percent of their crop. Higher proportions of the harvests of secondary pulse, root, cereal, and tree crops were sometimes sold, but peasants indicated that their first concern in production was to meet the subsistence needs of their families.

Income from crop sales ranged from zero to over 10,000 Ksh (or U.S. $1,250). The mean income during 1976 was 1210 Ksh (U.S. $151). This money (along with the income from wage labor, if any) is generally spent at local businesses for household necessities, tools, or seed. Some money also goes to meet school fees and medical or emergency expenses (for example, funeral costs).

Circulation also occurs outside these formal marketing structures. For example, crops can be given as gifts to friends and relatives who have not produced enough to meet their own needs. Crops may be distributed at funerals, weddings, or initiations. Wealth may also circulate as bride-price, or may be used to entertain neighbors.

During the long rains of 1976, 70 percent of the peasants interviewed distributed crops freely. They gave away an average of 75 kilograms of maize, or roughly 3 percent of their total harvest. Many used another 3 percent of their maize crop to entertain. In 1976, as much maize as was circulated informally as was sold in the formal markets.

Commoditization has affected the sphere of circulation in Wasweta I, and can be associated with a capitalist mode of production in operation there. Circulation also occurs outside the formal marketing structures, however, where it is guided, again, by generalized reciprocity.

ARTICULATING MODES OF PRODUCTION

The data from western Kenya reveal two modes of production in operation, one capitalist and the other noncapitalist. The capitalist mode of production is characterized by private ownership of land and the means of production, commoditization of the forces of production (including labor), commoditization within the sphere of circulation, and the establishment of relations of production in which owners control access to the forces of production while immigrants and submarginal producers become more heavily involved in wage labor.

The noncapitalist mode of production operates within a context of private ownership, but the forces of production are not treated as commodities by the peasantry. Instead, access is granted through gifts and donations, and labor is mobilized by engaging others in reciprocal exchange. Circulation occurs outside the market, mediated by gifts, donations, and the principle of reciprocity. Relations of production reflect ties of kinship and friendship which bind those who control more of the forces of production to those who control less.

Capitalism dominates the social formation in this area because the noncapitalist mode of production functions within its overall structure (for example, private ownership, commoditization, and wage labor). The point of articulation between capitalist and noncapitalist modes of production is the peasant household where decisions are made regarding which set of social relationships is to be activated at particular points in the production process.

Some argue that articulation of this sort is a temporary stage in the inevitable transition from a precapitalist to a capitalist mode of production (Bernstein, 1979; Dupre and Rey, 1973; Seddon, 1978: 64). This transformation is said to involve the intensification of commodity relations in society (Bernstein, 1979). Peasants are gradually drawn into production for the market, and the forces of production in peasant society ultimately become commodities themselves. It is only a matter of time before peasants are separated from their land and the means of production to form a true proletariat.

Others argue that the articulation is more stable. They contend that the transition to capitalism is blocked by international capital.[8] International capital, at times assisted by a state elite, is said to foster underdevelopment in order to maintain control over production and circulation. Peasant production is promoted rather than discouraged in order to provide capital with a source of inexpensive labor (that is, a labor force that feeds itself), and in order to undermine indigenous capitalists who might threaten the monopolists' control over the economy (Cowen, 1981a; Kahn, 1978).

Finally, the argument is made that the articulation of differing modes of production within a single social formation is caused by the resistance of the peasantry to change. They are able to maintain this resistance in the face of spreading capitalism due to the fact that they are still in control of the forces of production in most rural areas.[9]

Many who argue that the peasantry has yet to be captured seem to believe that at some point in the future they will be. Others remain unconvinced. What is certain, however, is that the transition to capitalism, if or when it occurs, will be shaped by both capital and the nature of the preexisting modes of production in those areas of the world undergoing change.

IDEOLOGICAL DIMENSIONS OF PEASANT PERSISTENCE

While we may accept that peasants have some control over what is happening in western Kenya, we need not accept that this is due only to their ability to maintain a certain degree of control over the forces of production. Control of the forces of production is important, but the data from Wasweta I reveal an ideological dimension to peasant persistence which is important as well.

Beliefs and values shape behavior in concert with the material conditions of life.[10] In Wasweta I Sub-Location, beliefs and values surrounding kinship, personal prestige, and autonomy underpin many of the behaviors observed within the noncapitalist mode of production which is operative in this area.

The obligation to assist kin who are in need is a key value which governs behavior in this area (Pala, 1980: 191-93; Shipton, 1984a: 621-22). People are bound to one another through generalized reciprocity which Hyden (1980a: 18) refers to as an "economy of affection." These ties create networks which can be utilized by those whose homestead production falls below a certain level due to low amounts of productive resources, illness, weather, or age. The ties ensure, as well, that people will be able to mobilize land, seed, ox-plow teams, labor, and food from among their relatives if they are without cash, and in need. In other words, obligations to kin may significantly affect production and circulation in ways that neoclassical economists might label irrational.

Kinship is hierarchical, with elders holding the senior positions (Ocholla-Ayayo, 1976: 39), but we do not see tribute of any kind being paid from junior to senior kinsmen. In fact, an ideology of egalitarianism is widespread, and underlies moral claims for aid from kin (Shipton, 1984b: 129). This has the effect of redistributing wealth among those in the kinship network (Goldenberg, 1982b; Parkin, 1978: 82-86). This ideology may occasionally cloud peoples' perceptions of wealth and power disparities (Goldenberg, 1982a), but both rich and poor peasants are bound up in relationships which are intended to promote the reproduction of the entire social group. One would not stand idly by observing the pauperization of kin, and this is sometimes generalized to include friends and neighbors.

Another ideological dimension of peasant persistence and strength is associated with the individual's desire for

personal   prestige.[11]   Prestige   is   sometimes   attained
through a process known as social investment (Johnson, 1983).
     When asked what they valued most highly, a majority of
the peasants who were interviewed responded that they preferred respect and social position to material wealth.   Many
small holders went on to indicate that the most valued and
respected positions in Wasweta I were to be found in the local
churches (Pentecostal and Seventh Day Adventist).   To be a
church committee member, an elder in the church, a leader of
the church's work team, or a lay preacher was what many peasants desired above all else.   These positions were more de-
sirable than being wealthy or being the best farmer in the
area.   Other respected positions which were highly valued
included membership on local school committees, membership on
area development committees, and control of the position of
headman (called the jaduongweng) of the area.
     These valued positions which give their holders a measure
of personal prestige are often obtained by means of social
investment, a process through which material wealth is translated into social position.[12]   Peasants who own enough land,
or who have an ox-plow team, allow others to use these resources free of charge.   In this manner, recipients become
indebted to their benefactors, almost as clients are beholden
to their patrons.   As a means of discharging their debts,
they support their benefactors' attempts to gain social position, for nearly all of these positions are filled through
local elections.
     A final ideological dimension to peasant persistence
involves the peasantry's desire to remain autonomous from the
market; to remain in control of land, provide for its subsistence needs, and reproduce itself as families or larger social
units (lineages or clans).   Gudeman (1978: 38) refers to this
as a "needs ideology" shared by peasants, while Hyden (1980a)
and Kongstad and Monsted (1980) think of it as an ideology
which focuses on the inseparability of humans from the land.
     Peasants who were interviewed in western Kenya indicated
that they thought first about meeting subsistence needs, and
only secondly about producing a saleable surfeit of crops.
The desire to control land is strong, even among those who
leave   the   countryside   for   the   cities   (Parkin,   1978).
Kongstad and Monsted argue that

> The will and right to possess one's own land, even if
> only a small holding, is the most fundamental element in
> rural ideology in present Kenya, and it is a more
> forceful political factor in the country than any other
> we can think of. (1980: 161)

     The importance of autonomy means that peasant producers
will always be wary of full participation in the market and a
capitalist mode of production.   This need for autonomy and a
strong sense of individualism are important aspects of Luo
society (Othieno-Ochieng', 1968: 5-6).
     The small holders of Wasweta I value kinship relations,
personal prestige, and autonomy, and they allocate their resources accordingly.   Instead of increasing levels of production so they can market more crops, gain cash, and reinvest
in land or productive resources, small holders grant to others
the right to use their land and resources.   They do this for

the reasons mentioned above. These values militate against the formation of either a class of capitalist farmers, or a pauperized rural proletariat. They provide ideological support for the persistence of the peasantry and a noncapitalist mode of production in western Kenya.

SUMMARY

A capitalist mode of production has penetrated western Kenya, but rural society has not been transformed. A noncapitalist mode of production is still operative.

Data from this region of Kenya suggest that the peasants themselves are partly responsible for containing the spread of capitalism. They have been able to do this because of their control of the forces of production, and because of certain ideological dimensions of social life in this area. Obligations to kin, desire for prestige, and the need for autonomy are values which underlie the continued existence of a noncapitalist mode of production. These ideologies, too, underlie the persistence of the peasantry in western Kenya.

NOTES

1. The field research upon which this chapter is based was conducted during 1976-1977 in southwestern Kenya. Partial funding was provided by the United States Department of Health, Education and Welfare in the form of a Fulbright-Hays Fellowship, and by Indiana University through a Grant-in-Aid of Research. Research was carried out in association with the Institute for Development Studies at the University of Nairobi.

2. This area of Kenya is occupied by the Luo-Abasuba. The Luo-Abasuba do not form a group whose members share a common history (see Butterman, 1979 and Lonsdale, 1977 on this feature of western Kenya). The Luo-Abasuba entered this region from at least three directions at three different points in time (Abuso, 1976; Ayot, 1979; Kenny, 1971, 1977; Ochieng', 1974; Ogot, 1967). Their economic history is similar to that described by Hay (1972) for the Nilotic Luo.

3. The average value for land in the 1960s was 771 Ksh (U.S. $96) per hectare. It rose to 1127 Ksh (U.S. $141) per hectare by 1976-1977. Land was rented for an average of 148 Ksh (U.S. $19) per hectare for a single planting season during 1976-1977.

4. An average of 74 Ksh (U.S. $9) was expended by sampled homesteads for seed to be used during the short rains of 1976.

5. In 1977, the cost of two oxen, a plow, and accessories was 1105 Ksh (U.S. $138). Teams were owned by 47.5 percent of the homesteads, and no homestead owned more than one team. See Johnson (1979a, 1979b) for a further discussion of relations between owners of plow teams and their neighbors, and how these relations affect productive activities.

6. The average amount expended by those hiring people to plow for them was 89 Ksh (U.S. $11).

7. The growing importance of wage labor in peasant agriculture is discussed by Cowen (1981a, 1981b), Kongstad and

Monsted (1980: 73-85) and Ng'ang'a (1981: 11-12) for other regions of Kenya.

8. This argument is made by many theorists, including Cowen (1981a, 1981b), Galli (1981), Grier (1981), Kahn (1978), Laclau (1971), and Wolpe (1972).

9. A point made recently by Berry (1980: 417); Heyer, Roberts, and Williams (1981: 5); Hyden (1980a, 1980b); Kahn (1978: 112); Long and Richardson (1978); Miller (1982); Weeks (1978); and Williams (1981: 29).

10. This point is made by a number of writers, including Clammer (1978: 253-54), Foster-Carter (1978: 240-43), Kongstad and Monsted (1980: 161-62), and N'yong'o (1981: 3). As Parkin (1978: ix) notes, "By ignoring or cursorily dismissing the meaning and potency for people themselves of their own belief systems, such views curiously exhibit a reactionary intellectual ethnocentrism." Cultural idealists contend that overly materialistic interpretations of human existence do not provide us with a complete understanding of social life, particularly of those people whose beliefs differ significantly from our own. When looking at change or transformation of a society, it may be true that in many instances culture does not provide the "kick" which sets the system in motion, but it most certainly shapes the resulting "projectile" and its trajectory.

11. "Prestige" and "power" sometimes go hand in hand. See Schiller (1982: 112-19) for a discussion of traditional routes to power, some of which involve social investment. See Kennedy (1964: 7) on Luo symbols of prestige which were preferred to "cash."

12. The translation of wealth into power and prestige is discussed by Hay (1976: 94), Odinga (1967: 7), and Whisson (1961, 1962).

BIBLIOGRAPHY

Abuso, P. A.
1976   A Survey of the Evolution of the Kuria C. 1500-1900. Kenya Historical Review 4(1): 111-23.
Ayot, Henry Okello
1979   A History of the Luo-Abasuba of Western Kenya: From A.D. 1760-1940. Nairobi: Kenya Literature Bureau.
Bernstein, Henry
1979   Concepts for the Analysis of Contemporary Peasantries. Journal of Peasant Studies 6(4): 421-44.
Berry, Sara
1980   Rural Class Formation in West Africa. In R. H. Bates and M. F. Lofchie, eds., Agricultural Development in Africa: Issues of Public Policy. New York: Praeger.
Butterman, Judith
1979   Luo Social Formations in Change: Karachuonyo and Kanyamkago C. 1800-1945. Unpublished Ph.D. Dissertation, Department of History, Syracuse University.
Clammer, John
1978   Postscript. In J. Clammer, ed., The New Economic Anthropology. New York: St. Martin's.

Cowen, Michael
1981a Commodity Production in Kenya's Central Province. In
      J. Heyer, P. Roberts, and G. Williams, eds., Rural
      Development in Tropical Africa. New York: St.
      Martin's.
1981b The Agrarian Problem: Notes on the Nairobi
      Discussion. Review of African Political Economy 20:
      57-73.
Dupre, G., and P. P. Rey
1973 Reflections on the Pertinence of a Theory of the
      History of Exchange. Economy and Society 2(2): 131-63.
Foster-Carter, Aiden
1978 Can We Articulate "Articulation?" In J. Clammer, ed.,
      The New Economic Anthropology. New York: St. Martin's.
Galli, Rosemary E.
1981 Columbia: Rural Development as Social and Economic
      Control. In R. E. Galli, ed., The Political Economy
      of Rural Development: Peasants, International Capital,
      and the State. Albany: State University of New York.
Goldenberg, David A.
1982a We Are All Brothers: The Suppression of Consciousness
      of Socio-Economic Differentiation in a Kenya Luo
      Lineage. Unpublished Ph.D. Dissertation, Department
      of Anthropology, Brown University.
1982b Liel-The Kenya Luo Funeral: Central Ritual in the
      Maintenance of Urban-Rural Ties. Paper presented at
      the 22nd Annual Meeting of the Northeastern Anthropo-
      logical Association, Princeton, N.J.
Grier, Beverly
1981 Underdevelopment, Modes of Production, and the State
      in Colonial Ghana. African Studies Review 24(1): 21-
      47.
Gudeman, Stephen
1978 The Demise of a Rural Economy: From Subsistence to
      Capitalism in a Latin American Village. London: Rout-
      ledge and Kegan Paul.
Hay, M. Jean
1972 Economic Change in Luoland: Kowe, 1890-1945. Unpu-
      blished Ph.D. Dissertation, Department of History,
      University of Wisconsin.
1976 Luo Women and Economic Change During the Colonial
      Period. In N. J. Hafkin and E. G. Bay, eds., Women in
      Africa: Studies in Social and Economic Change.
      Stanford: Stanford University.
Heyer, Judith, Pepe Roberts, and Gavin Williams
1981 Rural Development. In J. Heyer, P. Roberts, and G.
      Williams, eds., Rural Development in Tropical Africa.
      New York: St. Martin's.
Hyden, Goren
1980a Beyond Ujamaa in Tanzania: Underdevelopment and an
      Uncaptured Peasantry. Berkeley: University of
      California.
1980b The Resilience of the Peasant Mode of Production: The
      Case of Tanzania. In R. H. Bates and M. F. Lofchie,
      eds., Agricultural Development in Africa: Issues of
      Public Policy. New York: Praeger.

Johnson, Steven L.
1979a Changing Patterns of Maize Utilization in Western
      Kenya. Studies in Third World Societies 8: 37-56.
1979b Micro-Level Dependency Relations in Rural Kenya.
      Paper presented at the 55th Annual Meeting of the
      Central States Anthropological Society, Milwaukee, Wis.
1980a Production, Exchange, and Economic Development among
      the Luo-Abasuba of Southwestern Kenya. Unpublished
      Ph.D. Dissertation, Department of Anthropology,
      Indiana University.
1980b Changing Patterns of Labor Mobilization in Western
      Kenya. Paper presented at the 23rd Annual Meeting of
      the African Studies Association, Philadelphia, Penn.
1983 Social Investment in a Developing Economy: Position-
      holding in Western Kenya. Human Organization 42(4):
      340-46.
Kahn, Joel
1978 Marxist Anthropology and Peasant Economics: A Study of
      the Social Structures of Underdevelopment. In J.
      Clammer, ed., The New Economic Anthropology. New
      York: St. Martin's.
Kennedy, T. J.
1964 A Study of Economic Motivation Involved in Peasant
      Cultivation of Cotton. Conference Paper, East African
      Institute of Social Research, Makerere University
      College, Kampala, Uganda.
Kenny, Michael G.
1971 Report of the Expedition to Kenya (Lake Victoria).
      Bulletin of the Oxford University Exploration Club 18:
      1-12.
1977 The Relation of Oral History to Social Structure in
      South Nyanza, Kenya. Africa 47(3): 276-88.
Kitching, Gavin
1980 Class and Economic Change in Kenya. New Haven: Yale
      University.
Kongstad, Per, and Mette Monsted
1980 Family, Labour and Trade in Western Kenya. Uppsala:
      Scandinavian Institute of African Studies.
Laclau, Ernesto
1971 Feudalism and Capitalism in Latin America. New Left
      Review 67: 19-38.
Long, Norman, and Paul Richardson
1978 Informal Sector, Petty Commodity Production, and the
      Social Relations of Small-scale Enterprise. In J.
      Clammer, ed., The New Economic Anthropology. New
      York: St. Martin's.
Lonsdale, John
1977 When Did the Gusii (or any other group) Become a
      "Tribe?" Kenya Historical Review 5(1): 123-33.
Meillassoux, Claude
1978 "The Economy" in Agricultural Self-Sustaining Socie-
      ties: a Preliminary Analysis. In D. Seddon, ed., Re-
      lations of Production: Marxist Approaches to Economic
      Anthropology. London: Frank Cass (originally publish-
      ed in 1960 in Cahiers d'Etudes Africaines).
Miller, Frank C.
1982 Toward Self-Sufficiency in Basic Foods: The Political
      and Cultural Context of Mexican Food Policy. Culture
      and Agriculture 15: 7-12.

Ng'ang'a, D. Mukaru
1981 What is Happening to the Kenyan Peasantry? Review of
      African Political Economy 20: 7-16.
N'yong'o, P. Anyang'
1981 Editorial. Review of African Political Economy 20:
      1-6.
Ochieng', William R.
1974 An Outline History of Nyanza up to 1914. Nairobi:
      East African Literature Bureau.
Ocholla-Ayayo, A. B. C.
1976 Traditional Ideology and Ethics among the Southern
      Luo. Uppsala: Scandinavian Institute of African
      Studies.
Odinga, Oginga
1967 Not Yet Uhuru. London: Heinemann.
Ogot, Bethwell A.
1967 History of the Southern Luo, Volume 1: Migration and
      Settlement 1500-1900. Nairobi: East African Publish-
      ing.
Othieno-Ochieng', N. A.
1968 Luo Social System: With a Special Emphasis on Marriage
      Rituals. Nairobi: Equatorial.
Pala, Achola Okeyo
1980 Daughters of the Lakes and Rivers: Colonization and
      the Land Rights of Luo Women. In M. Etienne and E.
      Leacock, eds., Women and Colonization: Anthropological
      Perspectives. New York: Praeger.
Parkin, David
1978 The Cultural Definition of Political Response: Lineal
      Destiny Among the Luo. London: Academic.
Republic of Kenya
1974 Migori-Kihancha Regional Master Plan: Water and Land
      Utilisation. Ministry of Water Development.
Sahlins, Marshall D.
1965 On the Sociology of Primitive Exchange. In M. Banton,
      ed., The Relevance of Models for Social Anthropology.
      London: Tavistock.
Schiller, Laurence Dana
1982 Gem and Kano: A Comparative Study of Two Luo Political
      Systems Under Stress, C. 1880-1914. Unpublished Ph.D.
      Dissertation, Department of History, Northwestern Uni-
      versity.
Seddon, David
1978 Economic Anthropology or Political Economy? Ap-
      proaches to the Analysis of Pre-Capitalist Formation
      in the Maghreb. In J. Clammer, ed., The New Economic
      Anthropology. New York: St. Martin's.
Shipton, Parker M.
1984a Strips and Patches: A Demographic Dimension in Some
      African Land-Holding and Political Systems. Man 19
      (4): 613-34.
1984b Lineage and Locality as Antithetical Principles in
      East African Systems of Land Tenure. Ethnology 23(2):
      117-32.
Stichter, Sharon
1982 Migrant Labour in Kenya: Capitalism and African Res-
      ponse 1895-1975. Essex: Longman.

Weeks, John
  1978 Fundamental Economic Concepts and their Application to
        Social Phenomena. In J. Clammer, ed., The New Econo-
        mic Anthropology. New York: St. Martin's.
Whisson, Michael G.
  1961 The Rise of Asembo and the Curse of Kakia. Conference
        Paper, East African Institute of Social Research,
        Makerere University College, Kampala, Uganda.
  1962 The Journies of the JoRamogi. Conference Paper, East
        African Institute of Social Research, Makerere Univer-
        sity College, Kampala, Uganda.
Williams, Gavin
  1981 The World Bank and the Peasant Problem. In J. Heyer,
        P. Roberts, and G. Williams, eds., Rural Development
        in Tropical Africa. New York: St. Martin's.
Wolpe, Harold
  1972 Capitalism and Cheap Labour-power in South Africa:
        from Segregation to Apartheid. Economy and Society
        1(4): 425-56.

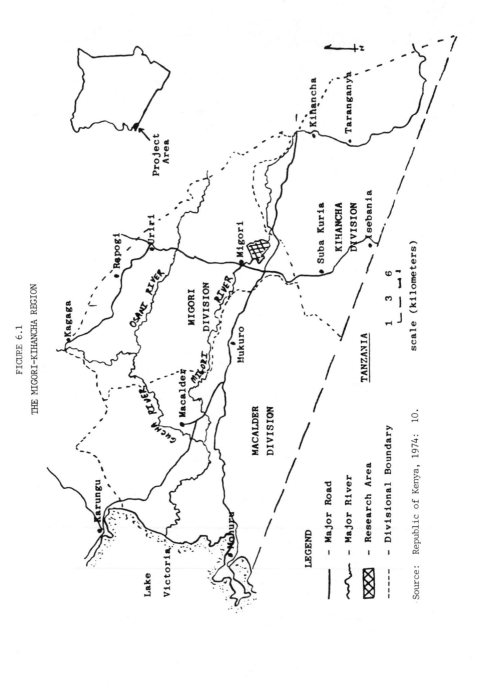

FIGURE 6.1
THE MIGORI-KIHANCHA REGION

LEGEND

— Major Road
— Major River
— Research Area
---- Divisional Boundary

Source: Republic of Kenya, 1974: 10.

scale (kilometers)

7

Conflict, Class, and the Urban Poor in the Third World

DEAN FORBES

One of the most significant developments in the literature on the political economy of poor countries in the last few years has been the growing call for a theory of underdevelopment which takes as its focus class analysis. In response to the critics of dependency, world systems, and allied macro theories of underdevelopment, scholars like Amin and Wallerstein have tried to write in more class analysis, which, in Amin's case has lead to the development of an "international class structure" (Amin, 1980). Others, such as Rey (1973), sought to reconcile the disparate strands of articulation theory and class analysis, while Brenner (1977) and, more importantly, Leys (1977, 1978) have tried to reconstitute a theory of underdevelopment around the linchpin role of the domestic bourgeoisie. The effects of this methodological reorientation have in some cases proved dramatic. When Leys (1975) used a dependency framework for an analysis of Kenya, he drew the conclusion that the persistence of underdevelopment in Kenya was likely due to structural forces. However, his later examination of the history of the capital accumulation of a domestic bourgeois class led him to the contrary belief that:

> capitalist production relations may be considerably extended in a periphery social formation, and the productive forces may be considerably expanded within and through them, for reasons having primarily to do with the configuration of class forces preceding and during the colonial period. (Leys, 1978: 216)

During the 1960s a precapitalist accumulating class reasserted their dominance. Combined with a proletariat that had evolved during the colonial period through the practices of the settler plantation owners, this created a set of economic relations in which the appropriation of surplus labor depended increasingly on augmenting the appropriation of relative surplus labor (by improving, for instance, labor productivity)

Nigel Thrift, Stephanie Fahey, Kathy Gibson, Peter Williams, Doug Porter, and Piers Blaikie have debated with me many of the issues raised in this paper and Richard Curtain provided useful comments on the manuscript. For all of these I am grateful.

rather than absolute surplus labor. Thus Leys demonstrated the critical importance of class structure and modes of surplus appropriation in an explanation of underdevelopment.

The significance of this sort of class-based analysis is that it shifts the focus of the development-underdevelopment debate away from the analysis of structures and the relationship between humans and nature (for instance, new technology) to relationships between humans themselves, human agency and political action. This is not to say that objective structures such as the laws of accumulation do not predetermine some and constrain other human behaviors, nor does it deny that the resource-base of a community, levels of technology, and other structural givens, are central to the underdevelopment issue. A class viewpoint highlights the development of a set of complex relationships between classes in a society by both the objective laws of the mode of production and the historical, spatially differentiated, semiautonomous social behavior of different strata within the society. As the Leys case study illustrates, these relationships take us a long way towards understanding patterns of underdevelopment, but they are also important in trying to understand development.

By this line of reasoning development is, to a large extent, the exercise of political power on behalf of the exploited. The analysis of class is, then, the analysis of conflict and the struggle for power, both historically and as a basis for social and economic change. While this shift of emphasis within development studies has been confined to the "radical" literature, it has had a growing impact on the ground. For example, the concientization of the poor seems to play an increasingly large role in the rhetoric, and sometimes the practice, of a number of nongovernmental aid organizations throughout the world. While this is not articulated as a class strategy, the effect has many parallels in awakening the poor and oppressed to the mechanisms of their oppression and offering local political solutions to their plight.

However, if we look critically at underdevelopment research in the last few years, we can quite legitimately question whether the general thrust of research has changed that much as a response to the mounting criticism posed by scholars like Leys, or in the light of the structure-agency debates which have been the preoccupation of many social theorists during the same period. Articles regularly appear (Fitzgerald, 1981; Smith, 1982) reaffirming the need for a theory of underdevelopment focussed on class analysis, class biographies, and the like, but the truth is that very little research of any substance expanding this theoretical framework has been published. Abandoning the structuralist universalisms of grand underdevelopment theory to become involved in the histories of class and place is all very well, but the danger is that theory is also put aside, and that was not the point of the exercise at all. The theoretical baby should not go the way of the universalist bathwater.

This chapter is intended as a contribution—a tentative methodological contribution—towards an analysis of proletarianization in the peripheral capitalist city. The first part of the chapter looks critically at a functionalist interpretation of urban class structure; the second part argues for the need to make considerations of human agency, particularly

resistance and conflict, central to concepts of class formation; and the third part considers proletarianization in
Jakarta, comparing and contrasting the behavior of the nonwage
labor-force, and suggesting how an emphasis on conflict and
resistance among these classes alters our conception of urban
class formation.

CLASS FORMATION IN THE CITY

The term "proletarianization" refers to two processes:
first, it is primitive accumulation, the separation of people
from the means of production, and second, it refers to the
absorption of people into wage labor, that is, the commoditization of labor.

> Capital development continually transforms the structure
> of places in the system of production and realization of
> capital as well as in the other manners of production
> that become dominated by capitalism. More precisely,
> the penetration of the capitalist manner of producing
> into all areas of economic activity results in the sepa-
> ration of various groups from the ownership of the means
> of production or from the effective capacity to trans-
> form nature into useful products. (Przeworski, 1977:
> 358)

Historically in Europe the two definitions of proletariat
overlapped because the theoretical connotation of the concept
of proletariat, which was defined in terms of separation from
the means of production, bore a close correspondence to the
intuitive concept of proletariat, which has been conceived in
terms of manual, principally industrial, laborers (Przeworski,
1977: 355). However, since then improvements in technology
have seen the growth of labor productivity and with this a
relative decrease in the capitalist utilization of labor
power. The speed with which capitalism historically destroys
small production exceeds the rate at which it is able to
generate places of productive capitalist employment. The
obvious outcome is that craftsmen, small merchants, and
peasants do not become transformed into productive manual
workers but remain trapped in an intermediate world, neither
peasant nor proletariat (Przeworski, 1977: 360-61).

> As a result, the process of proletarianization in the
> sense of separation from the means of production diverges
> from the process of proletarianization in the sense of
> creation of places of productive workers. This diver-
> gence generates social relations that are indeterminate
> in the class terms of the capitalist mode of production,
> since it leads to the separation of people from any
> socially organized process of production. (Przeworski,
> 1977:358)

Nineteenth-century conceptions of class formation have
in recent years been shaken by a series of processes which
are simply not explained by the proletarianization argument.
In capitalist societies this theoretical ambiguity has been
highlighted by interest in the power and wealth of the "new

middle class," by debates about the significance of the "labor aristocracy," by the conflict generated by the feminist movement and its arguments over gender and class, and by the enormous recent growth of unemployment in most capitalist countries.   Each of these issues has drawn attention to the complex and constantly changing nature of class formation in late capitalism, and the need for continuous monitoring of the changing circumstances of economy and society.   In the Third World, the persistence of a huge peasantry in Asia and the revolutionary role of the peasantry in China and Indo-china, the growth of a relatively small urban proletariat in these countries and their secondary role in revolutions, and the emergence of a large urban workforce of petty producers (protoproletarians) with an indeterminate place in most analyses of class formation, all likewise highlight the failure of our conceptions of class formation to keep pace with changing circumstances.

A number of useful studies, however, have tried to come to grips with class formation through an examination of the urban economy.   One key focus of this literature has been the significance of urban petty production.   "Petty commodity production" is the label generally used in the literature to define "that group of activities normally seen as lying outside the principal spheres of capitalist production in underdeveloped economies" (Gerry and Birkbeck, 1981: 128). Petty production,

> possesses no autonomous dynamic of its own and . . . the level of possible capital accumulation is constrained by structural factors embedded in the wider social formation.   The urban economy is conceptualized in terms of a continuum of economic activities with petty commodity production recognized as a form of production existing at the margins of the capitalist mode of production integrated into it in a dependent or subordinate fashion. The persistent feature of stagnating incomes in petty commodity production is linked to its important role within the capitalist mode of production of keeping down the reproduction costs of urban wage labour.   (Rogerson and Beavon, 1982: 250)

Petty production has existed historically in many different time periods and different economies in the form of family subsistence activities, "putting-out" schemes, petty trading, and the like.

> [T]he existence of vast layers of semiproletarianized labor accompanied the autonomous expansion of industrialism in the centers.   They gradually gave way to full proletarianization as the system was transformed by the rise of finance capital and imperialism.   Indeed, the capacity of the central economies to bring their working classes into fully commodified relations was, in part, dependent on their reach abroad and the exploitation of peripheral labor.   (Portes and Walton, 1981: 104)

Petty production today is not the same as it was in earlier periods:

It is impossible to assimilate the informal economy
as it exists today in peripheral countries to the
earlier "transitional" stage of advanced capitalism,
for the present situation is the deliberate and continuously reproduced consequence of a new world-wide
structure of accumulation. Thus, informal enterprise
is not a vestigial presence, a lag from precapitalist
times, but rather a very modern and expanding creation. It is an integral component of peripheral capitalist economies and its development is mandated by
the conditions in which these economies are incorporated into the contemporary world-system. (Portes and
Walton, 1981: 105)

Portes and Walton are primarily concerned with the conditions under which labor is reproduced in peripheral nations
in the world economy, and particularly with the low wage
levels characteristic of the periphery (they note that average
wage levels in Latin America are about one-fifth of those in
the United States). In the first place, they reject the
argument that it is the persistence of a rural subsistence
sector, apparently conserved in the face of capitalist expansion, which reduces payments to labor. This argument would
have it that the subsistence sector assumes

the costs of reproduction of new generations of workers
and absorb[s] those that have become redundant for the
capitalist sector. This "subsidy" paid by precapitalist
subsistence to capitalist production is translated into
wages lower than those that would be required for reproduction under fully proletarianized conditions. (Portes
and Walton, 1981: 70)

They depict this argument as functional dualism and reject it
on two grownds: first, because it oversimplifies labor utilization in the great majority of peripheral capitalist societies, the exceptions being perhaps South Africa and Zimbabwe.
Second, they argue that it is not possible that a stagnant,
and in many places declining, subsistence sector can reproduce
a large and growing urban wage labor force. They sum up the
argument thus:

whereas theories of accumulation on a world scale have
correctly   identified   subsistence   enclaves   and   the
process of return migration as mechanisms that lower
wage levels in the periphery, not all wage labor is
reproduced under traditional subsistence arrangements
nor do all those who leave this condition in search of
money wages return. Additional structural arrangements
for controlling returns to labor must exist. Unlike
traditional subsistence agriculture such arrangements
should not be based on a declining economic sector, but
on one that accompanies the very expansion of the
capitalist economy. (1981: 77)

Portes and Walton (1981) turn to urban informal sector
production as the key structural feature of contemporary
peripheral accumulation. Note that they use the term "informal sector production"--this is in fact an aggregate of all

the income-earning opportunities in urban areas outside capitalist wage labor, and includes petty production, subsistence
production, rents, transfer payments, and wages earned in
informal firms. While recognizing it as an individual's
strategy of survival, they stress that informal sector production as a whole is a large and growing feature of peripheral urban economies, constantly expanding into new areas of
production and showing no signs of declining with the expansion of capitalism. In other words, they stress that it is a
stable, structural component of peripheral capitalism.
    Informal sector production assists in the extraction of
maximal surplus value from the wage labor force in two ways.
First, unorganized production--subsistence household production, petty commodity production and trade, and informal land
occupation--contributes a subsidy to the wage bill of the
urban labor force by lowering the costs of reproduction of
labor below those that would occur if the labor were dependent
for reproduction on capitalist-produced goods and services.
Although the informal sector does not itself produce surplus
value, it affects the level of wages and the rate of extraction of surplus value from the workforce:

> It permits an average level of wages in formal firms
> that is above subsistence while being, at the same time,
> a fraction of those predominant in the centers. In this
> manner, the labor of unpaid family and informal workers
> eventually finds its way into the coffers of large in-
> dustrial corporations and finance houses. (Portes and
> Walton, 1981: 88)

Second, labor costs are further reduced by keeping the
size of the wage labor force as small as possible, which can
be done due to the existence of a large pool of unorganized
workers. Large and medium-sized firms in the garment and
footwear industries put out work to informal entrepreneurs,
who in turn organize mostly women workers in the home, who
use their own sewing machines and are paid piece-rates.

> Advantages of informal production include, first, cheaper
> cost per unit since workers subremunerate their own
> labor and that of kin and paid help. More important,
> informal production adapts to seasonal demand, permitting
> formal enterprises to hire and dismiss labor at will
> while avoiding unemployment compensation. (Portes and
> Walton, 1981: 99)

Likewise, petty traders provide for the cheap and efficient
circulation of commodities in peripheral economies, helping
to limit the size of the wage work force and reducing overall
costs of circulation.
    From this analysis, Portes and Walton (1981) argue that
the class structure of peripheral urban economies can be
described in terms of four broad categories--a bourgeoisie,
salaried labor, wage labor, and the various sub-categories of
petty production (the protoproletariat) (see figure 7.1).
The interests of the bourgeoisie rest in the maximal extraction of surplus value from the salaried and wage-earning
classes. Because this structure is set within a disarticul-
ated peripheral economy, the domestic market is relatively

insignificant and the export sector dominant, and therefore
surplus value extraction is maximized by keeping labor costs
down. As a result informal sector producers--the exploited
class--subsidize the costs of reproduction of the intermediate
classes, which in turn are subordinated to the extraction of
surplus value by the bourgeoisie.

FIGURE 7.1

CLASSES IN PERIPHERAL URBAN ECONOMIES

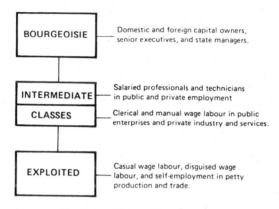

After Portes and Walton, 1981.

The problem with this account of class is that it rests
on a form of functional dualism which Portes and Walton (1981:
72) had already noted characterized those who advocated that
the rural sector played the key role in reducing labor costs.
Classes are defined purely in terms of relations of exploitation, and the four basic classes fit together with a tightness
and simplicity that would delight a systems theorist. The
protoproletariat are functional to the intermediate classes
and they in turn are functional to the survival of the bourgeoisie. While there is a clear indication that the informal
sector category is a very general one, there is no attempt to
differentiate between fractions within it in terms of class
and intraclass relations, or even to point to problems of
lumping together casual wage labor disguised wage labor, and
petty capitalists. Nor is there any consideration of the
role of consciousness and ideology in the formation and reproduction of the class structure. In other words, Portes and
Walton have put together a very general overview of the relations of exploitation within urban peripheral economies which
is both economistic and functionalist. Petty production is
functional to peripheral capitalism--it is a structural
feature of the economic organization of society. Functional-
ism of course is a risk--perhaps the major risk--in any
structuralist argument. After fleshing out the major structural forces in a society, it then becomes necessary to fit
people into the categories within the structure. Whereas
much of the work on petty producers in the 1970s stressed the

individualistic entrepreneurial talent of this group, the more recent work has tended to swing too far in the opposite direction, denying petty producers any economic or political independence.

CONFLICT AND CLASS

The underlying limitation of a functionalist interpretation of class formation is attributable to the nonrecursive definition of class it employs. In other words, determinations within functionalist interpretations are unidirectional: structure determines class and, by implication, structure determines behavior. This is an oversimplification of the argument, but it serves to highlight the key problem with this approach. It particularly overlooks the theory of structuration (Giddens, 1979, 1981, 1982) and the important debate on the relationship between structure and human agency and the crucial role of space-time mediations in this relationship (Gregory, 1981; Thrift, 1983; Forbes, 1984a).

In this section, I argue that class formation emerges from both the objective location of individuals within the general relations of production and the everyday practice--particularly that which is conflict-based--of those individuals. My thesis highlights the dialectical unity of these two processes, and the particular importance of intervening processes such as space-time relations.

Wright (1980: 365) has somewhat ironically noted that "the analysis of class structure is intended not as the end point of an investigation, but as the starting point." However, it is clear that there is little general consensus on the theoretical criteria for specific classes within the class structure of capitalist societies, nor is there agreement among Marxists on the precise class structure of contemporary capitalism.

There are quite a few approaches to class. Classes may be defined primarily in terms of:

    --gradation (for example, status or income)
    --relations of exchange (Weber)
    --relations of production
      --through a technical division of labor (occupation)
      --through authority (power) relations (for example,
        Dahrendorf)
      --in terms of exploitation (the Marxist approach)

We need not dwell upon critcisms of the first two approaches, as they have been dealt with elsewhere (Wright, 1980). Marxist definitions of class have at least three distinguishing features: first, they are relational rather than gradational definitions; second, they are focussed on the social organization and not on the technological organization of economic relations; and third, they deal with the social relations of production rather than relations of exchange (Wright, 1980: 325). However, even among Marxists, there are a number of different outcomes to the analysis of class formation, notably including on the one hand the social and labor history work of a number of English historians, especially E. P. Thompson, and on the other, the extensive debates about the political

consciousness of the contemporary working class, and particularly the "reform or revolution" question (Therborn, 1983:
37-38).

However, while a focus on exploitation and relationships
to the means of production might serve to differentiate
Marxist notions of class from many others, it by no means
constitutes an adequate definition. The critical missing
elements are struggle and conflict, and the historical and
spatial context in which these processes occur. Therborn has
argued that three important considerations must be taken into
account in the analysis of class formation. First, the degree
of "revolutionary ideology" of the working class is not important per se. Revolutions emerge out of particular situations which in themselves nurture a revolutionary ideology.
Second, all forms of revolutionary and reformist debate and
activity are important because of the way they change the
social relations of power. Third, "what is being done and
what is being achieved are more important than what ideas are
being held." Thus Therborn urges that we focus not on the
reformist-revolutionary dichotomy, but instead turn our attention to the notion of "class capacity" or "the capacities of
a given class to act in relation to others and the forms of
organization and practice thereby developed" (1983: 38).

As Poulantzas (who is sometimes held to epitomize the
structuralist view of class) has argued, there is an important
double articulation between form and behavior. He holds that
"economic, ideological, and political relations as a totality
impose a structure upon class struggles, but they become
transformed as effects of class struggles" (cited in
Przeworski, 1977: 368). Class is clearly not simply the
material form of a structural category: the structural
relations that constitute classes define class places, while
at any conjuncture, classes adopt positions. These positions
of course may not correspond to the attitudes and behavior we
might expect from the class places. Przeworski has taken
this proposition further:

> Classes are not given uniquely by any objective positions
> because they constitute effects of struggles, and these
> struggles are not determined uniquely by the relations
> of production . . . . Class struggles . . . are struc-
> tured by the totality of economic, political, and ideo-
> logical relations; and they have an autonomous effect
> upon the process of class formation . . . classifications
> of positions must be viewed as immanent to the practices
> that (may) result in class formation. The very theory
> of classes must be viewed as internal to particular
> political projects. Positions within the relations of
> production, or any other relations for that matter, are
> thus no longer viewed as objective in the sense of being
> prior to class struggles. They are objective only to
> the extent to which they validate or invalidate the
> practices of class formation, to the extent to which
> they make the particular projects historically realizable
> or not. (1977: 367)

Therborn makes a parallel (though certainly not identical)
point when he argues that class formation must be conceived
of as a "double process":

In its objective aspects, class formation is a socio-economic process accompanying the development of a mode of production: the process of agents moving into, being shaped by, and being distributed between the different kinds of economic practices which constitute the given mode of production . . . . In its subjective aspect, on the other hand, class formation is an ideological and political process of the tendential unification of class members into forms of common identity and of concerted action as conscious class members in relation to members of other classes. (1983: 39)

These arguments form the basis of a recursive class analysis, the elements of which are summarized in figure 7.2. It rests on three important principles: first, the fundamental "objective" nature of the social relations of production, especially exploitation or the means of appropriating surplus, defines class places; second, human agency has a determinate role in shaping and transforming these "objective structures," especially but not exclusively through conflict; third, the process is historical in the sense that it highlights the way in which human agency reproduces structure and society, and is space and time-specific in that it requires a conjunctural analysis in order to elucidate the nature of any given process.

FIGURE 7.2

STRUCTURE, AGENCY, AND CLASS

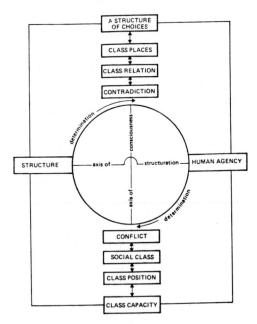

Human behavior, which has hitherto been located within the realms of class struggle and conflict, is related to the formation of social classes and class positions. In general terms this is an indicator of class capacity. These forces influence, reproduce, and sometimes transform the principally economic structure of society (the mode of production). This structure, then, contains contradictions which create class relations as well as defines class places: the structure of choices (or realms of possibility and impossibility) in turn has an influence on human behavior, and so on. The east-west axis is a double articulation which is structurationist: in the words of Gregory (1981: 13), and following Giddens, "social systems are both the medium and the outcome of the practices that constitute them: the two are recursively separated and recombined." The north-south axis is one of consciousness, in that the greater the degree of class consciousness, the more closely the two halves will appear to be mirror images of one another.

Classes cannot be simply read off from the mode of production, as if from a wall chart. As Therborn pointedly comments:

> Classes must be seen, not as veritable geological formations once they have acquired their original shape, but as phenomena in a constant process of formation, reproduction, re-formation and de-formation. (1983: 39)

The nature of capital accumulation, government policies and the particular role of the state, the "regime of accumulation" or the form of capital accumulation in a particular locality, the relationship of political time to economic time, human agency, social movements, and labor movements are all elements of a complex range of forces which bring about class formation and de-formation. However, although it is the relations of production which determine the class relation, it is human behavior and conflict which are the flesh and blood of class formation.

A specific illustration might aid in clarification. Working-class children are forced to attend school but, while there, many adopt a stance hostile to the school. They rebel against authority within the school as a sort of semiconscious rebellion against the structure of society as a whole, very much against the wishes of their teachers and middle-class society. A functionalist interpretation would say that they need to be educated to conform to society's need for a stable, educated labor force, but here they are struggling against "the system." Ironically, the end result of their struggle is to ensure the reproduction of their working-class identity because their lack of education practically ensures they will be unemployable or suited only to the worst-paid jobs (Willis, 1977). This argument tries to separate means from ends. In both a functionalist and nonfunctionalist interpretation the main ends are the same--the reproduction of a class-structured society--but the means toward those ends are quite different. In one, behavior is rigidly predetermined by objective structures, in the other, behavior both produces and reproduces the objective structure (Thrift, 1983).

This brings us to an important point about the meaning of conflict and its significance for the urban poor in the

informal sector of Third World cities. According to Nelson
(1979: 125-29), there are three main viewpoints on the political mobilization of the urban poor. The first is the theory
of the radical marginals, which argues that the lag between
urban growth and industrial progress radicalizes these "peri-
pherals"; the second is the theory of the available mass,
which argues that the urban poor are atomized and alienated,
and are therefore relatively easily mobilized; the third is
the theory of the passive poor, in which the "culture of
poverty" is a force for conservatism. In recent years the
general consensus has been that the urban poor have proved a
fairly conservative force. Communist Parties tend to draw
"virtually all their support from students, intellectuals,
and (often fairly elite) segments of organized labor," while
most revolutionary parties have focussed their mass revolutionary action on the proletariat, as in Latin America and
Vietnam prior to 1941, or the peasantry, as in China, Cuba,
and Vietnam) (Nelson, 1979: 344-45). There have been notable
exceptions, however: in Allende's Chile in the 1960s there
was a strong attempt to court the urban poor, while the
Turkish Labor Party also tried to mobilize this group. Clearly
the urban protoproletariat have not played a vanguard role in
revolutionary conflict, but that does not mean they have had
no role at all. For instance, strikes by pedicab drivers and
other urban workers during the 1920s and 1930s in Vietnam
played their part in leading up to the struggle for independence (Thrift and Forbes, 1983).

On the whole, though, this stress on the quiescence of
the urban poor has been part and parcel of the functionalist
interpretation of their role in Third World cities. There
are fragments of evidence which suggest that research on
petty producers has tended to underestimate the significance
of conflictual petty producer behavior. A chief reason for
this has been the use of what Cohen (1980: 8-22) has called
"formula dichotomies." Forms of conflict have tended to be
dealt with from polar positions. Fanon and some who followed
saw the lumpen proletariat as a revolutionary class, whereas
Marxists and non-Marxists alike have reacted by stressing the
political conservatism of the urban poor. The emphasis on
formula dichotomies forces us to take an "either/or" stand on
political conflict.

It is very clear that researchers have tended to ignore
the everyday forms of conflict--of consciousness, action, and
resistance. Cohen, Copans, and Gutkind (1978: 23) make the
point that historically much of the day-to-day struggle of
ordinary people is only poorly documented. Certainly there
is very little published social history of the urban poor;
nor, from what I have seen of the colonial records of Indonesia and Papua New Guinea at least, is there much source
material on the everyday existence of the urban poor. Nevertheless, it is the day-to-day conflicts and patterns of behavior which are the bread-and-butter of human history. As
Cohen (1980: 8) argues for the African working classes, "there
has been too much reliance on data relating to strike, unionization and overt political militance, and for the most part
a failure to discover and evaluate the silent, unorganized,
covert responses of African workers." Similarly, O'Malley
(1982) has discussed in a recent paper the underworld in
rural Java, juxtaposing the existence of bandits, criminals,

outlaws, robber gangs, gang leaders, and rascals with the perception of Javanese society as orderly and stable. Both non-Marxist and Marxist interpretations of Third World socie- ties have tended to ignore this type of behavior, implicitly dismissing it as insignificant. Conflict models have pointed to independence movements, break-away movements, labor strikes, religious movements, and riots, but have not reached down to encompass criminal behavior and everyday conflict, whereas these are the most common forms of conflict and the ones in which the urban poor are most likely to feature.

CLASS FORMATION AND THE URBAN POOR: AN INDONESIAN ILLUSTRATION

Some aspects of the conception of class formation out- lined above can be illustrated by looking at urban class formation in Indonesia, particularly Jakarta. Although not generally regarded in the same league as the "new industrial- izing countries" of Southeast and East Asia such as Singapore, South Korea and Hong Kong, the Indonesian economy has expanded steadily during the past decade. Real Gross Domestic Product grew by 9.9 percent in 1980 and 7.6 percent in 1981. However, the recession in the world economy during the last few years has taken its toll. Indonesia's dependence on oil meant that the government coffers were overflowing through much of the 1970s, but the glut in the world oil market in 1982 combined with a drop in the prices for agricultural products quickly changed that. Austere budgeting and cutbacks in government spending (for example, in fuel oil subsidies) in the 1982 and 1983 budget heralded a downturn in the economy.

Nevertheless, industrial development has continued, though growth rates are generally flattered by starting from low baselines (McCawley, 1981). From 1967 through 1983 the Capital Investment Coordinating Board (Badan Koordinasi Penanaman Modal) approved 809 foreign projects valued at U.S. $14.4 billion, and 4,050 domestic-financed projects valued at U.S. $19.9 billion (this does not include the oil, gas, banking, and insurance sectors). The distribution of these projects is worthy of note. First, the control of the major firms is overwhelmingly centered in Jakarta. For instance, out of 104 Australian firms operating in Indonesia, 101 had their head office in Jakarta (Forbes, 1984b: 63). Second, the largest portion of investment has gone into Jakarta and the neighboring province of West Java. Some 25.6 percent of foreign investment and 11.2 percent of domestic investment between 1967 and 1983 located in Jakarta, and 25.3 percent and 29.3 percent of foreign and domestic investment respec- tively went to West Java. Third, there are pockets of resource-related investment in the outer islands of Indonesia, particularly in the provinces of Aceh, North Sumatra, and East Kalimantan, which accounted for 24.9 percent of foreign and 20.6 percent of domestic investment (IDN, February 1984).

The result of the concentration of both the control and production of industry within Jakarta is a high rate of urbanization, increasing specialization in the work force, and a speeded-up process of proletarianization. The city more than doubled its size between 1961 (when its official population numbered almost 3 million) and 1980 (by which time

it had grown to 6.5 million, for an average rate of annual
growth of 4 percent or better). According to the 1978
National Labour Force Survey, 6.4 percent of the work force
of nearly two million were seeking work. Like most Asian
cities, tertiary sector employment predominates. Only 14.5
percent of the work force were employed in manufacturing
industry, electricity, gas and water, and construction,
whereas 83.9 percent were employed in trade, transport, and
services. In terms of employment status, 69.7 percent of the
work force were employees, while 24.9 percent were "own
account" workers or performed unpaid family labor. The key
occupational categories were sales workers (29.2 percent);
production, transport, and related workers (25.3 percent);
service workers (23.3 percent); and clerical and related
workers (14.1 percent) (Biro Pusat Statistik, 1982).

The aggregate statistics, however, are an imperfect guide
to class formation in the city, because they fail to reveal
the real importance of an emerging proletariat and the parallel growth of the urban informal sector. By way of illustration, Sethuraman (1975: 196) estimates that almost half the
Jakarta workforce is engaged in the informal sector, while a
recent estimate suggests that there are 65,000 trishaws operating in the Jakarta area alone (Far Eastern Economic Review,
March 8, 1984). However, it is readily apparent that in an
economic sense rapid urbanization is bringing about class
formation, and that the class structure in very general terms
is similar to that outlined by Portes and Walton (1981). The
urban class formation consists of a bourgeoisie, a proletariat
divided into a professional ("new class") and a laboring fraction, and an "exploited" class of peripheralized wage laborers
and informal sector workers. There remains a strong strand
in the political, social, and economic analysis of Indonesia,
however, which implicitly questions the significance of this
form of class analysis.

In the wake of the interest in urbanization stimulated
by initiatives like the International Labour Organization's
World Employment Programme (see Sethuraman, 1981) and researchers such as McGee (1967, 1976, 1982) in the late 1960s
and 1970s, there has emerged a growing bank of studies of
Indonesian cities, and especially of the urban poor in the
informal sector. This work has focussed on issues like rural-
urban migration, the formation of urban labor markets, urban
kampungs, housing issues, urban subsistence production and
petty commodity production (especially small-scale manufacturing, markets and trishaw riders). By and large these studies
(which, incidentally, focus overwhelmingly on Jakarta and
Yogyakarta) are essentially descriptive and fall within either
of two genres: the first is an account built around a statistical survey, and the second is a detailed personalized description of life in an urban village, among traders, trishaw
riders, and the like. Very little of this sort of material
is set within an explicit theoretical framework, but one
characteristic feature of all these studies is that they
argue the case in favor of the urban poor against their
enemies, real or perceived. Consequently, most play up the
stable, functional role of the urban informal sector and play
down conflict. This focus is not unexpected in the light of
the harsh and repressive legislation which has been directed
against the informal sector in most Indonesian cities. Indeed,

research of this orientation is divided between the need to protect informal sector workers from being squeezed out of their petty income-earning opportunities and recognition of the extreme poverty with which most of these people have to cope. The policy of toleration which emerges is not really a long-term solution to urban poverty, though, and neither is the enforced closure of the informal sector which urban administrators have often advocated. To return to the main point, however, research on the urban informal sector has tended to highlight its stability and functional role in the urban economy, in order to argue the case for toleration of the informal sector.

A parallel case can be argued for much of the research on the formal labor market. Here the emphasis is on the adequacy of data sources, migration, participation rates (for males and females), education, incomes, multiple job-holding, under- and unemployment, and labor-market segmentation, to name but a few themes (see, for instance, Manning, 1980; Soemantri, 1980; Jones, 1981). Like informal sector research, two strands are central to this approach: first, an analysis of the supply of labor and its suitability to the requirements of urban enterprises (for example, education and skills); second, an examination of the outcome of the development of the urban economy, highlighting the welfare of the urban workforce (incomes, underemployment, and multiple job-holding). Neither set of analyses adopts a conflict-oriented interpretation of the urban labor market, but instead orients research to the functionality of labor supply, and documents the outcome for the urban population. However, if we are interested in class formation, we need a dynamic perspective on the labor market which emphasizes the way in which human agency, particularly conflict, brings about change within the urban economy.

In fact, we have evidence of at least three different forms of urban conflict in Indonesia. First, there is evidence to suggest that urban informal sector workers and the urban proletariat have participated in broad social protest movements within the cities. There have been four periods of intensified conflict through the towns and cities of Indonesia in the last decade. These include the "Malari" riots in Jakarta in January 1974; the student riots protesting the likely reelection of President Suharto, which broke out in Surabaya and Bandung and throughout West Java in late 1977 and early 1978; the anti-Chinese disturbances in Ujung Pandang, Aceh, and various towns in East Java in 1980-1981; and the violence which accompanied election campaigning in Jakarta, Surabaya, and Yogyakarta in March and April 1982. Trishaw riders seemed to have played a back-up role to students in the anti-Japanese urban riots in Jakarta in the 1970s and early 1980s, but, more importantly, trishaw riders especially have links with semicriminal (prostitution) and criminal activities (Guinness, 1982).

We know more about patterns of migration among informal sector workers but still understand little about this as a form of conflict-avoidance and resistance. Rural depopulation in the province of South Sulawesi has not simply been a matter of rural-urban migration. Indeed, it seems that the Bugis-speaking population often move from rural Sulawesi to rural areas in other parts of Indonesia, especially Sumatra, and not to the regional primate city, Ujung Pandang (Forbes, 1981). This might or might not be interpreted as a manifestation of a hidden form of consciousness, but in any case it is the sort of question which we have not yet explored. Likewise, the illegal residents in urban villages in Indonesia, the orang gelap--that is, those without identification cards (Kartu Tanda Penduduk)--are usually seen as peripheral, but their numbers suggest they are not. (Sullivan [1980: 45] notes that 200 live semipermanently in a Yogyakarta ward of some 15.5 thousand, while many more wander in and out). If we were to shift the focus of our analysis of the urban poor away from a functional analysis and make these kinds of events central instead, we would begin to build a different sort of picture.

Furthermore, it is clear that petty producers come into conflict with the dominant forces in society in ways specific to this sector. It has recently been argued that petty and subsistence production may themselves be strategies for avoiding the wage labor relation. The corollary is that it is difficult to sustain empirically the argument that all informal sector production is functional to the cheaper reproduction of wage labor. The price of trishaw services, for example, is well above the price of transport on minibuses. In other words, it could be argued that there are significant components of informal sector production that may well be nonfunctional to the capitalist classes--if we were to focus on these groups then it would have to be as examples of strategies of employment independent of the wage labor relation. Resistance and conflict have also been central to the relations between the state apparatus and informal sector workers: trishaw riders avoid purchasing licenses, petty government regulations on traders are flouted and officials are bribed (Jellinek, 1975). Following encouragement by the ILO (International Labor Organization), World Bank and many independent consultants and scholars, urban governments are now urged to take a more conciliatory position towards petty producers. Many governments have accepted the functionalist proposition about petty production. As one glowing press report noted, the Jakarta government has adopted a new policy on the city's scavengers:

> Now they have come to realize the scavengers play an important economic role in not only supplying waste material to factories such as badly needed metal and glassware and provide jobs but also in keeping down the level of garbage in Jakarta. (The Canberra Times, January 16, 1980).

Should it be effectively implemented, however, this sort of policy will have no significant effect on petty producers as a whole, though it may aid the better-off. As with most policies of this sort, whether they be the upgrading of markets, the Kampung Improvement Programme, or Green Revolution technology, the poor are generally unable to capitalize on expensive government aid. Finally, there is significant conflict between different groups of petty producers. Often this conflict reflects ethnic divisions such as conflict in Ujung Pandang between trishaw riders from different regions within the province. (A hidden aspect of this is the closed-shop nature of much small-scale production--access to employment is only available to people with specific place-links, such as villages.) At the very least, the disruption that this form of violence creates represents significant resistance to the smooth operation of the urban economy (although fighting mainly occurs at night).

Third, there is evidence of growing conflict in Indonesia between labor and employers. While there have been a number of informative studies of strikes during the colonial period (Ingelson, 1981a, 1981b) and through the 1960s (Leclerc, 1972), there is rather less information available on conditions during the New Order. However, the Indonesian Documentation and Information Center (INDOC) in the Netherlands, which regularly scans newspapers for reports of industrial action, records details of 115 serious disputes between 1979 and 1982 (Borkent et al, 1981, 1983; Azies et al., 1982). These primarily involve protests over the loss of jobs and declining living standards; disputes resulting from action taken by employers to prevent the work force from unionizing or joining the All-Indonesia Labor Federation (Federasi Buruh Suluruh Indonesia-FBSI); and protests arising from undue employer involvement in the appointment of union delegates. Dismissals frequently result from any labor activity, while regional governments and police have in a number of cases sided with employers in enforcing solutions to labor protests. One of the main criticisms by INDOC is that because the FBSI is a government-sponsored union monopoly, it violates International Labour Organization Convention 98, which gives workers the right to organize freely. The absence of free unions is in itself a cause of industrial conflict in Indonesia.

Contrary to the view of Indonesian society which emphasizes conflict avoidance, there is ample evidence of resistance and conflict in the workplace and beyond in contemporary urban Indonesia. The facts cited above are merely indicative of more substantial evidence that awaits extraction and analysis. This discussion underlines the point, however, that considerations of the functioning of the labor market in Indonesia which overlook this important process are partial at best. They generally give an incomplete picture of the proletariat and protoproletariat in urban Indonesia, implying a false acquiescence to a social and economic order which has provided far fewer benefits to the working classes than it has done to those in positions of power. Furthermore, it contributes to our understanding of class formation by demonstrating the active struggles in which proletarians and protoproletarians alike are engaged, a process which itself significantly shapes the class formation. Finally, it imbues our conception of class formation with a sense of dynamism. The urban poor are not simply the passive bearers of their lot in life, they are active agents in the reproduction and transformation of the society to which they belong. At the present time the orbit of human agency, manifest in resistance and conflict, reproduces a cycle geared to reform rather than revolution. Strikers struggle for better conditions or to unionize, not to overthrow the existing order; as argued earlier, however, this does not preclude revolutionary activity should the conditions warrant and permit it.

If we accept the argument that conflict both reproduces and transforms--and in this case, hopefully reforms--the structural composition of the economy and society, what evidence is there in Jakarta to substantiate the proposition? This is not the sort of question that can be answered in any depth here, but isolating two features of contemporary Indonesia allows us to raise some questions about the sorts of relationships for which we should look. First, there is evidence of the repressive nature of the state in New Order Indonesia (Amnesty International, 1977; Feith, 1980), its persistence evident in the last few years in the wave of government-initiated killings in Java (Lane, 1983). Although ostensibly directed at habitual criminals, it has clearly terrorized many of the urban poor.

What is the relationship between this sort of repressive action, the government refusal to sanction free unions, and repressive legislation such as that which now seeks to clear all trishaws out of Jakarta? Furthermore, what is the relationship, if any, between the urban conflict discussed earlier and these different forms of repressive government action? Second, how has the process of class formation in Jakarta contributed to the redefinition of the city's place within the Indonesian and world economies? After 1974 there was a marked decline in foreign investment in Indonesia, but in contrast, right through the period since 1965, foreign and domestic investment has concentrated in Jakarta and West Java. To what extend has conflict within the labor force shaped the pattern of location of manufacturing industry and services in Indonesia in recent years? To date these questions are unanswered, but they are important nevertheless, for they shift our focus from functional integration within the urban area and its related static, economistic perspective, to broader questions of the interlocking nature of economy, state, and society.

CONCLUSION

This chapter began by arguing that we need to develop a better and more structured understanding of class formation and the distribution of power within the Third World city if we are to understand the process of underdevelopment and strategies for tackling development. It argued that the discussion of class formation offered by Portes and Walton (1981) was functionalist in structure and economistic in the stress that it placed on the significance of the informal sector in reducing the costs of reproduction of urban wage labor. Posing a model of class formation based on the need to recursively combine structure and agency (expressed, for instance, through resistance to the domination of capital), it was suggested that we need to pay greater attention to the social economy and the everyday forms of conflict which have in the past been overlooked both in radical-theoretical and empirical research on the urban poor. These are significant because they are evidence of an embryonic class consciousness among the urban "exploited" class--the informal sector workers and the proletariat--while the different forms of resistance and conflict in turn help shape class formation. This led me to dispute the "politically conservative" label which has been assigned to the urban poor--instead, it has been the case that the political action of the urban poor has taken forms different from those we have been expecting. It remains well beyond the scope of this chapter to analyze whether this form of behavior is "part of an incremental chain of consciousness" (Cohen, 1980: 2) or simply a disorganized and individualistic response; regardless, it is something that must be considered. Overall, the aim of this chapter has been to argue for a new methodological viewpoint in our analysis of Third World cities. Now that there is a literature that is beginning to sketch in some detail the broad characteristics of class formation in these cities, it is time for us to look critically at our tools of analysis, particularly those that have led to a crudely functional interpretation of class formation. A focus on resistance and conflict and the interdependence of structure and agency is one way of trying to achieve this.

BIBLIOGRAPHY

Amin, S.
1980 Class and Nation, Historically and in the Current Crisis. New York: Monthly Review.
Amnesty International
1977 Indonesia; an Amnesty International Report. London: Amnesty International.
Azies, M. Van Doorn, J. Hadjar, et al.
1982 Indonesian Workers and their Right to Organise. Leiden: Indonesian Documentation and Information Center.
Biro Pusat Statistik
1982 Statistik Indonesia 1980/1981. Jakarta, Indonesia.
Borkent, H., M. Van Doorn, I. Farjoh, J. Hadjar, J. Leclerc, Satyawan, R. Van Yderen
1981 Indonesian Workers and their Right to Organise. Leiden: Indonesian Documentation and Information Center.
1983 Indonesian Workers and their Right to Organise. March 1983 Update. Leiden: Indonesian Documen- tation and Information Center.
Brenner, R.
1977 The Origins of Capitalist Development; a Critique of Neo-Smithian Marxism. New Left Review 104: 25-93.
Cohen, R.
1980 Resistance and Hidden Forms of Consciousness among African Workers. Review of African Political Economy 19: 8-22.
Cohen, R., J. Copans, and P. C. W. Gutkind
1978 Introduction. In Gutkind, Cohen and Copans, eds., African Labor History. Sage Series on African Modernization and Development (2). Beverly Hills, Calif.: Sage.
Feith, H.
1980 Repressive-Developmentalist Regimes in Asia; Old Strengths, New Vulnerabilities. Prisma 19: 39-55.
Fitzgerald, F. T.
1981 Sociologies of Development. Journal of Contemporary Asia 11 (1): 5-18.

Forbes, D. K.
  1981 Petty Commodity Production and Underdevelopment; the
        Case of Pedlars and Trishaw Riders in Ujung Pandang,
        Indonesia. Progress in Planning 16. Oxford: Pergamon.
  1984a The Geography of Underdevelopment; a Critical Survey.
        London: Croom Helm.
  1984b Corporate Relocation; Australian Companies in Indone-
        sia. In M. J. Taylor, ed., The Geography of Austra-
        lian Corporate Power. Sydney: Croom Helm.
Gerry, C., and C. Birkbeck
  1981 The Petty Commodity Producers in Third World Cities:
        Petit Bourgeois or "Disguised" Proletarian? In F.
        Bechhofer and B. Elliott, eds., The Petite Bour-
        geoisie; Comparative Studies of the Uneasy Stratum.
        London: Macmillan.
Giddens, A.
  1979 Central Problems in Social Theory; Action, Structure
        and Contradiction in Social Analysis. London:
        Macmillan.
  1981 A Contemporary Critique of Historical Materialism.
        Vol. I, Power, Property and the State. London:
        Macmillan.
  1982 Profiles and Critiques in Social Theory. London:
        Macmillan.
Gregory, D.
  1981 Human Agency and Human Geography. Transactions,
        Institute of British Geographers 6 (1): 1-18.
Guinness, P.Y.
  1982 Rukun Kampung; Social Relations in Urban Yogya-
        karta. Unpublished Ph.D. thesis. Canberra:
        Australian National University, Department of
        Anthropology, Research School of Pacific Studies.
Indonesia Development News
        Indonesia; Development News. Various issues.
Ingelson, J.
  1981a Bound Hand and Foot; Railway Workers and the 1923
        Strike on Java. Indonesia 31: 53-87.
  1981b Worker Consciousness and Labour Unions in Colonial
        Java. Pacific Affairs 54 (3): 485-502.
Jellinek, L.
  1975 The Life of a Jakarta Street Trader. Working Paper
        9. Melbourne: Monash University, Centre of Southeast
        Asian Studies.
Jones, G. W.
  1981 Labour Force Developments Since 1961. In A. Booth and
        P. McCawley, The Indonesian Economy During the
        Soeharto Era. Kuala Lumpur: Oxford University.
Lane, M.
  1983 Soeharto's Strong-Arm Man Sends in the Death Squads.
        National Times, August 19: 15-17.
Leclerc, J.
  1972 An Ideological Problem of Indonesian Trade Unionism in
        the Sixties: "Karyawan" versus "Buruh." Review of
        Indonesian and Malayan Affairs 6 (1): 76-91.
Leys, C.
  1975 Underdevelopment in Kenya; the Political Economy of
        Neo-Colonialism. London: Heinemann.
  1977 Underdevelopment and Dependency; Critical Notes.
        Journal of Contemporary Asia 7 (1): 92-107.

1978 Capital Accumulation, Class Formation and Dependency; the Significance of the Kenyan Case. The Socialist Register: 241-66.
McCawley, P.
1981 The Growth of the Industrial Sector. In A. Booth and P. McCawley, eds., The Indonesian Economy During the Soeharto Era. Kuala Lumpur: Oxford University.
McGee, T. G.
1967 The Southeast Asian City. London: Bell.
1976 The Persistence of the Proto-proletariat. Progress in Geography 9: 1-38.
1982 Urban Systems, Labour Markets and the Urbanization Process in Southeast Asia; Research Priorities for Government Policy. In R. P. Misra, ed., Regional Development. Singapore: Maruzen Asia.
Manning, C.
1980 Dualism in Labour Markets and Labour Market Segmentation in Indonesian Manufacturing. In J. J. Fox, R. Garnaut, P. McCawley and J. A. C. Mackie, eds., Indonesia; Australian Perspectives. Canberra:
      Australian National University, Research School of Pacific Studies.
Nelson, J. M.
1979 Access to Power; Politics and the Urban Poor in Developing Nations. Princeton: Princeton University.
O'Malley, W.J.
1979 Liberal, Structural and Radical Approaches to Political Economy; an Assessment and an Alternative. Contemporary Crises 3: 109-47.
1982 The Underworld in Rural Java. Unpublished paper. Canberra: Australian National University, Department of Political and Social Change, Research School of Pacific Studies.
Portes, A., and J. Walton
1981 Labor, Class and the International System. New York: Academic.
Przeworski, A.
1977 Proletariat into a Class; the Process of Class Formation from Karl Kautsky's The Class Struggle to Recent Controversies. Politics and Society 7 (4): 343-400.
Rey, P. P.
1973 Les Alliances de Classes. Paris: Maspero.
Rogerson, C. M., and K. S. O. Beavon
1982 Getting by in the "Informal Sector" of Soweto. Tijdschrift voor Economische en Sociale Geografie 73 (4): 250-65.
Sethuraman, S. V.
1975 Urbanisation and Employment; a Case Study of Djakarta. International Labour Review 112: 191-205.
1976 Jakarta; Urban Development and Employment. Geneva: International Labour Office.
Sethuraman, S.V. (ed.)
1981 The Urban Informal Sector in Developing Countries. Geneva: International Labour Office.
Smith, S.
1982 Class Analysis versus World Systems; Critique of Samir Amin's Typology of Under-development. Journal of Contemporary Asia 12 (1): 7-18.

Soemantri, S.
 1980 Study of Indonesia's Economically Active Population.
       Yogyakarta: Gadjah Mada University.
Sullivan, J.
 1980 Back Alley Neighbourhood; Kampung as Urban Community
       in Yogyakarta. Working Paper 18. Melbourne: Monash
       University, Centre of Southeast Asian Studies.
Therborn, G.
 1983 Why Some Classes are More Successful than Others. New
       Left Review 138: 37-55.
Thrift, N. J.
       1983
On the Determination of Social Action in Space and Time.
Society and Space 1 (1): 23-58.
Thrift, N., and D. Forbes
 1983 A Landscape with Figures; Political Geography as Human
       Conflict. Political Geography Quarterly 2 (3): 247-63.
Willis, P. E.
 1977 Learning to Labour; How Working Class Kids Get Working
       Class Jobs. Farnborough: Saxon House.
Wright, E. O.
 1980 Varieties of Marxist Conceptions of Class Structure.
       Politics and Society 9 (3): 323-70.

Conclusion:
Notes on Theory and Method
for Third World Studies
NOVELLA ZETT KEITH

It is always a risky undertaking to isolate for commentary ideas, issues, positions, and the like from any collection. The difficulty arises from the fact that each idea or position nearly always has a legitimate claim to exclusive treatment. How, for instance, does an editor choose "fairly" between the issues of ethnicity raised so compellingly by Howard and Skinner and the insights on the subjective dimensions of consciousness derived from Dean Forbes?

Nonetheless, invoking editorial privilege, I will close this volume with a few observations on the broad concept of ideology. My specific reference points will be the phenomenon of religion and the so-called "moral economy" question analyzed respectively by Tom Bamat and Steve Johnson. Why so? It appears that the choice is timely, given the outpouring of scholarly writings on these questions; indeed, religion becomes even more central because of the existence of two contemporary upheavals in which its role is quite marked: the Sandinista revolution and the Iranian revolution under Khoemeni.

These comments are prompted by the crucial reevaluations taking place with respect to analyses of the theory and concept of ideology within advanced capitalist societies. In fact, during 1982 and 1983, a very sophisticated project-- Rethinking Ideology--was undertaken in West Germany to analyze and reevaluate the relevance of the concept to Marxism. It was apparent then that the ebb and flow of social and societal phenomena has simply drifted past these explanatory theories. As Andre Gorz (1986) has so correctly informed us, contemporary capitalism is rendering obsolete such Marxist constructs as the labor theory of value and exploitation (and, by implication, the derivative concepts). We are also in need of similar reevaluations with regard to the place of ideology in contemporary society.

While the extensive question of ideology is ramified, its main dimensions appear to revolve around the following headings:

1. how to define social classes, the so-called "boundary question" (Meiksins, 1986; Wright, 1985; Laclau and Mauffe, 1985);

2. how to assess the significance of commodity production in the determination of class consciousness
(Katznelson, 1981; Wright, 1985; Nielsen, 1985); and

3. how to define ideology to excise that irritating
"omnibus" quality (Hamilton, 1987).

These rethinkings and revisitations are healthy and
timely for the efficacy and morale of Third World research
and scholarship. When scholars of Third World studies insist that their analyses of social phenomena in the periphery won't fit, they should now expect to hear less deterministic arguments and see fewer ad hoc formulations. It is
no longer correct to say that the peasants are suffering from
"false consciousness" because they have not been sufficiently
brought into intimate contact with the consciousness impart-
ing characteristics of commodity production. If in the
matter of class definitions, we still have to cope with the
declaration that "the urban masses . . . comprise a real, if
distinctive, proletariat" (Gutkind, 1984), we take courage in
the fact that many countervailing responses will follow.
In an oblique, yet definitive way, the existence of the
Journal of Peasant Studies testifies to the independence,
particularity, and centrality of the class and mode of production approach in the global study of social class relations. Of course, the true measure of the journal rests in
the high quality scholarship for which it has become justi-
fiably well known.
For another reason--once again using the example of the
peasantry--contentions to the effect that peasant struggles
are often interdependent with broad-based mass movements and
often define social, political, and economic outcomes will be
taken as strong evidence against certain forms of crude
generalizations (Mallon, 1983). I see Dean Forbes' insights
on class consciousness within "informal sectors" of Third
World cities to be similarly worthy of such recognition.
Howard and Skinner, two other contributors, should now feel
more comfortable declaring their findings that ethnicity is
not epiphenomenal. There is certainly more productive evidence of center-peripheral dialogue and cooperation, especially as research at the center is compelling identical
conclusions (see Nelson Keith's chapter).
Let me now address the two themes singled out for comment. First, I will discuss the "moral economy" theme found
in Steve Johnson's "Ideological Dimensions of Peasant Persistence in Western Kenya." This chapter, supported by
fieldwork in Kenya, emerges as a challenge or a reminder in
the sense that it presents some empirical validity to theories still experiencing a rough passage. It is clear to me
that this piece raises some fundamental issues which I will
discuss under the headings of conceptualization and methodology.
Conceptually, the main themes of Johnson's chapter draw
their lifeblood from the so-called "moral economy" thesis.
Briefly, the thesis states that between peasants and their
landlords, there exists a traditional pact which helps to
determine what is a just demand. This tradition, which can
have strong associations with kinship, inserts an obligation
which dulls the edge of capitalist exploitation (Scott, 1976,
1977; Klein, 1980).[1]

William Roseberry (1986), in reference to the Venezuelan peasantry, and now Steve Johnson--though the latter has done so far more elaborately--have raised the issue anew. As the former has enunciated it, tradition can create the basis for more inclusive theorizing on consciousness. The phenomenon, he continues, exists "not as a dead weight of the past, but as the active, shaping force of the past in the present" (Roseberry, 1986: 149-50). As a timely caveat, however, I would endorse the critical observations of Cooper (1981: 314) who warns that an accurate definition of the social formation in question needs to precede other definitional and analytical exercises.[2]   Nevertheless,   there   is   compelling   evidence that tradition, moral economy, and the like are not merely cultural relics.

I will comment briefly on some encouraging formulations geared to the theoretical integration of these and similar phenomena within historical materialism, but before proceeding with that exercise, an additional point should be raised. Just as ideology has become a frightful catchall basket of cognitive shards and splinters (Hamilton, 1987), so could the more enveloping concept of consciousness, if the proper conceptual and methodological reins are not placed upon the passion to strain the limits of the imagination. In a derivative way, Young (1982) implies much that could be of use here. Without confusing or dulling the efficacy of precapitalist phenomena, he makes the oblique point that "fellow feeling" (which could be scoffed at as humanism) cannot be imposed as a national ideal through incantations and exhortations--the twaddle of nationalism. The implicit message is hardly against the crucial role of these phenomena as it is directed to the task of accurately determining their origins, locations, and interplay with class relations and social change. Not every dog that barks has teeth! On an aside, we can now further correct the unintended damage of Hobsbawm who posits a two-class model for capitalism in industrial England: precapitalist forms had little chance of survival as "the ancient ways and practices . . . brought from the countryside or the pre-industrial town became irrelevant or impracticable" (1975: 212-13).

My comments on methodology are less innovations than reminders. The novelty of the call, if any, rests more in an ideological challenge: court the charge of eclecticism, as in the end the benefits to theoretical development will offset the torture to the ego. If the more palatable term is "synthesis," let us increase the pace of these endeavors. When Herder or D'Annunzio utterly bore us with their weary processions of romantic epithets on tradition (Volk) and nationalism--both nonproperty and noneconomic variables--our response should not be a rejection based on disgust or ideological requirements. These phenomena emerge from deep-seated cognitive structures, molded to the worldview of a Herder, a D'Annunzio or a Michelet. In fact, espousal of the Volk was successful (less so for reasons of propaganda) in offsetting the attack of the philosophes on the laboring classes, the aristocracy, and the society in which they lived (Lunn, 1986: 481).

This brings me to the more direct task of synthesis and reformulation within the framework of historical materialism. The real challenge thrown down by these precapitalist

forms is that of properly integrating subjectivity with a
materialist conception of history in ways that avoid the element of dependence suggested in all modifications and variations of the base-superstructure schema. The notion of
"relative autonomy" formulated and popularized by Althusser
and Poulantzas are encouraging refinements but remain quite
incomplete and unsatisfactory.

Of the various attempts made at solving this pivotal
epistemological problem, I find the contributions of Lucien
Seve, the French philosopher, to be most encouraging. Among
the seminal ideas raised by Seve (see Carl Shames' lucid and
insightful 1981 article, which I have used liberally), is the
need, in a sense, to go back to the basics. We need to
reassess the interplay of matter and motion in the definition
of human beings in a complex social world. Seve sees the
problem as one created by the separation between the ongoing
metamorphosis of motion (that is, thought) and that of
substance (or human beings). This separation lies at the
heart of the epistemology of the natural sciences.

For a considerable period of time the separation per-
sisted, giving rise to mechanical and organismic formulas for
the conceptualization and development of the whole. Under
the influence of the natural sciences--with their immense
success built upon objective laws -- the development of substance subordinated and shoved aside the dynamics of motion
(it will be recalled that Marx himself, in the _Grundrisse_,
showed tendencies to positivism). However, the natural
sciences gradually came to recognize the complex interdependence of phenomena. In biology and physics, appropriate
theoretical refutation gave rise to systems theories and the
concept of field, respectively.[3]

For the social sciences and historical materialism,
these developments are enormously important. As Shames
(1981: 5) put it, "just as physics learned to overcome the
theological laments of the 'death of matter' and developed
new concepts to study laws of matter-in-motion that unite
complexity and development, so too must the human sciences
develop the understanding of people-in-relations." (To
reinforce the point, I would add the necessity of overcoming
secular laments of "epiphenomena" and developing new concepts
to study the laws of phenomena-in-motion).

As Seve continues, the task cannot involve mechanistic
approaches such as structuralism which "divorce[s] material
reality from the relations and motion of that reality"
(Shames, 1981: 5). In the end the logic of structuralism
emerges as one that underpins a system without living, productive activity. Structuralism also fails to retain the
dialectical character of theory, as it "absolutizes" relations
of exchange over production relations.

The virtue of this form of theorizing is that it
cogently and suggestively argues for the personality as an
integral part of a materialist conception of history. A
further step in this line of discourse is the integration of
the so-called "epiphenomena" that are now crucially related
to the development of class consciousness in the periphery.

Now I will turn to the issue of religion that Tom Bamat
highlights for us in this volume. One of the many points
raised by Bamat's contribution is that the Catholic Church,
given its constitution, political ties with state apparatuses,

and doctrinal commands, cannot be expected to support a Marxist revolution. First, it faces the inordinate difficulty of supporting the species of violence likely to emerge from that event.   Second, its articulation to the state is one of its real sources of temporal power.

It is evident that liberation theology has not diminished the tensions surrounding it. Indeed, violence is only one of the problematic areas, which many theologians have found not incompatible with social justice: if not resorting to the ebb, flow, and definition of history, they take refuge in Aquinas' theory of "just war." On the other hand, others have even adopted Marxism with its substantial commitment to violence.   In 1971, for example, a large group of Italian priests of the diocese of Bolzano-Bressanone made such a declaration--a renunciation of capitalism and its profit motive while stressing that Marxism is "more attuned to God's plan than capitalist society."[4]

On the question of private property--another problem area--others have linked it to the very "realization of one's human condition" (Segundo, 1968: 577). It emerges in language in which natural rights claims are couched. Even so, less reverence is paid to the metaphysical God who serves to prop up the status quo and legitimate oppressive political systems (Segundo, 1984).

Then there is the matter of atheism. Indeed, the famous position of Archbishop Hurtado de La Paz continues to hold some sway. The Archbishop pursued a line somewhat close to Marxism but vigorously denounced violence and atheism. Perhaps most representative of this position--and indeed quite a sophisticated work--is Rene Coste's Marxist Analysis and Christian Faith, which systematically analyzes these tensions and discrepancies but opts in the end for the Christian doctrine.

These examples do not make the whole case, but they strongly suggest an imperative. The various discussions surrounding faith, violence, and private property give rise to minidiscourses within the general framework of religion, which must be resolved if religion is to be furthered as an effective instrument of fundamental social change. It can hardly be contested that in the Third World countries where religion flourishes, only change of a fundamental nature will provide the needed equity and social justice. The task is even more urgent, from a practical standpoint, as both Christianity and Marxism share a common humanistic origin, with common approaches (up to a point) to dehumanization and political oppression.

In spite of the oft-repeated statement that Christianity is socialist in its essence (Dussel, 1976), no one would seriously dispute that it lacks a scientific grounding. Fideism takes the place of science, as proof (as in the case of Catholicism) always resides in the faith pronouncements of the Pope. With the stroke of the pen, Pope John XXIII elevated private property to the state of natural right "which the state may by no means suppress."[5]

I will not be as cavalier as Fierro (1977: 80) and Currier (1987: 38) in suggesting that theology in search of a legitimating science must adopt the principles of Marxism. For one, I am not so sure that Marxism, with its continuing spate of antireligion propaganda, is constitutively ready for such a project. It does appear however, due to the commonalities reflected by these agendas, that such a suggestion should be pursued with vigor. That religion is not epiphenomenal (Gismondi, 1986: 30) should now be obvious to many Marxists. What Bamat's chapter and others who have focussed on the Sandinista revolution have shown is that the revolution occurred substantially without an industrial working class but with the aid of a consciousness steeped in Christian principles.

Whither goes Marxism! It is clear that while a great deal has been accomplished in the name of synthesis, more is required, especially as, broadly speaking, both camps can point to successful social revolutions (for example, Cuba and Nicaragua). Somehow I feel compelled to return to my earlier comments on the epistemological crisis in Marxism. The promising formulations that I suggested then would assist in opening the way for integrating religion and other epiphenomena into a materialist framework, providing the wherewithal around which people could mobilize, like wages.

On the other hand, how should liberation theology accept or deal with, say, violence? I do not think that the related difficulties are philosophically or theologically forbidding as they are delicate in strategic and political senses. The traditional power garnered over the ages by the Catholic Church vis-a-vis the state will not be abandoned easily. On the other hand, the Church has throughout history thrown its weight behind wars, and even the Sandinista revolution had its share of this kind of support from the lower clergy. The fact is that in spite of the supranatural claims made on behalf of religion, the movement of history has shown it to be naturally influenced by the social context in which it is located. Consequently, it can be put in the service of the kind of violence contemplated by Marxism while maintaining its credibility with theological and philosophical systems (see the enlightening collection of essays edited by Ginsberg, 1970).

Now that the dust is beginning to settle, many writers, Marxists and non-Marxists alike, are beginning to grasp the historical peculiarities emerging from the Sandinista revolution and the epochal strains between Marxism and Christianity. As Montgomery (1983) put it, the seeming continuous lines leading from the purely religious to the political are "paradigmatic," and not unique to given experiences. As a further step along the path to synthesis, Giulio Girardi, one familiar with the old debate on religion and Party in Italy, has suggested that the collaboration between Christians and Marxists is not, as most commentators have suggested, only a practical convergence existing within (or even in spite of) fundamental theoretical divergencies. He posits the existence of a theoretical convergence founded on the basic epistemological choices of liberation theory and Marxism: the one exerts a "preferential option for the poor," the other espouses a "proletarian point of view." Inevitably, the "criticism by Marx toward the moralism of religious socialists no longer holds when these are socialists whose utopia is articulated with a class analysis and proletarian practice (Girardi, 1983: 180). Reformulations of the kind I recommend bear a close association to this new, evolving line of theoretical reasoning.

NOTES

1. For the most part, the merit of Scott's challenge rests less in analytic strength than in its accuracy of description; he appears to infer, for example, that the moral economy might be susceptible to capitalist forces.
2. I cannot agree, however, with Cooper's additional suggestion that "we will do better" to examine the responses of various classes to the expansion of world markets to determine the origins and extent of systems of production, class structures, and political conflicts. This directive smacks of the old materialist approach which has progressively become more and more obsolete.
3. Wiegele's collection of essays (Biology and the Social Sciences: An Emerging Revolution. Boulder Colo.: Westview, 1982) raises a number of interesting issues relating to the integration of paradigms. See also Heiner Flohr, "The Importance of Biology for the Social Sciences," Ratio 28 (1), June 1986.
4. New York Times, March 10, 1971.
5. John XXIII, "Mater et Magistra." Boston: St. Paul, 1961. Cited in Foroohar (1986).

BIBLIOGRAPHY

Cooper, Frederick
1981 Peasants, Capitalists, and Historians: A Review Article. Journal of Southern African Studies 7 (2): 248-314.
Coste, Rene
1985 Marxist Analysis and Christian Faith. Maryknoll, N.Y.: Orbis.
Currier, Fred J.
1987 Liberation Theology and Marxist Economics. Monthly Review 38 (January): 23-39.
Dussel, Enrique
1976 History and the Theology of Liberation: A Latin American Perspective. Maryknoll, N.Y.: Orbis.
Fierro, Alfredo
1977 The Militant Gospel. Maryknoll, N.Y.: Orbis.
Foroohar, Manzar
1986 Liberation Theology; the Response of Latin American Catholics to Socioeconomic Problems. Latin American Perspectives 13 (3): 37-57.
Ginsberg, Robert, ed.
1970 The Critique of War. Chicago: Henry Regnery.
Girardi, Giulio
1983 Il Marxismo di Fronte alle Esperienze Religiose Revoluzionarie. Critica Marxista 21 (2-3): 155-86.
Gismondi, Michael A.
1986 Transformations in the Holy Religious Resistance and Hegemonic Struggles in the Nicaraguan Revolution. Latin American Perspectives 13 (3): 13-36.
Gorz, Andre
1987 The Socialism of Tomorrow. Telos 67 (Spring): 199-206.
Gutkind, Peter C. W.
1984 A Case Against Class Models. Third World Book Review 1 (1): 55-56.

Hamilton, Malcolm B.
1987   The Elements of the Concept of Ideology.   Political
       Studies 35: 18-38.
Hobsbawm, Eric J.
1975   The Age of Capital 1848-1875.   New York: Charles
       Scribner's Sons.
Katznelson, Ira
1981   City Trenches: Urban Politics and the Patterning of
       Class in the United States.   New York: Pantheon.
Klein, Martin A.
1980   Peasants   in   Africa: Historical   and   Contemporary
       Perspectives.   Beverly Hills, Calif.:   Sage.
Laclau, Ernesto and Chantal Mauffe
1985   Hegemony and Socialist Strategy: Toward a Radical
       Democratic Politics.   London: Verso.
Lunn, Eugene
1986   Cultural Populism and Egalitarian Democracy: Herder
       and Michelet in the Nineteenth Century.   Theory and
       Society 15 (4): 479-517.
Mallon, Florencia E.
1983   The Defense of Community in Peru's Central Highlands:
       Peasant Struggles and Capitalist Transition, 1860-
       1940.   Princeton: Princeton University.
Meiksins, Peter
1986   Beyond the Boundary Question.   New Left Review 157
       (May/June): 101-20.
Montgomery, Tommy Sue
1983   The Church in the Salvadorean Revolution.   Latin
       American Perspectives 10 (1): 62-87.
Nielsen, Francois
1985   Ethnic Resurgence in Advanced Countries.   American
       Sociological Review 50 (April): 133-49.
Roseberry, William
1986   Images of the Peasant in the Consciousness of the
       Venezuelan Proletariat.   In Michael Hanagan and
       Charles Stephens, eds., Proletarians and Protest:
       Roots of Class Formation in an Industrializing World.
       New York: Greenwood.
Scott, J.
1976   The Moral Economy of the Peasant: Rebellion or
       Subsistence in Southeast Asia.   New Haven: Yale.
1977   Hegemony and the Peasantry.   Politics and Society 7:
       267-96.
Segundo, Juan Luis
1968   Social Justice and Revolution.   Americas (April 27):
       574-77.
1984   Faith and Ideologies.   London: Sheed and Ward.
Seve, Lucien
1975   Marxism and the Theory of Human Personality.   London:
       Lawrence and Wishart.
1978   Man in Marxist Theory and the Psychology of Personal-
       ity.   Atlantic Highlands, N.J.: Humanities.
Shames, Carl
1981   The Scientific Humanism of Lucien Seve.   Science and
       Society 45 (1): 1-23.
Wright, Erik Olin
1985   Classes.   London: Verso.

Young, Crawford
  1982 Nationalizing the Third World State: Categorical Im-
        perative or Mission Impossible? <u>Polity</u> (Amherst) 15
        (2).

Index

Contributors

THOMAS BAMAT is currently Education Coordinator for Ecuador's Ecumenical Human Rights Commission (CEDHU) in Quito. He received a Ph.D. in sociology from Rutgers University in 1978. He has published articles in Latin American Perspectives and the Latin American Research Review. His most recent works are Los Derechos Humanos: El Caso Ecuatoriano (Human Rights: the Ecuadorian Case), co-edited with Elsie Monge and Raul Borja in 1985; and Salvacion o Dominacion? Las Sectas Religiosas en el Ecuador (Salvation or Domination? Religious Sects in Ecuador), published in 1986.

RICHARD CURTAIN completed a doctorate at the Australian National University in Canberra, Australia. He has published a number of articles arising out of his research in Papua New Guinea, including "Labor Migration in Papua New Guinea," in Migration and Development, edited by Helen Safa and Brian DuToit, and several articles on related topics in Pacific Viewpoint, Singapore Journal of Tropical Geography, and others. Currently, he directs a research project on manpower needs for the Australian Department of Labour in Canberra, Australia.

DEAN FORBES is an aid program analyst with the Australian Development Aid Bureau and a Visiting Fellow in the Research School of Pacific Studies of the Australian National University. He has undertaken research and development project work in Indonesia, Papua New Guinea, Vietnam, China, and the Philippines. His most recent books are The Price of War: Urbanisation in Vietnam, 1954-1985 and The Socialist Third World: Urban Development and Territorial Planning (both jointly with Nigel Thrift).

ALLEN M. HOWARD is Associate Professor of History at Rutgers University of New Jersey. He is co-author of Community Leadership and the Transformation of Freetown, 1801-1976 and of articles in the Journal of African History, African Urban Studies, Africa, and elsewhere. Formerly he was co-editor of the African Studies Association's Annual Review of Books. He is currently completing a book on Freetown and the Sierra Leone-Guinea commercial system, from 1780 to 1930.

STEVEN L. JOHNSON is a Program Officer with the New Jersey Department of Higher Education. Prior to joining the Department he was an Assistant Professor of Anthropology at Gettysburg College. His research and publications fall within the areas of African political economy, Native American ethnohistory, and urban anthropology. His articles have appeared in Human Organization, Current Anthropology, and elsewhere. He is also the author of a bibliographic work, Guide to American Indian Documents in the Congressional Serial Set: 1817-1899.

NELSON W. KEITH is an international development consultant who was for a number of years a member of the faculty at the School of Urban and Regional Policy of Rutgers University in New Jersey. He has written extensively on Third World issues. His latest work, co-authored with Novella Z. Keith, is National Popularism in Jamaica. He is currently completing a critical study of Marxist analyses of social classes in the Third World.

NOVELLA Z. KEITH is currently directing an educational evaluation project at Glassboro State College in New Jersey and was formerly a member of the Sociology faculty at Stockton College. She has published a number of articles based on her research in the Caribbean and expertise with Third World development issues. Her most recent work, in addition to the volume co-authored with Nelson Keith, is in the areas of interdependence and Third World development and the relationship of Third World development to peace issues.

JAY R. MANDLE is Professor of Economics at Temple University. He has published extensively in the area of Third World development studies, with special reference to Third World socialist countries. His most recent book is Big Revolution Small Country: The Rise and Fall of the Grenada Revolution. Together with Joan D. Mandle, he has recently completed a study of the basketball communities in Trinidad and Tobago, which emphasizes ideology and consciousness.

DAVID E. SKINNER is Associate Professor of History at Santa Clara University. He is co-author of Community Leadership and the Transformation of Freetown, 1801-1976 (1978), of Thomas George Lawson: African Historial and Administrator in Sierra Leone (1980), and of articles in The International Journal of African Historical Studies, Canadian Journal of African Studies, Africa, and elsewhere. Currently he is doing research for a book on Islamic education in West Africa during the twentieth century.